T0352968

GOLD

About the Authors

Charles "Chic" Cicero was born in Buffalo, New York. An early love of music and the saxophone resulted in Chic's many years as a lead musician in several jazz, blues, and rock ensembles, working with many famous performers in the music industry. Chic's interest in Freemasonry and the Western Esoteric Tradition led him to become a member of several Masonic, Martinist, and Rosicrucian organizations. He is a Past Grand Commander of the Grand Commandery of Knights Templar in Florida (2010–2011) and a 9th Degree in the Masonic Rosicrucians (SRICF). He was also a close personal friend and confidant of Dr. Israel Regardie. Having established a Golden Dawn temple in 1977, Chic was one of the key people who helped Regardie resurrect a legitimate, initiatory branch of the Golden Dawn in the United States in the early 1980s. He is currently the G.H. Imperator of the Hermetic Order of the Golden Dawn (www.hermeticgoldendawn .org), an international Order with temples in several countries.

Sandra "Tabatha" Cicero was born in rural Wisconsin. After graduating from the University of Wisconsin–Milwaukee with a Bachelor's Degree in Fine Arts in 1982, Tabatha worked as an entertainer, typesetter, editor, commercial artist, and computer graphics illustrator. She is currently the Supreme Magus (Imperatrix) of the Societas Rosicruciana in America (www.sria.org) as well as the G.H. Cancellaria of the Hermetic Order of the Golden Dawn.

Edited & Annotated by Chic Cicero
& Sandra Tabatha Cicero

GOLD

ISRAEL REGARDIE'S
LOST BOOK OF
ALCHEMY

Llewellyn Publications
Woodbury, Minnesota

FIRST EDITION
Fifth Printing, 2024

Cover art: 2285229/©James Steidl/Shutterstock.com
166564175/©Yure/Shutterstock.com
Cover design by Kevin R. Brown
Interior art credits on page xi

Llewellyn Publications is a registered trademark of Llewellyn Worldwide Ltd.

Library of Congress Cataloging-in-Publication Data
Regardie, Israel.
 Gold : Israel Regardie's lost book of alchemy / by Israel Regardie,
Chic Cicero, and, Sandra Tabatha Cicero.
 pages   cm
 Includes bibliographical references and index.
 ISBN 978-0-7387-4072-0
1. Spirituality—Miscellanea. 2. Alchemy—Religious aspects. 3.
Alchemy—Miscellanea. 4. Regardie, Israel. Philosopher's stone. 5.
Alchemy. 6. Regardie, Israel. Tree of life. 7. Magic. 8. Occultism.
I. Title.
 BF1999.R4155 2015
 540.1'12—dc23
                                        2014049773

Llewellyn Worldwide Ltd. does not participate in, endorse, or have any authority or responsibility concerning private business transactions between our authors and the public.
 All mail addressed to the author is forwarded but the publisher cannot, unless specifically instructed by the author, give out an address or phone number.
 Any Internet references contained in this work are current at publication time, but the publisher cannot guarantee that a specific location will continue to be maintained. Please refer to the publisher's website for links to authors' websites and other sources.

Llewellyn Publications
A Division of Llewellyn Worldwide Ltd.
2143 Wooddale Drive
Woodbury, MN 55125-2989
www.llewellyn.com

Printed in the United States of America

Other Books by the Authors

By Israel Regardie, Chic Cicero, and Sandra Tabatha Cicero

A Garden of Pomegranates: Skrying on the Tree of Life

The Middle Pillar: The Balance Between Mind and Magic

The Philosopher's Stone: Spiritual Alchemy, Psychology, and Ritual Magic

The Tree of Life: An Illustrated Study in Magic

By Chic Cicero and Sandra Tabatha Cicero

Creating Magical Tools: The Magician's Craft

The Essential Golden Dawn: An Introduction to High Magic

Experiencing the Kabbalah: A Simple Guide to Spiritual Wholeness

The Golden Dawn Enochian Skrying Tarot: Your Complete System for Divination, Skrying, and Ritual Magick, with Bill and Judi Genaw

The Golden Dawn Journal: Book I—Divination

The Golden Dawn Journal: Book II—Qabalah: Theory and Magic

The Golden Dawn Journal: Book III—The Art of Hermes

The Golden Dawn Magical System: A Complete Tarot Set

Golden Dawn Magical Tarot and Deck

The Magical Pantheons: A Golden Dawn Journal

The New Golden Dawn Ritual Tarot: Keys to the Rituals, Symbols, Magic, and Divination

Ritual Use of Magical Tools: The Magician's Art

Secrets of a Golden Dawn Temple

Self-Initiation into the Golden Dawn Tradition: A Complete Curriculum of Study for Both the Solitary Magician and the Working Magical Group

Tarot Talismans: Invoke the Angels of the Tarot

By Sandra Tabatha Cicero

The Babylonian Tarot

The Book of the Concourse of the Watchtowers

To Donald Michael Kraig

with much love and appreciation
for your work and friendship

Contents

Illustrations

FOREWORD

by Chic Cicero and Sandra Tabatha Cicero

"Francis" Israel Regardie (1907–1985) was the author of several notable books on ceremonial magic. Although he was born in England, he spent most of his life in the United States. As a young man, Regardie studied every text on magic and mysticism that he could get his hands on. In 1932, Regardie was a twenty-five-year-old published author, with two of his most important books in print that year: *A Garden of Pomegranates*, which describes the mystical system known as the Qabalah, and *The Tree of Life*, a comprehensive textbook covering virtually every aspect of magic from the perspective of a practicing magician. This later book is still considered to be Regardie's magnum opus.

Publication of *The Tree of Life* brought Regardie an invitation into the Stella Matutina, the most viable remaining offshoot of the Hermetic Order of the Golden Dawn. He was initiated into the order in January of 1933 and made rapid progress through the grades. However, Regardie was very disappointed with the state of affairs within the group. He left the Stella Matutina at the end of 1934, having concluded that much of the order's teachings would soon be lost due to neglect. Three years later, he published much of the order's teachings in four volumes titled *The Golden Dawn*. This was a game-changing event in the world of ceremonial magic.

In 1938, Regardie published *The Philosopher's Stone*, a work on spiritual alchemy. At the time of its writing, Regardie was convinced that medieval alchemy was a thinly veiled psycho-spiritual process— that the laboratory operations of alchemy said to work on various substances in order to change "lead into gold" were in reality focused solely on man's mind, soul, and spirit.

The manuscript of *Gold* was written sometime between 1938 and 1941, as indicated by the date at the end of the original introduction. The subject of *Gold*, like *The Philosopher's Stone*, is spiritual alchemy. However, *Gold* takes up exactly where the earlier book left off, comparing the Great Work of alchemy to the goals of Eastern mysticism— *samadhi* of yoga and *satori* of Zen Buddhism. It was during this period that Regardie immersed himself in the study of psychology and psychotherapy, a fact that is clearly evident in *Gold*.

We were presented with this unpublished Regardie manuscript by a source who wishes to remain anonymous. The lone copy of this text was damaged, and because of the poor condition of the paper, it was necessary to reconstruct one or two sentences. Such occurrences are very minimal, however, and are clearly indicated in our footnotes.

Israel Regardie is often credited as the person most responsible for removing the veil of secrecy surrounding ceremonial magic and Western occultism. For decades, students have appreciated Regardie's expertise and wisdom. His reader-friendly style of writing is a cherished hallmark of all his works. Therefore, it is with great pleasure that we present *Gold*. We have no doubt that Regardie's fans will come to cherish this little treasure as much as we do.

—Chic Cicero & Sandra Tabatha Cicero
Metatron House
Autumnal Equinox 2013

INTRODUCTION
TO REGARDIE'S TEXT
by Chic Cicero and Sandra Tabatha Cicero

Quintessence, which is a virtue or power that is imperishable, permanent, and perpetually victorious, nay it is a clear
light, which sheds true goodness into every Soul that once
has tasted of it. It is the knot and link of all the Elements,
which it contains in itself, as being also the Spirit which
nourishes all things, and by the assistance whereof Nature
works in the Universe. [...] Know then, my dear Son, that
the ignorant man cannot comprehend the secret of the Art,
because it depends upon the Knowledge of the true Body,
which is hidden from him.

—FROM *THE TRUE BOOK OF THE LEARNED GREEK ABBOT
SYNESIUS* (BY ANONYMOUS)

The history of alchemy is a tale of knowledge discovered, nearly lost,
rediscovered, and reinterpreted. The "Royal Art," the "Hermetic
Art, and "the Philosophy of the Wise" are just a few of the epithets associated with the spiritual science of alchemy, a word composed of the
Arabic words *al* and *khemi*, referring to "the Egyptian matter." Alchemy

traces its roots to Bronze Age Egypt, where the prevailing religious beliefs and practices surrounding mummification led to an elementary understanding of chemistry, which in turn became linked to magic and the concept of eternal life. Beginning in the sixth century BCE, Greek philosophers such as Heracleitus, Pythagoras, Aristotle, and Plato began to incorporate alchemical ideas into their teachings. Over time, Greek thought and Egyptian spirituality merged into Hermeticism and Neo-Platonic philosophy, which spread across the Greek-speaking world. Some of the earliest surviving texts on alchemy, including works by Zosimos of Panoplis, date from the Hellenistic period (roughly 300 BCE–300 CE).

In legend, the founder of alchemy was reputed to be none other than the fabled master Hermes Trismegistus. "Hermes the Thrice Great" was said to be an ancient Egyptian priest and magician credited with writing forty-two books collectively known as the Hermetic literature. These books, including the *Emerald Tablet* and the *Divine Pymander*, describe the creation of the universe, the soul of humanity, and the way to achieve spiritual rebirth.

In the latter stages of the Roman Empire, alchemical principles found their way into works by Plotinus and Proclus. However, by the fourth and fifth centuries, the Church's persecution of all non-Christian religions and pagan academies resulted in scholars fleeing en masse into Persia. An important school founded in the city of Harran during this time was instrumental in preserving all manner of Hellenistic knowledge. After the Muslim conquest of Egypt in the seventh century, the Arabs absorbed the knowledge of the Alexandrian alchemists and carefully preserved many Greek and Arabic texts on the subject. Thus the Islamic world became the caretaker of the alchemical arts and all other ancient sciences, which they brought to Spain in the eighth century. From the ninth to the eleventh century, Spain became a repository of alchemical knowledge; notable Arabic alchemists included Jabir ibn Hayyan (known by the Latinized name "Geber") and Ibn Sina ("Avicenna").

The Crusades, as well as the Christian reclamation of Moorish Spain, brought the knowledge of alchemy back into Europe, and a good number of alchemical texts were translated from Arabic into Latin. Important medieval alchemists who benefited from having access to this information included Albertus Magnus, or "Albert the Great" (1200–1280), the most prolific author of his day and a champion of natural science; Englishman Roger Bacon (1220–1292), a chief advocate of experimental science in the Middle Ages; and Frenchman Nicolas Flamel (1330–1418), who studied astrology and Qabalah in addition to alchemy. Other scholars such as Raymond Lully (1235–1315) and Arnold of Villanova (1235–1311) probed the spiritual side of alchemy.

The Renaissance period was the golden age of European alchemy. It was during this time that Cosimo de' Medici commissioned Marsilio Ficino (1433–1499) to translate the *Corpus Hermeticum*. The works of Hermes Trismegistus were considered so important that Ficino had to put aside translation of the entire works of Plato until after the *Corpus Hermeticum* had been tackled. Another Renaissance figure, Basilius Valentinus (or Basil Valentine), wrote several important treatises including *The Triumphal Chariot of Antimony* (1604) and *The Twelve Keys* (1599). Possibly the greatest alchemist of all was German-Swiss physician Paracelsus (1493–1541), who maintained the Hermetic view that human life was inseparable from the life of the cosmos. Paracelsus is credited with starting what would later become the science of pharmacology.

By the sixteenth and seventeenth centuries, alchemists and philosophers such as John Dee, Robert Fludd, Jean Baptiste van Helmont, and Sir Isaac Newton were regularly studying the practical and mystical aspects of the spagyric art. However, by the eighteenth century the once-revered science was being steadily usurped by its prodigy—interest in alchemy declined as modern chemistry gained popularity and respect. In time, only mystics sought out alchemy's hidden wisdom. To the general public, alchemy became unfairly tarnished as a primitive pseudo-science.

What is alchemy? The "separative art" is an early form of sacred chemistry that explores the nature of various substances. It is a multifaceted natural science–philosophy rooted in a spiritual worldview in which everything in the cosmos contains a universal spirit that is the origin of all matter, which is a living thing. Alchemy teaches that by combining the four basic qualities of living matter (earth, fire, air, and water) in certain ratios, the alchemist can "speed up" the processes of nature, with the goal of perfecting and transforming a substance to its highest possible potential as a universal medicine, the elixir of life, or the Philosopher's Stone. At its core, alchemy is concerned with purification, transformation, and growth. Its objective is to bring all things, especially humanity, to their preordained state of perfection.

Alchemy has always had a dual nature and two lines of approach. Practical alchemy is concerned with transforming a base material into a higher, more purified substance, such as the turning of lead or a lesser metal into gold, or the extraction of a medicinal substance from a plant in order to create a healing elixir. This is the type of alchemy readers traditionally think of when they encounter the term—a laboratory stocked with furnaces, bellows, stills, condensers, and glass beakers.

While many alchemists worked in a lab, the principal interest of many alchemical philosophers was spiritual. These alchemists did not look merely for the substance of gold; they sought to give the quality of gold to their own being, to transmute the base metals—the gross and impure parts of their own nature—into spiritual gold, or divine wisdom.

Spiritual or inner alchemy is concerned with the transformation of the human soul from a state of baseness to one of spiritual enlightenment. In mystical terms, alchemy is symbolic of a conversion from the heavy, leaden, physical, earthbound consciousness to the refined gold of the divinely inspired being. It creates a road map of the internal energies that can affect the purification of body, mind, and soul.

The goal of alchemy is called the *Magnum Opus*, or the "Great Work." This refers to the purification and evolution of something lesser and baser into something greater and more exalted—whether the practitioner is working with metals, vegetable matter, or human consciousness. The process of alchemy is often symbolized by the transformation of lead, the darkest, heaviest, and least valuable of the metals, into pure gold, the most brilliant and valuable of metals.

The classical texts of alchemy are rich in symbolism and allegory. Some of these books contained little more than alchemical prints and illustrations. Others had few illustrations but were filled with cryptic language, enigmatic rhymes, and perplexing metaphors and allegories. The practical reason usually given for this coded language is that the alchemists wished to hide their laboratory techniques from those who would profane the sacred art. However, it was also thought that only those who were spiritually pure could decode the message and unlock the divine secrets of the art. "Alchemy is not merely an art or science to teach metallic transmutation, so much as a true and solid science that teaches how to know the center of all things, which in the divine language is called the Spirit of Life."[1]

Alchemy has gained popularity in recent years through the works of Swiss psychologist Carl G. Jung, who construed alchemy as an age-old method of psychological transformation clothed in the terminology of metalworking. The system developed by Jung, known as analytical psychology, became one of the most common mechanisms for the interpretation of occult phenomena in the twentieth century. The main thrust behind Jungian psychology is that all occult and religious phenomena are psychological in nature and are connected to the relationship between the individual and the realm of the collective unconscious. The primary inhabitants of the collective unconscious are the archetypes—pre-existent ideas or basic categories of human awareness. They are centers of psychological energy that tend to surface in human consciousness through similar forms and images. These images are timeless and universal.

Jung was intrigued by the fate of Austrian psychoanalyst Herbert Silberer, whose magnum opus, *Problems of Mysticism and Its Symbolism* (1917),[2] represented the first serious attempt to correlate the methods of psychoanalysis with the literature of alchemy, Rosicrucianism, and Free-

---

1. Pierre-Jean Fabre, *L'abregé des secrets chymiques* (1636), quoted in Stanislas Klossowski de Rola, *Alchemy: The Secret Art* (New York: Bounty Books, 1973), 8.

2. Dr. Herbert Silberer, *Problems of Mysticism and Its Symbolism* (New York: Moffat, Yard and Company, 1917); republished as *Hidden Symbolism of Alchemy and the Occult Arts* (New York: Dover Publications, 1971).

masonry. Unfortunately, Silberer's work was thoroughly rejected by his mentor Sigmund Freud and he later committed suicide because of it.

Jung was influenced by the work of Silberer and the fact that alchemical symbolism kept appearing in the dreams of patients who had no knowledge of alchemy at all. Jung came to believe that these symbols originated from the collective unconscious of humanity, and that the work of alchemy was a process of individuation, or self-realization toward a fully integrated personality. In 1926, Jung had a remarkable dream in which he saw himself as a seventeenth-century alchemist engaged in the Great Work. This dream led Jung to a revelation that alchemy was a connecting link between the spiritual wisdom of the ancient Gnostics and the modern science of psychology. Jung described his revelation in his autobiography:

> [Alchemy] represented the historical link with Gnosticism, and [...] a continuity therefore existed between past and present. Grounded in the natural philosophy of the Middle Ages, alchemy formed the bridge on the one hand into the past, to Gnosticism, and on the other into the future, to the modern psychology of the unconscious. First I had to find evidence for the historical prefiguration of my own inner experiences. That is to say, I had to ask myself, "Where have my particular premises already occurred in history?" If I had not succeeded in finding such evidence, I would never have been able to substantiate my ideas. Therefore, my encounter with alchemy was decisive for me, [...] Only by discovering alchemy have I clearly understood that the Unconscious is a process and that ego's rapports with the unconscious and his contents initiate an evolution, more precisely a real metamorphoses of the psyche.[3]

Beginning in the 1940s, much of Jung's work focused on the psychological implications of alchemy as revealed in his text *Psychology and Alchemy* (1944). Jung's view became very popular, particularly in the twentieth century, because it provided a way for alchemy to be explored in a manner that did not directly contradict the theorems and

---

3. Carl G. Jung, *Memories, Dreams, Reflections*, edited by Aniela Jaffé, translated by Richard and Clara Winston (New York: Vintage Books, 1963), 192–193, 200.

principles of modern science. As a result, alchemical symbols, metaphors, and concepts have been extensively adopted into a wide variety of psychological and spiritual endeavors in ways that the medieval alchemists could have scarcely imagined. In a series of filmed interviews he gave in 1957, Jung reiterated his basic alchemical theory:

> Of course I cannot tell you in detail about alchemy. It is the basis of our modern way of conceiving things, and therefore it is as if it were right under the threshold of consciousness. It gives you a wonderful picture of how the development of archetypes, the movement of archetypes, looks when you see them as if from above. From today you look back into the past, and you see how the present moment has evolved out of the past. Alchemical philosophy—it sounds very curious. We should give it an entirely different name. It does have a different name, it is called Hermetic philosophy, though of course that conveys just as little as the term alchemy. It is the parallel development, as Gnosticism was, to the conscious development of Christianity, of our Christian philosophy, of the whole psychology of the Middle Ages.[4]

Israel Regardie's education in alchemy began early. In 1926, the same year that Jung dsreamt he was an alchemist, a nineteen year-old Regardie joined the Washington College of the Societas Rosicruciana in America, where he studied many aspects of Hermetic philosophy. By the end of 1929, Regardie was living in London. At this time he was "studying mysticism in all its phases, branches and variations."[5] Having served for a time as Aleister Crowley's secretary in Paris, Regardie became an esoteric author in his own right with the publication of *A Garden of Pomegranates* and *The Tree of Life* in 1932. Publication of the latter opened the way for Regardie's initiation and advancement into various grades of the Stella Matutina. After leaving the order in 1934, Regardie continued to study and write books, including *The Golden*

---

4. Transcripts of these interviews were published in *Conversations with Carl Jung and Reactions from Ernest Jones* by Richard I. Evans (Princeton, NJ: D. Van Nostrand Reinhold Co., 1964).

5. Israel Regardie, *The Eye in the Triangle: An Interpretation of Aleister Crowley* (Las Vegas, NV: Falcon Press, 1989), p. 6.

Dawn (1937), *The Art of True Healing* (1937), and *The Philosopher's Stone* (1938).

The study of the human psyche was also a subject that was close to Regardie's heart. He underwent a lengthy Freudian analysis and studied psychotherapy with Dr. E. Clegg and Dr. Laurence J. Bendit in London. In 1937, Regardie returned to the United States and turned his attention to psychology. He studied with Dr. Nandor Fodor in New York and entered the Columbia Institute of Chiropractic (CIC, today's New York Chiropractic College), graduating in 1941 with a doctorate in psychology. In his application to the CIC, Regardie wrote:

> Since 1931 I have done a good deal of journalism on philosophical and psychological topics, and have written eight books, five of which so far have been published. [...] I had read widely on Psycho-Analysis and Analytical Psychology. In 1935 I began studying it from a practical point of view, and have received about 150 hours of analysis with three leading Harley and Wimpole Street psychologists. I practiced Massage in London for two years under London County Council license. [...] Was trained in hypnotic procedure by the superintendent of an English mental hospital and by a private practitioner. I have used, as a lay practitioner, both the methods of Analytical Psychology and hypnosis ever since.[6]

After graduating, Regardie established a clinical practice and taught anatomy for a time while at CIC before enlisting in the United States Army in 1942. In 1944, he relocated to California and set up practice as a chiropractor and a Reichian therapist. He also taught psychiatry at the Los Angeles College of Chiropractic. During this time he contributed articles to various psychology magazines, including the *American Journal of Psychotherapy* and *Psychiatric Quarterly*.

Regardie's first text on alchemy, *The Philosopher's Stone*, was written over a two-week period in the winter of 1936–37 when he was bedridden in London with a severe bout of bronchitis. To make the best use of this time, he was determined to tackle a lengthy and difficult text on

---

6. Nicholas T. Popadiuk et al., "From the Occult to Chiropractic Psychiatry: Francis Israel Regardie, D.C.," *Chiropractic History* 27, no. 2 (2007): 39.

alchemy, Mary Anne Atwood's *A Suggestive Inquiry into the Hermetic Mystery* (1850), which documented the enormous impact of Hermetic philosophy on human spirituality. The essence of Atwood's hypothesis was that alchemy was actually a method for transforming the human soul through altered states of consciousness, and that all mention of metals, minerals, and alchemical processes were merely symbols and metaphors for spiritual alchemy.

It was during his illness, spent studying Atwood, that Regardie experienced his eureka moment concerning alchemy. He was convinced that alchemy was in reality a thinly veiled psycho-spiritual process, and that all alchemical operations concerning the transmutation of various substances were focused solely on man's mind, soul, and spirit. In other words, "practical" laboratory alchemy was simply wrong-headed, and only theoretical, spiritual, or psychological alchemy was valid. In *The Philosopher's Stone*, Regardie admitted that while a certain number of alchemical texts could be construed as having a literal, "primitively chemical" interpretation, he was adamant that alchemical writings should be "interpreted solely in terms of psychological and mystical terms." At this period in his life, Regardie felt that laboratory alchemy was at best a blind that veiled sublime spiritual truths through symbolism, and at worst a shell game perpetrated by "puffers."

In *The Philosopher's Stone*, Regardie presents three seventeenth-century alchemical treatises—"The Golden Treatise of Hermes," "The Six Keys of Eudoxus," and "Coelum Terrae"—documents infused with riddles and emblematic language used to communicate to fellow alchemists in secret. In the intervening chapters, Regardie skillfully pulls the psychological import from the symbols and metaphors of these three cryptic texts, drawing upon his own inspiration as well as knowledge gained though the writings of Silberer, Jung, and others. His approach was to analyze these seventeenth-century texts emblematically, using the symbol systems of magic, Qabalah, and Jungian psychology to explain how the laboratory operations of alchemy were really psychoanalytical methods for self-realization and spiritual attainment.

Gold, written between 1938 and 1941, is a direct follow-up to *The Philosopher's Stone*, containing many of the same assertions about alchemy. In the present book, which might well be called called "Volume Two" of *The Philosopher's Stone*, Regardie continues to shed light on the psycho-spiritual meaning behind the cryptograms of the spagyric art. This time, only one alchemical treatise is presented for dissection and analysis, *The True Book of the Learned Synesius, a Greek Abbot, Taken Out of the Emperour's Library, Concerning the Philosopher's Stone*, written by an anonymous alchemist who could not have been Synesius of Cyrene, bishop of Ptolemais. As in his previous book, Regardie discusses this treatise in the language of Jungian psycho-analysis, magnetism, and hypnosis. But here the discussion is more specific, with Regardie citing his own experiences as a therapist, as well as some examples from pioneers in hypnosis and the study of the human aura. He also explores the similarities between alchemy, Taoist philosophy, yoga, and Zen Buddhism.

Approximately thirty years after writing *The Philosopher's Stone* and *Gold*, Regardie completely reversed his thinking about laboratory alchemy. This change of heart was a result of his having attended a seminar by Albert Riedel, acclaimed founder of the Paracelsus Research Society in Salt Lake City, Utah, which offered instructional courses in practical alchemy. The work of Frater Albertus, as Riedel was known, was instrumental in reviving the laboratory practice of alchemy in the latter half of the twentieth century. In his introduction to the second edition of *The Philosopher's Stone*, Regardie describes his meeting with Albertus and his next eureka moment concerning alchemy:

> It took only a few minutes to realize that I was talking to the first person I had ever met who knew what he was talking about on the subject of Alchemy. We promised to keep in touch—and we did.
>
> This promise later eventuated in an invitation to attend a seminar on Alchemy that he was conducting at the newly instituted Paracelsus Research Society in Salt Lake City. Most of the material presented in the Seminar concerned Alchemy, Qabalah, Astrology, etc.—with which I was already theoretically familiar—though even there some radically new and stimulating viewpoints were

obtained. But the piece-de-resistance was the laboratory work. Here I was wholly dumbfounded.

It took no more than a few minutes to help me realize how presumptuous I had been to assert dogmatically that all Alchemy was psycho-spiritual. What I witnessed there, and have since repeated, has sufficed to enable me to state categorically that, in insisting solely on a mystical interpretation of Alchemy, I had done a grave disservice to the ancient sages and philosophers.[7]

Admitting that he had to eat crow with regard to his previously held beliefs, Regardie was happy to do so, although he decided against rewriting his earlier texts on alchemy. Nevertheless, he still felt that a mystical and psychological interpretation of some alchemical texts was legitimate. "There is unequivocally this aspect of the subject." Some alchemical texts "cannot be interpreted except in these terms."[8] Therefore, he let his original texts on spiritual alchemy stand as they had been written and suggested that students supplement their readings with alchemical texts "of more recent vintage."

This continues to be good advice. Today there are several good books on practical alchemy, which is undeniably an important part of the hermetic art. Should students be inclined to learn more about the laboratory methods of alchemical work, they should consult *The Alchemist's Handbook* by Frater Albertus, *The Practical Handbook of Plant Alchemy* by Manfred Junius, *The Path of Alchemy* by Mark Stavish, and *Real Alchemy* and *The Way of the Crucible* by Robert Allen Bartlett. Additionally, articles by practicing alchemists are included in the second half of the latest edition of Regardie's *The Philosopher's Stone: Spiritual Alchemy, Psychology, and Ritual Magic*.

Why has *Gold* not been published until now? The manuscript has been held in the hands of a friend of Regardie for several years. By the time Regardie wrote the second introduction to his classic text *The Golden Dawn* in 1968, his interaction with the Paracelsus Research Society caused him to drastically rethink his belief that practical labo-

---

7. Israel Regardie, *The Philosopher's Stone: Spiritual Alchemy, Psychology, and Ritual Magic* (Woodbury, MN: Llewellyn Publications, 2013), 17–18.

8. Ibid.

ratory alchemy was specious. He was absolutely stunned at the revelation that alchemy was a bona fide physical science and not merely a metaphoric structure for mysticism. Since Regardie no longer agreed with his previous approach to the subject of alchemy, he no longer wished to see *Gold* published. Thus the manuscript remained locked away in a drawer for decades.

However, with the passage of time, the owner of the document realized the inherent value of Regardie's original thoughts, and while the psycho-spiritual approach to alchemy was certainly not the only way to tackle the spagyric art, the alchemical information as well as the Jungian approach presented in *Gold* was still valid, vital, lucid, and practical. Rather than let this important book continue to crumble away into dust, the owner decided to let it be published and made available to interested readers, students of alchemy, and admirers of Regardie's writings. So when we were contacted by the document's steward, we were thrilled and honored to be able to serve the esoteric community by saving this significant text.

The subject of *Gold* is spiritual alchemy, an important topic in its own right. Although Regardie was wrong in his initial assessment of laboratory alchemy, he was right to lavish high praise on inner alchemy.

A spiritual alchemist is the subject of his own alchemical experiments; he analyzes, identifies, or separates the various parts of his own psychic makeup. Nothing can remain repressed or shoved into the cellar of the subconscious mind. No portion of the psyche can remain buried. The tools and substances described in alchemy represent the various states of consciousness and the methods for achieving them. The alchemical metals of lead, iron, copper, tin, mercury, silver, and gold, as well as other substances enshrined in alchemical literature, are emblems of the numerous life experiences the soul must endure in order to build a worthy spiritual body—a sturdy vehicle for the Divine Light. The internal quest for the Stone of the Wise brings us to the crossroads of science and religion—to the junction between the mind and the soul. And it is here that we find the connection that exists between ancient magic and modern-day psychology.

Franz Hartmann put it this way:

Alchemy is that science which results from a knowledge of God, Nature, and Man. A perfect knowledge of either of them cannot be obtained without the knowledge of the other two, for these three are one and inseparable. Alchemy is not merely an intellectual, but a spiritual science; because that which belongs to the spirit can only be spiritually known. Nevertheless, it is a science dealing with material things, for spirit and matter are only two opposite manifestations or "poles" of the eternal one. Alchemy is an art, and as every art requires an artist to exercise it, likewise this divine science and art can be practiced only by those who are in possession of the divine power necessary for that purpose. It is true that the external manipulations required for the production of certain alchemical preparations may, like an ordinary chemical process, be taught to anybody capable of reasoning; but the results which he would accomplish would be without life, for only he in whom the true life has awakened can awaken it from its sleep in the prima materia, and cause visible forms to grow from the Chaos of nature. Alchemy in its highest aspects deals with the spiritual regeneration of man.[9]

Changes Made to Regardie's Text

As we pointed out in the foreword, the only surviving copy of *Gold* was in poor condition, and as a result one sentence had to be reconstructed as indicated in the relevant footnote.

Gold, like Regardie's other early works, featured Qabalistic words written with an Ashkenazic dialect. This is a form of Hebrew pronunciation used in central Europe wherein the Hebrew letter *tau,* or *tav,* is sometimes pronounced as an "s" rather than a "t" or "th." Although Ashkenazic may have been the Hebrew pronunciation that Regardie grew up with, and was probably the dialect spoken by his Hebrew tutor in the early 1920s, it was not the dialect preferred by the Hermetic Order of the Golden Dawn and its offshoots, all of which employed the more common Sephardic, or Mediterranean dialect. The Sephardic version is used almost exclusively by Western magicians today. With this in mind, we have changed *Sephiros* to *Sephiroth, Keser* to *Kether, Daas*

---

9. Franz Hartmann, *In the Pronaos of the Temple of Wisdom* (Kila, MT: Kessinger Publishing, n.d.), 85. Originally published in 1890.

to *Daath, Tiphares* to *Tiphareth, Malkus* to *Malkuth,* and so on, to reflect the modern usage. In his later years, Regardie also turned to Sephardic spellings and pronunciations, so we are confident that he would have approved of these changes to his text.

Explanatory titles have been added to the various chapters that Regardie had originally listed as numbered "commentaries." Because of this change, readers will have a better preview of what is contained within the chapters. Additionally, all British spellings have been changed to American, which, in the original manuscript, were not consistently one way or the other.

Readers should note that Regardie's use of the term "man" or "men" to represent humanity as a whole was common for the time period in which *Gold* was written and was not intended to be sexist or to refer only to males. It was conventional for authors of Regardie's era to use these terms to reference all humankind, regardless of gender.

The following is a description of the various chapters and sections of *Gold.*

Regardie's Introduction examines claims and theories around the authorship of *The True Book of the Learned Greek Abbot Synesius,* as well as the social and spiritual environment in which the book was written.

Following the Introduction, *The True Book of the Learned Synesius, a Greek Abbot, Taken Out of the Emperour's Library, Concerning the Philosopher's Stone* is given in its entirety.

Chapter One: Alchemy and Psychology continues the discussion that Regardie started in his book *The Philosopher's Stone* concerning what he believed to be the true nature of alchemy and its relation to spirituality, philosophy, and psychology. To be concise, Regardie thought that descriptions of chemical operations in alchemy constituted a smoke screen designed to conceal the real subject of the Royal Art: the human mind: "Since the advent of modern psychological knowledge," he writes, "we have been given a key to the understanding of myths, epics, legends and dreams of every kind … It is to this branch of scientific research that we must first turn in seeking an elucidation of the enigmas and obscurities of the alchemical works."

Chapter Two: The Universal Agent, Polarity, and the Collective Unconscious examines the animating principle of the universe known by many names: Spirit, Mercury of the Wise, *anima mundi*, First Matter, Quintessence, etc. This Agent is divided into the two great universal polarities of masculine and feminine within the processes of alchemy, just as it is within the human psyche.

Chapter Three: The Mystical Experience explores the one thing that lies "at the foundation of every great religion" and is shared by mystics the world over, regardless of which faith they ascribe to: enlightenment, illumination, or union with God. Visualization, devotional exercises, and prayer are cited as some of the techniques whereby the mystic can achieve this state of mind, with particular emphasis on the experience of *satori* in Zen Buddhism.

Chapter Four: The Great Work investigates the various processes that the alchemist must undergo in order to complete the Great Work of integration. Awareness of this Living Mercury must be "widened, enhanced and heightened." This is neither an easy nor a quick process.

Chapter Five: The Secret Fire examines how alchemical change is accomplished in the human psyche, mainly through harnessing and directing the spiritual forces of the libido, "the power and active side of the psyche, the energy which must be released from the primordial deeps." Through conscious effort, training, and voluntary disintegration, the mind's root essence is laid bare and the "libido or vital stress normally resident in the Unconscious is activated, welling up to the surface to heat or stir up the contents of the mind."

Chapter Six: Magnetism, Visualization, and Healing looks at the manipulation of vital life force using mesmerism, hypnotism, relaxation, and the concerted use of the imagination and will.

Chapter Seven: Alchemical Symbolism and the Aura explores the rich symbology that fills the pages of alchemical treatises such as *The True Book of Synesius*. Implications of alchemical color symbolism and the color attributions of the planets are examined with special regard to how these symbols can be used to effect change within the human aura.

Chapter Eight: In Conclusion summarizes Regardie's analysis of all the preceding chapters in plain language, stripped of its alchemical symbolism and metaphor.

The sections that follow contain elements that we have added to supplement Regardie's text of *Gold*, beginning with *Appendix I: The Art of True Healing*. In chapter six, Regardie mentions a meditative method that he had developed for the control and transmission of vital life force—a therapeutic technique that could be utilized for healing oneself as well as others. Regardie published this in 1937 in a little book called *The Art of True Healing: A Treatise on the Mechanism of Prayer, and the Operation of the Law of Attraction in Nature.*[10] This text provides a practical application of the principles discussed in *Gold*, particularly with regard to the conscious manipulation of the Secret Fire in spiritual alchemy. Therefore, it seemed appropriate to add this paper as an appendix to the present book. The version of *The Art of True Healing* provided here is taken straight from the author's personal copy, signed "I Regardie, advance copy, April 1st, 1937. 11 am," complete with Regardie's own corrections penciled in the margins. It is also much shorter than later versions of this paper. Nevertheless, Regardie's ingenuity shines through even in this early version.

The Art of True Healing provides readers with a healing ritual based on the Middle Pillar exercise, a Golden Dawn method for charging energy centers within the aura. Regardie, more than any other individual, saw the vast potential of the Middle Pillar exercise that was given, albeit in an incomplete form, in the papers of the Stella Matutina. He realized that this simple ritual could be adapted for a variety of exercises with different levels of complexity and purpose, and consequently provided an outline of his therapeutic technique in *The Art of True Healing*. It is through rituals and exercises like this that students can accomplish the internal work of spiritual alchemy.

---

10. Israel Regardie, *The Art of True Healing: A Treatise on the Mechanism of Prayer, and the Operation of the Law of Attraction in Nature* (London: Leaf Studio, 1937).

In *Appendix II: Correspondences for Healing Rituals*, we provide lists of Qabalistic, elemental, planetary, and zodiacal attributions that can be employed by readers who wish to use Regardie's ritual technique from appendix I. A basic Middle Pillar exercise and sample healing ritual is given. This can easily be adapted for many different therapeutic purposes.

The latter portion of this book contains a glossary, bibliography, and index.

Contemplation of alchemical symbolism—conscious as well as subconscious—is meant to captivate and inspire the student on many levels. This emblematic language speaks directly to the human soul on the true nature of the alchemist's "gold." However, eternal wisdom remains dormant in humanity so long as a mundane state of ignorance and superficiality exists. Inner alchemy is the uncovering of this interior wisdom and the removal of obstacles between the human mind and its intrinsically pure divine source. Throughout his lifetime, Israel Regardie did much to remove blinds and obstacles to students' understanding of important spiritual truths. His work in *Gold* helps to further this objective in no small way.

Gold is an important addition to the collective corpus of the alchemical arts. This is because the science of alchemy cannot be adequately understood if the reader approaches it from one perspective only. It is no simple thing, but rather a coherent, holistic system, similar to Qabalah or astrology. The student of Qabalah cannot hope to grasp the magnitude of that mystical tradition by studying the Hebrew alphabet *without* internalizing the Sephiroth of the Tree of Life. Similarly, one cannot understand astrology by mechanically delineating a zodiacal chart without understanding the philosophical ideas that help to explain the spiritual milestones of human life. The same is true of alchemy. To understand alchemy correctly, the practitioner cannot *just* do laboratory work or *only* perform the exercises of spiritual alchemy— the true alchemist must do both. This is why alchemy stands beside Qabalah and astrology as one of the foundational pillars of Hermetic philosophy.

The laboratory approach can no longer be ignored by the knowledgeable reader, and so the works of modern alchemists such as Frater Albertus, Mark Stavish, and Robert Allen Bartlett must be consulted if one is to have any hope of attaining a full comprehension of the matter. However, Mary Anne Atwood's *A Suggestive Inquiry into the Hermetic Mystery* and Herbert Silberer's *Problems of Mysticism and Its Symbolism* should also be consulted, because they provided crucial early links in the study of dream and myth interpretation of alchemical symbolism. Works such as these foreshadowed Carl Jung's breakthrough psychological viewpoint as set forth in his work *Psychology and Alchemy*. And it was Atwood's text, along with the Jungian approach, that inspired Israel Regardie to pen first *The Philosopher's Stone* and then *Gold*.

Regardie's experience as a practicing Golden Dawn magician and psychotherapist provided him with a unique perspective on the symbolism and language of the spagyric art. *Gold* provides readers first and foremost with a *magical interpretation* of alchemy—a perspective that is based on Regardie's study of Qabalah and magical imagery; the powers of the human mind and psychic vitality; visualization and prayer; color and planetary magic; yoga and zen; magnetism and the manipulation of the vital life force; the focused use of human willpower and imagination; and the mystical goal of the Great Work of alchemy—often referred to as enlightenment, illumination, or union with God.

It would indeed be difficult to have a complete and thorough understanding of alchemy without exploring Regardie's unparalleled insights as set forth in *Gold*.

The history of literature abounds with tales of forgotten writings —texts lost to the ages through fateful mistakes, deliberate destruction, or simple carelessness. Israel Regardie's writings played a central role in shaping modern ceremonial magic and establishing the connections between magic, alchemy, and psychology. Therefore, it is a privilege for us to be able to help save this previously unpublished work by Regardie from becoming just another missing manuscript. Admirers of "Francis" will no doubt agree.

—Chic Cicero & Sandra Tabatha Cicero
Metatron House
Autumnal Equinox, 2013

GOLD

BY ISRAEL REGARDIE

Hermes Trismegistus and the Book of Knowledge

INTRODUCTION

Synesius, the author of this text, was born during the fourth century A.D., at Cyrene, a Greek-colony in Africa. His environment was the lurid world of Gnosticism and Neo-Platonism. Various forms of mystical thought, some outrageous in the fantastic proportions they reached, were openly flourishing in the intellectual center of the Western world of that day, Alexandria. It was about 311 B.C. that there Alexander the Great had founded his colony. Almost immediately the little community had established a Ptolemaic school of philosophy where the prevailing ideas, modified by later influences, were essentially Platonic and Aristotelian.

From her founding, the city had been the heir and protector of a stern philosophy. Gradually she had become rich and commercial, very worldly and very attractive. Because of her wisely chosen situation on the coast and because of the canal system by which the produce of Upper Egypt found an outlet to the sea, the city became very significant and important. That is, she developed into the one port through which flowed the riches of the Mediterranean cities, of India, and of the fertile granary of the Nile Valley. Each consignment contributed its toll in commissions and duties to her merchant princes and to the city government. In consequence, wealth had so accumulated there that, within one or two hundred years after the date of her foundation, there had arisen already many famous buildings, including the celebrated library.

She was a cosmopolitan city. We would have found there many racial divisions, with many and diverse interests. A large native population crowded certain districts—a native population which still held to the world of the ancient Egyptian gods and beliefs. In the northeast, another section was set off as the Jewish quarter, where we would have seen a motley crowd of Hebrew traders and merchants and scholars. An unyielding Jehovistic faith struggled with an advancing world for right of continuance. From the date of the martyrdom of St. Mark, the Christian infiltration had been making gradually increasing progress both from the numerical and social points of view. Greeks, Jews, Egyptians and the Christians—each perhaps differing from the other in many ways, with nevertheless an agreement in one particular at least. They agreed on the religious particular of the existence of God. Though here, even in this single agreement, were several important theological differences based on racial temperament and varying psychological needs.

The craze of the time, possibly a deep and urgent psychological necessity in view of the insecure nature of social and political life, comparable in many ways to the present day, was a syncretism. The Pauline attempt of some three hundred years earlier to wed Greek thought to Jewish Messianism by means of an intellectual or spiritual vision is a particular instance of that tendency. Everywhere, and on every hand, people were extravagantly undertaking synthetical combinations of all the existent religions, cults, and philosophies. It was a mad confused world this, just prior to the victory of Church authority over independent inspiration and religious experience in anticipation of the complete extinction of intellectual effort and spiritual initiative in the Dark Ages.

Synesius was educated in all that characterized Neo-Platonism. It is evident that some of his writings, the essay *De Insomniis*, for example, were profoundly influenced by Plotinus, Later, however, he evolved to the viewpoint that his personal pagan philosophy was not necessarily incompatible with Christianity. He was a man of great determination and many talents with a robust common sense. Synesius was not in reality a mystic, even although a strain of mysticism peers out here and there from his writing. Historically he appears to us rather as of a very positive extraverted character. The role of philosopher was one which, perhaps in moments of over-ambition and aspiration, he had imposed upon himself, guided more by personal predilection than by inherent capacity. It is difficult to imagine that it was one assigned to him by nature. Such a role, it is evident to us now, rested upon a very fragile and shallow foundation. As a bishop, he was militant, and a deep patriot. But he was neither a profound nor an original thinker, as is evidenced by his essays and letters. The volume *The Essays and Hymns of Synesius*, edited and introduced by A. Fitzgerald and published by the Oxford University Press, is ample proof of this assumption. He was, in fact, something of a dilettante, a man moderately well-versed in the culture of his age. The charm of his writing rests in the intimate contact and sympathy that his writings establish with the reader, rather than in any spontaneity or originality of thought or expression.

I have written thus far about Synesius and his *milieu* to convey some slight picture of the bishop of Ptolemais who is supposed to have been the author of this text. Quite apart from the intrinsic evidence of the writing which I propose to examine soon, it is more or less obvious that Synesius of Cyrene, a Christian abbot during the fourth century, could not have been its author. The nature of his very few extant writings as evidenced by the volumes I have cited above, depict him as of another nature than a writer on alchemy. Scholarship maintains that whilst he occasionally wrote in a mystical vein he himself was no mystic. And this is not difficult to understand. A more or less educated man of today would unwittingly express himself, should he essay expression in writing, in the scientific and conventional clichés of our time. This would not necessarily indicate that this person was a scientist—a logical empiricist. In such of his literary output as we possess, we clearly may detect the strains of Platonism and Neo-Platonism in addition to the pre-dominant Christian feeling. He was simply expressing himself in the ideology and intellectual clichés of his age. But that is to say quite another thing than that such a man could have been capable of writing alchemical obscurities.

Yet at the same time, another viewpoint is most certainly not impossible. I do not wish to be a partisan. A critic, above all, must be impartial, weighing such evidence, large or otherwise, as makes its way into his ken. We know that the jargon of alchemy is one that has persisted more or less in the same basic form throughout the centuries. Greek alchemy displays fairly much the same characteristics as later European alchemy. Chinese texts, *au fond*, are very similar to those of Byzantium and of India, of Persia and Arabia. It is not at all impossible that in Alexandria at Synesius' day were alchemists and alchemical writers. It is not even impossible, though this we do not definitely know, that he himself had met them and had been influenced by them. In fact, it is highly probable that he did. But speculation will tell us nothing of this, and I must not force the issue. It simply makes it very difficult to determine the author of the text, if such determination is considered important.

The entire evidence presented makes me feel dubious in accepting Synesius as the author of *The True Book*. Actually, the message conveyed by the title itself—that it is the *true* book of the abbot, having been taken or stolen out of the Emperor's library—by the mere fact of its insistence arouses suspicion that all is not well. The emphasis, it seems to me on psychological grounds, is slightly overdone. It is as though a psychotic with marked paranoic symptoms were to walk into a psychiatric consulting room and say, without prompting or justification, "Oh no; I was not really being followed here. I don't actually believe I am being spied upon." Suspicion would immediately be aroused by such spontaneous and uninvited denial. You would wonder why it was necessary to give assurance in advance of the absence of paranoic symptomatology. Likewise here. The title alone would have been enough—sufficiently interesting or convincing by itself—without having had to add that it had been taken from the Emperor's library.

There are, furthermore, several references to alchemical authorities of a much later age. A former colleague of mine, a scholar with a profound and unrivalled knowledge of alchemical literature and history, does not believe however that such references necessarily prove the spurious nature of the text. It is his contention that these alchemi-cal manuscripts may have been privately distributed and circulated for generations. It may well have been that some over-zealous owner of the text in, let us say, the fourteenth century, interpolated quota-tions from alchemical writings of his day in order to buttress up his own belief in the art. In so doing, he failed to recognize that he had almost completely ruined an authentic text of an earlier age.

Be that as it may, the treatise mentions Geber twice, and Alphidius once. The date of Geber, the Arabian prince alchemist, is difficult to place. It ranges anywhere from the sixth to the tenth century. We may therefore hazard a safe guess in the assumption that he lived about the eighth century. Alphidius dates considerably later. If we except the theory that there may have been an original Greek manuscript writ-ten by the abbot Synesius in which several centuries afterwards inter-polations were inserted—and this of course may never be proved—then we are obliged to consider *The True Book of the Learned Synesius* as having an origin at the earliest in the thirteenth century, or it may be a little later. Some may feel inclined to posit the theory that Syn-esius was gifted with prevision.

Who the author of this text was, we do not really know. His mod-esty in bestowing the fruits of his pen and the cloak of his erudition on a Neo-Platonic abbot defeats us in our search into origins. But whoever he was, he must have felt that the system he was attempting to delineate had certain points of contact with that espoused by Syn-esius. Otherwise, why should he have taken the trouble to mention Synesius by name? Why not Plotinus or Iamblichus—or anyone of the host of celebrities who, so far as the authority of mere name values is concerned, might have answered to his purpose equally? Possibly his name was chosen to render the work more acceptable to those of the Christian faith. Nevertheless, when attempting to widen our under-standing of this treatise, we must remember this allusion to the doc-trines of Neo-Platonism, where we are confronted with fundamental religious doctrines.

So far as the actual text and its bibliography is concerned, there is little to say. In the year 1678, the first English edition was published in

London, as may be seen by the imprint on the title page reproduced herein. (See illustration on page 30.) *The True Book of Synesius*, in that edition, was inconspicuously tucked away at the back of a much larger and better known alchemical treatise by Basil Valentine, *The Triumphal Chariot of Antimony* with annotations by Theodore Kirkringius, M.D. Prior to this, the most easily accessible copy of the text was a Latin version, one edition of which was published from Amsterdam in 1671. The French edition appeared in Paris in the year 1612, in a volume entitled *Traites de la Philosophie, etc.*

Whether or not there was a Greek original from which the Latin and French editions were rendered is open to question. There is so little trustworthy evidence of any kind that one hesitates to express any opinion. For sooner or later, some of the larger libraries in Europe, in which ancient manuscripts have resided for long centuries without being pored over and disturbed by inquisitive minds and roaming hands, may be opened to research and investigation, if they are not previously destroyed by vandals. Possibly then some sort of original text may come to light. Meanwhile I am inclined to doubt that there is an original Greek text, for the style and tenor betray quite a late period of expression.

So far as I personally am concerned, however, it does not matter a rap who really wrote the book. This matter may be left to scholars of the future to decide. Why should we be bothered about abstract problems of this type? What I am interested in, however, is a purely practical consideration. That is to say, is there anything in this text which is of any importance to us? I claim there is.

I may as well take my stand here at the outset, and express my fundamental platform. It is my contention that alchemical writing is of a peculiar type. It belongs to that vast realm of expression which has a close kinship with mythology, religion, poetry and dream. In a word, it is material that has issued from the hidden depths of man's unconscious psyche. Not only so, but I believe that we can learn a very great deal from it. The alchemists have much to give us. If we are humble and receptive, there is much that we may obtain—information by way of a psychological technique of psychic integration and illumination that make our modern therapeutic systems look like the dabblings of triflers and dilettante. So serious am I in this belief, and so convinced am I from prolonged investigation of this branch of knowledge and its application above all to my own psychological practice, that I propose to examine this text of Synesius in terms of the general principles underlying its assumptions. Whether Synesius wrote it or not is unimportant. What Synesius or the real author has said, that for me is significant. It is this inner kernel of value that I have always sought irrespective of where it was that the search has led me. And here in *The True Book* there are discoveries to be made. I should like to share the book with other minds of equal eagerness and intentness and open earnest heart.

—ISRAEL REGARDIE
New York
August, 1941

BASIL VALENTINE

HIS

Triumphant Chariot

OF

ANTIMONY,

WITH

ANNOTATIONS

OF

Theodore Kirkringius. M. D.

WITH

The True Book of the Learned *Synefius* a
Greek Abbot taken out of the Emperour's
Library, concerning the Philofopher's
Stone.

LONDON.
Printed for *Dorman Newman* at the Kings Arms
in the *Poultry.* 1 6 7 8.

Title Page of Basil Valentine's The Triumphal Chariot of Antimony

THE TRUE BOOK OF THE LEARNED GREEK ABBOT

SYNESIUS

TAKEN OUT OF THE EMPEROR'S LIBRARY

Though the Ancient Philosophers have written diversely of this science, concealing under a multitude of names the true principles of the Art; yet have they not done it but upon important considerations as we shall hereafter make appear. And though they are different in their expressions, yet are they not any way discordant one from another, but aiming all at one end, and speaking of the same thing, they have thought fit (above all the rest) to name the *proper Agent*, by a term, strange, nay sometimes contrary to its nature and qualities.

Know then, my Son, that almighty God together with this Universe, created two *Stones*, that is to say, the *White* and the *Red*, both which are under one and the same subject, and afterwards multiplied in such abundance, that everyone may take as much as he please thereof. The matter of them is of such a kind, that it seems to be a mean between *Metal* and *Mercury*; and this matter is the instrument whereby our desire is accomplished, if we do but prepare it. Hence it comes that those who bestow their endeavors in this Art without the said *medium*, lose their labor, but if they are acquainted with the *Medium*, they shall find all things feasible and fortunate. Know then that this Medium, being aerial, is found among the celestial Bodies, and that it is only there are found the Masculine and Feminine Gender (to speak properly) having a constant, strong, fixed and permanent Virtue, of the essence whereof (as I have told thee) Philosophers have expressed themselves only by Similitudes and Figures. This they did, that the science might not be discovered by the Ignorant, which if it should once happen, all were lost: but that it might be comprehended only by those patient souls, and subtilized understandings, which being sequestered from the soyliness of this world, are cleansed from the filth of that terrene dunghill of Avarice, whereby the ignorant are chained to the earthiness of this World, which is (without this admirable quintessence) the receptacle of poverty; it being certain, that those divine souls, when they have div'd into Democritus's Fountain, that is to say, into the truth of Nature, would soon discover what confusion might happen in all estates and conditions, if everyone could make as much Gold as he would himself. Upon this ground was it that they were pleased to speak by figures, types, and analogies, that so they might not be understood but by such as are discreet, religious, and enlightened by (divine) Wisdom. All which, notwithstanding, they have left in their writings a certain method, way and rule, by the assistance whereof the wise man may comprehend whatever they have written most obscurely, and in time arrive at the knowledge of it, though haply wading through some error, as I have done, praised be God for it. And whereas the Vulgar ignorant person ought to submit to these reasons, and consequently adore, what is too great, to enter into his Brain, he on the contrary accuses the Philosophers of imposture and impiety, by which means, and the scarcity of wise men, the Art falls into contempt.

But for my part, I tell thee, they have always expressed themselves according to certain Truth, though very obscurely, and sometimes fabulously, all which I have discipher'd in this little Treatise, and after such a manner that the earnest desirer of Science shall understand what hath been mystically delivered by the Philosophers. And yet if he pretend to understand me and know not the nature of the Elements and things created, as also our rich Metal, he doth but lose his Labor: but if he understand the Concord and Discord of Natures, he will by God's assistance arrive to the rest. It is therefore my suit to God, that he who shall understand the present Secret may work to the glory and praise of the sacred Divinity.

Know then, my dear Son, that the ignorant man cannot comprehend the secret of the Art, because it depends upon the Knowledge of the true Body, which is hidden from him. Know then, my Son, *pure* and *impure*, the *clean* and *unclean* Natures, for there cannot come from any thing that which it hath not. For things, that are not or have not, cannot give but their own Nature: make use then of that which is most perfect and nearest in kind, thou shalt meet with, and it shall suffice. Avoid then that which is *mixt*, and take the *simple*, for that proceeds from the Quintessence. Note that we have two bodies of very great perfection, full of *Mercury:* Out of these extract thy Mercury, and of that thou shalt make the *Medicine*, called by some *Quintessence*, which is a Vertue or Power that is imperishable, permanent, and perpetually victorious, nay it is a clear Light, which sheds true goodness into every Soul that hath once tasted of it. It is the knot and link of all the Elements, which it contains in itself, as being also the Spirit which nourisheth all things, and by the assistance whereof Nature works in the Universe. It is the force, the beginning and end of the whole work, and to lay all open to thee in a word, know that the *Quintessence* and the hidden things of our Stone is nothing else than our viscous, celestial and glorious Soul drawn by our Magistery out of its Mine, which engenders itself, and that it is not possible for us to make that water by Art, but Nature alone begets it, and that water is the most sharp Vinegar, which makes Gold to be a pure spirit, nay it is that *blessed Nature* which engenders all things, which through its putrefaction is become a Triunity, and by reason of its Viridity causes an appearance of diverse colors. And I advise thee, my Son, make no account of any other things (as being vain), labor only for that *water* which *turns to blackness, whitens, dissolves* and *congeals.* It is that which putrifies, and causes germination, and therefore I advise thee, that thou wholly employ thyself in the decoction of this water, and quarrel not at the expense of time, otherwise thou shalt have no advantage. Decoct it gently by little and little, until it have changed its false color into a perfect, and have a great care at the beginning that thou burn not its Flowers and its vivacity, and make not too much haste to come to an end of thy work. Shut thy Vessel well, that what is within may not breathe out, and so thou mayst bring it to some effect. And note that to *dissolve*, to *calcine*, to *tinge*, to *whiten*, to *renew*, to *bathe*, to *wash*, to *coagulate*, to *imbibe*, to *decoct*, to *fix*, to *grind*, to *dry*, and to *distill*, are all one, and signify no more than to *concoct* Nature, until such time as it be perfect. Note further that to extract the soul, or the spirit, or the body, is nothing else than the above said Calcinations, in regard they signify the operation of *Venus*. It is therefore through the fire of the extraction of the soul that the spirit comes forth gently, understand me. The same may also be said of the extraction of the soul out of the Body, and the reduction of it afterwards upon the same Body, until the whole be drawn to a commixtion of all the four Elements. And so that which is below, is like that which is above, and consequently there are made therein two luminaries, the one fixt the other not, whereof the fix'd remains below, and the volatile above, moving itself perpetually, until that which is below, which is the male, get upon the female, and all be fixed, and then issues out an incomparable Luminary. And as in the beginning, there was only one, so in this Matter, all proceeds from one and returns to one, which is called a conversion of the Elements, and to convert the Elements, is as much as to make the humid dry, and the volatile fixed, that so that which is thick may be made thin, and weaken the thing that fixeth the rest, the fixative part of the thing remaining entire. Thus happens the life and death of the Elements, which compose, germinate and produce, and so one thing perfects another and assists it to oppose the Fire.

The Practice

My Son it is necessary that thou work with the *Mercury of the Philosophers* and the wise, which is not the *Vulgar*, nor hath anything of the *Vulgar*, but, according to them, is the *first Matter*, the *Soul of the World*, the *cold Element*, the *blessed Water*, the *Water of the Wise*, the *Venemous Water*, the *most sharp Vinegar*, the *Mineral Water*, the *Water of celestial grace*, the *Virgin Milk*, *our Mineral and corporeal Mercury*. For this alone perfects both the stones, the White and the Red. Consider what Geber sayes, that our Art consists not in the multitude of several things, because the *Mercury* is but one only thing, that is to say, one only Stone wherein consists the whole Magistery; to which thou shalt not add any strange thing, save that in the preparation thereof thou shalt take away from it whatsoever is superfluous, by reason that in this matter, all things requisite to this Art are contained. And therefore it is very observable that he saies, we must add nothing that is strange, save the Sun and Moon for the red and white Tincture, which are not strange (to it) but are its Ferment, by which the work is accomplished. Lastly, mark my Son, that these Suns and Moons are not the same with the Vulgar Gold and Silver, for that our Suns and Moons are better in their nature than the Vulgar Suns and Moons. For our Suns and Moons are in their nature living, and those of the Vulgar are dead in comparison of ours, which are existent and permanent in our Stone. Whence thou mayest observe that the Mercury drawn out of our Bodies, is like the aqueous and common Mercury, and for that reason enjoys itself and takes pleasure in its like, and is more glad of its company, as it happens in the simple and compound, which thing hath not been discovered by the Philosophers in their Books. And the advantage therefore which is in this Art, lies in the Mercury, Sun and Moon. *Diomedes* saith, make use of such a matter as to which thou must not introduce any strange thing, neither pouder nor water, for that several things do not improve our Stone, and thereby he sufficiently instructs him, who understands him, that the tincture of our Stone is not drawn from any thing but the Mercury of the Philosophers, which is their principle, their root, and their great Tree, sprouting forth into boughs and branches.

The First Operation
Sublimation

It is not Vulgar but Philosophical whereby we take away from the Stone whatever is superfluous, which, in effect is nothing else, but the elevation of the not-fixed part by fume and vapor, for the fixed part should remain in the bottom, nor would we that one should be separated from the other, but that they remain and be fixed together. Know also that he, who shall sublime our Philosophical Mercury (wherein is all the vertue of our Stone) as it ought to be done, shall perfect the Magistery. This gave *Geber* reason to say that all perfection consists in *Sublimation*, and in this Sublimation all other operations, that is to say, *Distillation, Assation, Destruction, Coagulation, Putrefaction, Calcination, Fixation, Reduction* of the White and Red Tinctures, procreated and engendered in one furnace and in one Vessel and this is the ready way to the final Consummation whereof the Philosophers have made divers chapters, purposely to amuse the Ignorant.

Take then in the name of the great God the venerable matter of the Philosophers, called the first *Hyle* of the Sages, which contains the above named Philosophical Mercury, termed, the first matter of the perfect Body, put it into its Vessel, which must be clear, diaphanous and round, and closely stopped by the *Seal of Seals*, and make it hot in its place, well-prepared, with temperate heat, for the space of a *Philosophical Month*, keeping it six weeks and two days in the sweat of sublimation until it begins to be putrefyed, to ferment, to be colored and to be congealed with its metallick humidity, and be fixed so far, that it do no more ascend in *aiery fumous substance*, but remains fixed in the bottom, turned from what it was, and divested of all viscous humidity, putrefyed and black, which is called the Sable Robe, Night, or the Crowe's-head. Thus when our Stone is in the Vessel, and that it mounts up on high in fume, this is called Sublimation, and when it falls down from on high, *Distillation*, and *Descension*. When it begins to participate of the fumous substance, and to be putrefyed, and that by reason of the frequent ascent and descent it begins to coagulate, then it is *Putrefaction* and devouring Sulphur, and lastly through the want or privation of the humidity of the radical water is wrought *Calcination* and Fixation both at the same time, by decoction alone, in one only Vessel, as I have already said. Moreover in this sublimation is wrought the true separation of the Elements, for in our Sublimation the *Elixir* is turned from Water into a terrestrial Element dry and hot, by which operation it is manifest, that the separation of the four Elements in our Stone is not Vulgar but Philosophical. Hence also is it, that in our Stone there are but two *for-*

mal Elements, that is to say, Earth and Water; but the Earth hath in its grossness, the virtue and drought of Fire; and the Water contains in it self the air with its humidity. Thus we have in our Stone visibly but two elements, but effectually there are four. And by this thou maist judge, that the separation of the four Elements is absolutely physical not vulgar and real, such as the ignorant daily employ themselves in. Continue therefore its decoction with a gentle fire, until all the black matter appearing in the superficies be quite dissipated by the Magistery, which blackness is by the Philosophers called the dark mantle of the Stone, which afterwards becoming clear is termed the cleansing water of the earth, or rather the Elixir. And note, that the blackness which appears is a sign of putrefaction. And the beginning of the dissolution is a sign of the conjunction of both natures. And this blackness appears sometimes in forty dayes, more or less, according to the quantity of the matter, and the industry of the Operator, which contributes much to the separation of the said Blackness. Now my Son, by the grace of God thou art acquainted with one Element of our Stone, which is the black earth, the Raven's head, by some called the obscure shadow, upon which earth as upon a base all the rest is grounded. This terrestrial and dry Element, is called, *Laton*, the *Bull, black Dreggs*, our *Metall*, our *Mercury*, And thus by the privation of the adult humidity, which is taken away by Philosophical sublimation, the volatile is fixed, and the moist is made dry and earth; nay, according to *Geber*, there is wrought a change of the complexion, as of a cold and humid Nature, into dry choler; and according to Alphidius, of a liquid into a thick. Whence is apprehended what the Philosophers mean when they say, that the operation of our Stone is only a transmutation of Nature and a revolution of Elements. Thou seest then how that by this incorporation the humid becomes dry, the volatile fixed, the Spiritual corporeal, the liquid thick, water fire, air earth, and that there happens an infallible change in their true nature, and a certain circulation of the four Elements.

The Second Operation
Dealbation [1]

It converts our *Mercury* into the *white* Stone, and that by decoction only. When the earth is separated from its water, then must the Vessel be set on the Ashes, as is usual in a distilling furnace, and the water be distilled by a gentle fire at the beginning, so that the water come so gently that thou mayst distinctly number as far as forty names, or pronounce fifty-six words, and let this order be observed in all the distillations of the black earth, and that which is in the bottom of the Vessel, that is, the *Faeces* remaining to be imbided, with the new water, will be dissolved, which water will contain three or four parts more than those Feces, that so all may be dissolved and converted into Mercury and *Argent vive*. I tell thee that this must be done so often, that there shall remain nothing but the Murc. For this distillation there is no time limited, but it is done sooner or later according to the greater or lesser quantity of the water, proportionably to the quantity of the fire. Then take the earth which thou shalt have reserved in a Vessel of Glass, with its distilled water, and with a soft and gentle fire, such as was that of Distillation, or purification, or rather one somewhat stronger, continue it, till such time as the earth be dry and white, and by reason of its drought, drunk up all its water. This done, put to it some of the abovesaid water, and so, as at the beginning, continue on the same decoction, until that earth is become absolutely white, cleansed and clear, and have drunk all its water. And note that the said earth will be washed from its blackness by the decoction, as I have said, because it is easily putrefyed by its own water, and is cleansed, which is the end of the Magistery, and then be sure to keep that white earth very carefully. For that is the *White Mercury, White Magnesia, Foliated earth.* Then take this white earth rectified as abovesaid, and put it into its vessel upon the ashes, to a fire of Sublimation, and let it have a very strong fire until all the coagulated water, which is within, come into the Alembick, and the earth remain in the bottom well calcined: then hast thou the earth, the water, and the air, and though the earth have in it the nature of the fire, yet is it not apparent

---

1. To make white.

in effect, as thou shalt see, when by a greater decoction thou shalt make it become red; so that then thou shalt manifestly see the fire in appearance, and such must be the proceeding in order to Fermentation of the white earth, that the dead body may be animated and enlivened, and its vertue be multiplied to infinity. But note, that the Ferment cannot enter into the dead body, but by the means of the water, which hath made a contract and a marriage between the Ferment and the white earth. And know that in all Fermentation the weight is to be considered, that so the quantity of the volatile exceed not the fixed, and that the marriage pass away in fume. For, as *Senior* sayes, If thou convert not the earth into water and the water into fire, there cannot be a conjunction of the spirit and body. To do this take a *Lamen* or plate red hot and cast on it a drop of our Medicine, which penetrating, it shall be of a perfect color, and will be a sign of perfection. If it happen it do not tinge, reiterate the dissolution and coagulation, until it do tinge and penetrate. And note, that seven imbibitions, at the most, are sufficient, and five at the least, that so the matter may be liquifyed, and without smoak, and then the matter is perfect as to whiteness, for as much as the matter sometimes requires a longer time to be fixed, and sometimes is done in a shorter, according to the quantity of the Medicine. And note that our Medicine from the creation of our Mercury requires the term of seven months to compass the whiteness, and, to arrive at the redness, five; which put together make twelve.

Of the Third Operation
Rubification

Take of the white Medicine, as much as thou wilt, and put it with its Glass upon the hot ashes, till it becomes as dry as the ashes. Then put to it some water of the Sun, which thou hast kept purposely for that end, and continue the fire to the second degree, until it become dry, then put to it again some of the abovesaid water, and so successively imbibe and dry, until the matter be rubified, and fluxible as wax, and cover with it the red *Lamen*, as hath been said, and the matter shall be perfect as to redness. But note that at every time, thou needs put no more of the water of the Sun than is barely necessary to cover the body, and this is done that the Elixir sink not and be drowned, and so the fire must be continued unto dessication, and then must there be made a second imbibition, and so proceed in order to the perfection of the Medicine, that is to say, until the force of the digestion of the fire convert it into a very red pouder, which is the *true Hyle* of the Philosophers, the bloody Stone, the purple red Coral, the precious Ruby, red Mercury and the red Tincture.

Projection

The oftner thou shalt dissolve and coagulate it, the more will the Vertue of it be multiplied to infinity. But note that the medicine is multiplied later by *Solution*, then by Fermentation. Wherefore the thing dissolved operates not well if it be not before fixed in its ferment. Nevertheless the multiplication of the Medicine by Solution is more abundant than that of the Ferment, by reason there is more subtilisation. Yet I advise thee that in the multiplication thou put one part of the work upon four of the other, and in a short time there will be made a pouder, all Ferment.

The Epilogue According to Hermes

Thus art thou to separate the *earth* from the *fire*, the *gross* from the *subtil* gently, with great Judgment, that is to say, separate the parts that are united to the Furnace, by the dissolution and separation of the parts, as the earth from the fire, the subtile from the gross &c., that is to say, the more pure substance of the Stone, until thou hast got it clean, and free from all spots or filth. And when he saith, *it ascends from the earth up into Heaven and returns again into the earth,* there is no more to be understood by it than the *Sublimation* of the Bodies. Further, to explain what distillation is, he sayes *the Wind carryes it in its belly,* that is, when the water is distilled by the Alembick, where it first ascends by a wind full of Fume and Vapor, and afterwards returns to the bottom of the Vessel in water again. When he would also express the congelation of the matter, he says, *Its force is absolute, if it be turned into earth,* that is to say, be converted by decoction. And to make a general demonstration of all that hath been said, he says, *It shall receive both the inferior and Superior force,* that is to say that of the Elements, far as much as, if the

Medicine receive the force of the lighter parts, that is to say, air and fire, it shall also receive that of the more grave and weighty parts, changing itself into water and earth, to the end, that the Matters being thus perpetually joined together, may have permanence, durance, constancy, and stability. Glory be to God.

FINIS.

CHAPTER ONE

ALCHEMY AND PSYCHOLOGY

In the Middle Ages, alchemy was a body of knowledge accorded the utmost respect and veneration. It had penetrated every form of learning. Before its shrine the savants of philosophy and theology paid humble homage. Nowadays the various histories of chemistry which are considered authoritative look askance at the noble parent of their science. It is an object of derision and contempt. Few modern historians, however, realize that it is not from alchemy proper that the chemical art was derived. Rather it was from the mistaken efforts of uninitiated operators—those who despite clear instruction, worked with actual vulgar materials. These, came derisively to be known as the Puffers. It is from these pseudo-alchemists, and not from the accredited philosophical authorities, that we have inherited the earliest chemical discoveries.

To this day, the real nature of alchemy—or rather an intelligible interpretation of alchemical texts—remains a dark mystery to academic scholarship. It is claimed by some that a crude and archaic form of chemical practice and metal working indubitably underlies these texts. And to understand them, we must therefore apply a primitive chemical and scientific interpretation. In a very penetrating and erudite work entitled *Alchemy, Child of Greek Philosophy*, the author, Arthur John Hopkins, ventures a theory and posits statements which, whilst in harmony with the currently accepted ideas on the subject, are in my estimation erroneous. He says, "But because the true theory

43

of alchemy, the original Egyptian theory, was no longer understood, the writers of Western Europe were never able to carry out in practice the promises expressed in their books. The actual gold which was looked for was never produced." [1]

Though it is not my intention to labor upon the idea of a physical transmutation of metals, since that is a subject calling for special treatment by specialists, nevertheless the issue raised here requires some little discussion. The contention is that the evidence we have from the past is not only untrustworthy but that the alchemists themselves were knaves and liars. It suggests that the testimony of these alchemists that actually they did produce gold, is false testimony. The assumption, I contend, is false. Its psychology is undoubtedly fallacious. The factor involved in so sweeping a statement is due no doubt not only to the widespread extraverted attitude of the day, but to the sense of antagonism experienced by our modern scientists to the means by which the alchemists are said to have produced that gold. No matter how produced, and regardless of the unacceptableness or the repugnance of the transmuting mechanism to us today, the fact is that Flamel, Van Helmont, Sendivogius, and many another claimed not only to have produced gold artificially but to have had it tested and accepted as currency. We have evidence as valid as any of that of past times that this gold was tried thoroughly by all the acid tests of the jewelers. There was no question merely of tinting or of a surface plating of a metal to suggest solid gold, as Hopkins suggests. Chemical tests had already been sufficiently well developed for the goldsmiths to have seen through so superficial a metallurgical artifice.

Hopkins' theory is that originally alchemy grew out of a simple artisanship. Here he repeats the celebrated French scholar Berthelot, and it is obvious that Arthur Edward Waite, who propounds a simi-

---

1. Arthur John Hopkins, *Alchemy, Child of Greek Philosophy* (New York: Columbia University Press, 1934), 10–11. Online version at http://babel.hathitrust.org/cgi /pt?id=uc1.b4566948.

lar view in *The Secret Tradition in Alchemy*,[2] derives his conclusions from the same source. In Egypt, where the art is said to have had its inception, the colors of nature were drab, and meagre. The sun, hot and glaring and cruel, burned the life and color out of the vegetation, and the environment in consequence appeared but dull and monotonous and uninteresting. Sand and desert stretched for miles about the Egyptian cities. As a result, the people were moved to improve upon nature. This they did by employing in their building operations stones and bricks of different colors and textures in order to relieve the wide neutrality and boring monotony about them. Also they painted designs and pictures of bright and varied hue in their interiors, as compensation for the drabness and lifeless appearance of nature in which they lived.

They loved clothes colored with rich bright dyes, and the so-called "royal purple" intrigued them enormously. Theirs was a distinct leaning towards jewelry. Bracelets and necklaces and rings of gold and silver, exquisitely worked and chased, were especially desirable. Since gold and silver, precious metals, were beyond the reach of the simple inhabitant of those days, the desire for ornamentation gave impetus to the alloying of metals. These were cunningly mixed and tinted by a bronzing surface treatment so as to give the appearance of the "genuine article." "The first appearance of these colored metals on the market," suggests Hopkins, "must have come as a novelty and created a demand very encouraging to the manufacturer."[3]

At the beginning therefore there was apparently no deliberate deception or disgrace involved in the practice of tinting metals. Nevertheless it was from this need to give cheap and tawdry baubles to the common people that arose alchemy with its aspiration towards the real transmutation of metals.

---

2. A. E. Waite, *The Secret Tradition in Alchemy: Its Development and Records* (London: Kegan Paul, Trench, Trubner & Co., Ltd., 1926).

3. Hopkins, 48.

Such a view, while no doubt a correct one in the main, is faulty in at least one particular. It takes no cognizance of the view that long prior to such a commercial exploitation of alloyed metals, was a long tradition of mystical and high religious thought. To ignore this is at once to knock away the foundations from under one's feet. And without such a realization all one's speculations partake of modernity in its worst sense—of theories deprived of all substance, suspended in mid-air, timeless because not grounded in our history and intellectual evolution. Earlier in his work, Hopkins had mentioned the established fact that for at least a couple of thousand years before the Christian era, the Egyptians had evolved a very profound religious culture. This was centered about Osiris, the resurrection God. By the psychological mechanism of portmanteau symbolism, displacement and condensation—mechanism so clearly operating in those spontaneous irruptions of psychic activity, dreams and fantasies, mechanisms with which the genius of Freud has familiarized us—he became associated with the solar Gods Ra and Khephra. Consequently there developed too the association with yellow, the physical golden color of the sun. Hence to *become* Osiris by the various religious means of the ancient Egyptians, implied a species of union or identification with the Sun, or that ultimate reality of life implied by the Sun, the source of light and life and virtue. And it is evident that to a religious people, the body-consciousness with its down-tending desires and predilections came to be symbolized as dark, heavy, and leaden in nature. The spirit represented by the Sun and by Osiris was considered as light, activity, and the purest gold. It was the lead consciousness of which they wished to be relieved, with its burden of guilt, fear and anxiety. It was this that they wished to open up, and thus transmute, to the pure gold of the heavenly Osiris, the Redeemer and Mediator. From this elementary and primitive reasoning the sacerdotal classes had developed an imposing superstructure of mystical realization. It is evident that the priests, who we know had already evolved a complex spiritual scheme, noble and fine in many ways, would have been able to develop a psychological technique whereby such a transmutation from the lead of corruption to the gold of psychic incorruptibility could be accomplished.

Osiris

I believe that the Hopkins or generally accepted scientific view is certainly valid in respect of a certain class of texts. Alchemy has of course several planes of interpretation, and an equal number of classes of texts. Nevertheless his view is not one that can be over-zealously or too widely applied. The present text, for example, is a case in point. No doubt it is spurious in the sense that *The True Book of the Learned Synesius* cannot be the work of Synesius the abbot of Ptolemais in the fourth century. It must therefore be considered a mediaeval forgery. On the other hand it is typical of a distinct class of alchemical literature. The very definitions employed—and I must mention the fact that this work is famous for its classical and almost perfect definitions—lead one to suppose that another level of interpretation must be sought.

Excluding the idea that this particular book is an early chemical text-book, as I maintain we are *forced* to exclude, then we are confronted by the problem as to what other direction we may turn for a solution. I may say briefly here that there are several other interpretations possible. There is the religious or moral viewpoint, and the mystical and occult. Naturally each of these exegetical approaches applies its own norm of interpretation to certain parts of certain texts to confirm its own particular hypothesis.

Since the advent of modern psychological knowledge, with particular reference to the clinical findings of those great pioneers Sigmund Freud and C. G. Jung, we have been given a key to the understanding of myths, epics, legends and dreams of every kind, whether racial or individual. These findings are so tremendous in implication that to ignore them would be unwise—even stupid. It is to this branch of scientific research that we must first turn in seeking an elucidation of the enigmas and obscurities of the alchemical works. Since these, like dreams and myths, issue from the dark submerged levels of the human psyche, and inasmuch as they do not seem to respond to any of the ordinary interpretations along scientific mechanistic lines, then we are forced to turn the psychological key. And the lock opens!

Because they were humanly penned, these obscurities *must* have some meaning in terms of human consciousness. Everything humanly created has meaning and significance of some kind. Even nonsense has some significance in that it is an outpouring of a particular human mind. We have only to discover the hidden motive of that mind, and the nonsense at once becomes intelligible. I am convinced that the attempt to employ the psychological key to these dark mysteries of alchemy will yield significant material and ideas. A technique is yielded, moreover, which indicates that these early writers whoever they may have been, so far from having been lost in a meaningless maze of gibberish, as most modern critics unjustifiably have come to think, knew very well what they were writing. And that, moreover, they possessed a very profound and extensive knowledge of the deeps and intricacies of the various levels of man's own mental, moral and spiritual nature. This knowledge I believe to have some value even for us today.

Such a point of view is imperative. Not only is it so for the reasons I have stated, but because we find it infuriating and injurious to our sense of self-esteem to be baffled by the intellectual or literary expression of our fellows. I contend this must be true for several reasons. Even if we assume that this especial text is spurious and could never have been penned in the early centuries of the Christian era, yet the mere fact that some ten centuries later its actual composer did attribute it to Synesius must have some particular meaning, some psychic significance of no little import.

Synesius, as we know, was a Neo-Platonist who converted to Christianity, becoming eventually a pillar of the Church. It was his belief that Paganism and the newer dispensation, so far from being antagonistic, had a very great deal in common one with another. He held that they should unite to form a single religious and philosophical unit. Accordingly, in the mere accident of attribution alone I am inclined to seek a spiritual or philosophical signification. I suggest the text must be interpreted on a high philosophical or mystical level, using the symbolism and technique of Analytical Psychology as the means whereby the quasi-religious or philosophical interpretations may be rendered acceptable to modern thought and scholarship. That some spiritual or inward and not a chemical interpretation is imperative is borne in upon us by one or two of the definitions provided in the text itself.

For example, the first sentence of the second section reads: "My son, it is necessary that thou work with the *Mercury of the Philosophers* and the Wise, which is not the Vulgar, nor hath anything of the Vulgar."

Here is a direct injunction not to stoop down into the mineral world. How, in view of such a caution, could one confuse metallurgical processes with those of philosophy? What is the Mercury of the wise? Our text suggests the answer. "It is the first Matter, the Soul of the World." At once we are plunged into the deeps of early philosophy and religion, a late reflection of Platonic speculation. According to archaic philosophy, the Soul of the World is the one reality. It is the ideal world, of which the actual physical world susceptible to the physical senses is the negation or phenomenon. Likewise it is considered as an omnipresent life principle, pulsating throughout all space, and permeating every living thing. It is life itself, and without it no thing could be. Life and consciousness, in mystical philosophy throughout the ages, are identical. Where the one is, there may we find the other. Hence to work with the Mercury of the Philosophers is to confine one's labors metaphysically to the ever-present spirit of life, ubiquitous and infinite, pulsing in the core of the human heart.

Though the human psyche is a whole or unity, it has its own various compartments or functions which roughly we may designate as Conscious and Unconscious. That is to say, that certain of our thinking processes are consciously performed, whilst at the same time there is a vast field of cerebration and psychic activity of which normally we have not the vaguest awareness. The appearance of dream and fantasy is eloquent proof of this unconscious activity.

The enormously wide field of hypnotic experiment, unacceptable though it may be to some who prefer the comfort of dogmatic theories to actual indisputable facts, stands as eloquent proof of the concept of the Unconscious and unconscious psychic activity. Modern psychology and psychological technique owe their very existence to Mesmer and to the pioneer work of great hypnotists such as Janet, Charcot, Bernheim and Liébault. These labored with suggestion therapy and trance-states to indicate that the individual in his waking state may be influenced by a multitude of ideas and feelings, of the existence of which he has not the least conscious awareness whatsoever. For example, Dr. J. Milne Bramwell, possibly the greatest living authority on hypnotism, records a vast number of Experiments that he made. A series of them were with a Miss D. She was, he says, a very ordinary girl of board school education.[4] Her arithmetical powers were in keeping with this. She could do ordinary examples in multiplication and subtraction only if permitted

---

4. J. Milne Bramwell, *Hypnotism: Its History, Practice and Theory* (London: J. B. Lippincott, Co., 1903), 119–121.

to do them with pencil and paper. Mental arithmetic was beyond her. There was no particular aptitude for appreciating the passage of time.

On one particular occasion she was placed deeply under hypnosis at 3:55 p.m. Dr. Bramwell gave the suggestion that at the expiration of 5 hours and 20 minutes after she awoke she was to make a cross on a piece of paper and to write down the time she believed it to be. At about 9:15 the mother of the girl noticed that Miss D. was restless. Five minutes later the girl wrote rapidly on a piece of paper "20 minutes past 9." [5] The French psychologist Delboeuf made innumerable similar experiments to this one many years before with similar satisfactory results. [6]

These and a host of like experiments seem to indicate that the subliminal consciousness or the Unconscious, or any other name that you may prefer to use for this dark hidden side of one's being, possesses a remarkable time sense. Or else that it can calculate and function totally in independence of what consciously we think and do.

If suggestions implanted in the mind from without may so affect the individual, may it not be also that from within the psyche there may be evolved a certain content the effect of which may not be too dissimilar to post-hypnotic suggestions? It is on this hypothesis that Freud and others have labored at great length. And it is this hypothesis that they have proved.

Just as human physiology is based upon universal principles, so also it seems is human psychology. In the collective universal sense, we are confronted then with what Plato would have called the world of Ideas, and with what the very eminent psychologist C. G. Jung has chosen to call the Collective Unconscious. This postulate is not a matter of speculation nor a necessity imposed upon our thinking by any philosophical dialectic. It is a matter of everyday clinical experience. Symbols and ideas and inspirations charged with exuberance and vitality appear constantly in dreams, and influence the personality in a profound and lasting way. When all the superfluities and personal aspects are explained or analyzed away, these are seen to belong wholly

---

5. Ibid.

6. Ibid., 116–119.

or in part to that mythological world in which the ancients lived. This same world of the Unconscious still lives in each one of us, albeit deeply buried. It is the world of universals which Jung has named the Collective Unconscious—that which all men have in common and share, unknown to themselves, with each other. He defines it more particularly in these terms: "As a common human heritage it transcends all differences of culture and consciousness and does not consist merely of contents capable of becoming conscious, but of latent dispositions towards identical reactions. Thus the fact of the collective unconscious is simply the psychic expression of brain-structure irrespective of all racial differences. By its means can be explained the analogy, going even as far as identity, between various myth-themes and symbols, and the possibility of human understanding in general. The various lines of psychic development start from one common stock whose roots reach back into the past. Here too lies the psychological parallelism with animals."[7] It is this world too, or this psychological principle, which Synesius or our mediaeval forger has termed the Mercury of the Wise, or the Soul of the World.

Moreover, this same text gives us such a definition of the alchemical art as to indicate beyond the possibility of doubt that no chemical interpretation can be sought. Assuming the reality or tangibility of the First homogeneous Matter which is to be coagulated after purification into the so-called Philosopher's Stone, what then is the object of alchemy? "Consider what Geber sayes," counsels our text, "that our Art consists not in the multitude of several things, because the *Mercury* is but one only thing, that is to say, one only stone wherein consists the whole Magistery; to which thou shalt not add any strange thing, save that in the preparation thereof thou shalt take away from it whatsoever is superfluous, by reason that in this matter, all things requisite to this Art are contained."[8]

---

7. Richard Wilhelm, *The Secret of the Golden Flower: A Chinese Book of Life* (London: Kegan Paul, Trench, Trubner & Co., 1962), 83–84.

8. See page 35.

The philosophical meaning is indisputable. Since all particulars spring from, or are contained in the Universals, or since the physical world is a falling away from the reality of God but is nevertheless contained in God, all we have to do is to eliminate the superfluities, the unrealities, in order to become aware of Reality. Looking at it again from another viewpoint, the sole object required by the art is the latent root of consciousness, using this term in its widest sense as the all-inclusive Self, and this is possessed by every man and woman alike. Therein are contained in potentiality all the factors and instruments necessary to perfection. Furthermore, Synesius says, "Know, that the Quintessence and the hidden thing of our stone is nothing else than our viscous, celestial and glorious soul drawn by our magistery out of its mine."

In modern clinical psychology, if the analysand would recover his mental and physical well-being and live healthily and sanely, the deeper levels of his own being must be recognized and expressed. Thus the value of attention to dreams, which are the spontaneous activities and workings of the unconscious aspect of the psyche. To live wholly and completely we must take cognizance of the Unconscious, and admit of the validity of its existence together with the rational superficial side of us. We must accept the emotional and feeling side of us as well. It is this part of us which modern life tends to make us repress, inhibit and forget from childhood on. But this cannot be. It is an unrighteous condition of things. For our very being is then disrupted and torn too terribly asunder by such a deliberate denial to be endured. Our lives become sterile and insignificant. All ease and meaning and beauty in life vanish in the same measure as integrity is lost. And this psychic affliction is responsible for the vast increase today of ill-health and neurotic manifestation, both physical and mental.

By resurrecting this shadow side of us—which alas it seems to have become when actually it is the Light world of surpassing brilliance and divine beauty—and letting our smaller selves, our superficial egos, be immersed or baptized in that mystical sea of the Wise, then are we restored and made whole. Such is the elixir of life—the rediscovery of the operation of natural law in the inner spiritual world, the recovery of a hitherto lost part of ourselves. It consists in the "extraction of our celestial and glorious soul from its mine." That is the terminology of Synesius. Should we attempt a translation of the "glorious and viscous soul" that he speaks of into the terminology of the Jungian psychology we have more than interesting parallels. In Jung's book *Modern Man in Search of a Soul* there is a very important and significant essay "Postulates of Analytical Psychology." In that essay he makes some statements about the Unconscious which, in time to come, may be considered as classical definitions. For my purpose here, they are illuminating, giving us some idea of what it is that we are to excavate from our alchemical mine. In that book, Jung writes: "While consciousness is intensive and concentrated, it is transient and is directed upon the immediate field of attention; moreover, it has access only to material that represents one individual's experience, stretching over a few decades ... It (the Unconscious) is not as concentrated and intensive, but shades off into obscurity; it is highly extensive and can juxtapose the most heterogeneous elements in the most paradoxical way. More than this, it contains, besides an indeterminable number of subliminal perceptions, an immense fund of accumulated inheritance-factors left by one generation of men after another, whose mere existence marks a step in the differentiation of the species. If it were permissible to personify the Unconscious, we might call it a collective human being combining the characteristics of both sexes, transcending youth and age, birth and death, and, from having at his command a human experience of one or two million years, almost immortal."[9]

To have discovered a "being" such as this within one's heart would be an event of supreme and paramount significance in any individual's life. It is a concept enough to inspire us with an entirely new vision of existence. It is a vision of the whole of the universe, making possible a full and unconditioned acceptance of, and compliance with, the eternal laws of life which after all are the laws of the Unconscious. This is in its widest sense the Philosopher's Stone. Man is glorified by

---

9. Carl G. Jung, *Modern Man in Search of a Soul,* trans. W. S. Dell and C. F. Baynes (New York: Harcourt, nd.), 186. First published in 1933.

the integration of the personality into one entire unit during some psychic process in which the ego gradually becomes reconciled to and united with its dynamic stem and root, the Unconscious or the Soul of the World. And his every psychic principle, permeated anew with life and vitality, perfected through free and complete expression of its own innate superior wisdom, is made golden and glowing like some rare psychic jewel. The magnetic emanations so to speak, issuing from such an individual, become purified and engender themselves anew. Their colors, to the sensitive able to feel and perceive them, become alive and flashing, capable of exerting powerful effects on whomsoever and whatsoever is brought into vital contact with them.

It is this conception, briefly, rather than chemistry, which underlies, I think, the willful deliberate obscurantism of alchemy.

CHAPTER TWO

THE UNIVERSAL AGENT, POLARITY, AND THE COLLECTIVE UNCONSCIOUS

It is not my intention to provide a complete or systematic commentary to this text. I feel it would be wiser for the reader to work out his own lengthy reactions to its stimulus. But I should like to indicate in a slightly fuller fashion certain of the ideas dominating the philosophy and practice of alchemy. Principal amongst these, and common to the whole range of alchemical literature, regardless of the age or clime in which that literature first appeared, is the belief in some universal agent, some homogeneous medium into which the ego, the unpurified Stone, is to be dissolved and then reconstructed according to another pattern. In the *Aurea Catena Homeri*[1] it is said, "A medium of union is wanting. They (the students) should look for such a medium. One metal does not and cannot enter into a radical union with another without their medium of union; this medium they may have lost at the melting furnace, near the mines. Go there and look for it, or take its like."[2]

---

1. Anton Josef Kirchweger, *Aurea Catena Homeri* (1723). Available at www.levity .com/alchemy/catena1.html. A German edition by Hermann Kopp, published in 1880, can be found at Google Books.

2. R. W. Councell, *Apollogia Alchymiae: A Restatement of Alchemy* (London: John M. Watkins, 1925). See "Section I: Prefatory Remarks." This text can be found online at www.levity.com/alchemy/counsel1.html and www.rexresearch.com/alchemy2 /councell.htm.

Ingenuity of the most fertile kind has been exercised throughout the ages in naming this medium in such a guise that it shall not be recognizable save to those whose intellectual and spiritual gifts have elevated them above the herd. Fantastic and arbitrary some of the definitions may seem to have been, but meditation will reveal to the enquiring mind that reality to which they point. I propose dilating upon this topic more fully a little further on. As Synesius says of the alchemists of all time, and their spagyric expositions: "And though they are different in their expressions, yet are they not in any way discordant one from another, but ayming all at one end, and speaking of the same thing, they have thought fit (above all the rest) to name the *proper Agent* by a term, strange, nay sometimes contrary to its nature and qualities." [3]

The True Book further states: "*My Son*, it is necessary that thou work with the *Mercury of the Philosophers* and the Wise, which is not the *Vulgar*, nor hath any thing of the Vulgar, but, according to them, is the *First Matter, the Soul of the World, the cold element, the blessed Water, the Water of the Wise, the Venemous Water, the most sharp Vinegar, the water of celestial grace, the Virgin Milk, our mineral and corporeal Mercury.*" [4]

With this clue provided by our author almost any true alchemical treatise may readily be understood. The basic formula has been defined and we may go forward from the dark towards the light. It is assumed in alchemical metaphysics that throughout space there is diffused a universal and homogeneous sub-stratum of a very subtle, fine and tenuous spiritual principle. "It is not possible for us to make that water by Art, but Nature alone begets it." [5] This must be postulated or experienced before anything else may be done. Some have called it Hyle, others have termed it spirit, and the moderns name it the Collective Unconscious: and we have already read by what names our text has so eloquently described it. The entirety of alchemical literature,

---

3. See page 31.

4. See page 34.

5. See page 33.

as I have said, is replete with enigmatical descriptions of this ethereal substance, this universally pervasive medium into which they seek to reduce their working metals. From this substance, if name it such we must, mind and matter have their origin. Or, shall I say, these two extreme functions of the psyche are but opposite poles of its homogeneity, male and female, positive and negative. "Know then, my Son," asserts Synesius, "that almighty God together with this Universe created two Stones, that is to say, the *White* and the *Red*, both which are under one and the same subject."[6]

The duality here of the white and the red is similar to the reference on another page of this treatise to the Sun and the Moon. There is the specific caution that they are not the Vulgar Gold and Silver nor the Vulgar Sun and Moon. This latter is explicable on the ground that the metals and the planets in alchemy are attributed one to another. Not only so but they are frequently used interchangeably as surrogate symbols. The caution therefore suggests a subjective transcendental line of psychological enquiry—more along the Jungian lines.

If the luminaries are not the vulgar objective luminaries, then what are they? To answer this, philosophy and religion must be called to our conference. Traditionally, the Sun and consequently Gold, refer, as previously I have intimated, to the freed human consciousness. Free association on dream material confirms this. The Freudians have a vast series of correspondences or associations to gold. At first sight these seem entirely opposed to the meaning dilated upon here. Their attitude is to reduce the content of the dreams to basic infantile experience, or rather to the memory of such experiences. Gold to an infantile consciousness would refer to its own excreta. For one thing the color of its faeces would be the determining factor, and for another the idea of value.

---

6. See page 31.

Sun and Moon

Value in faeces, you may ask in amazement? But the child, you must remember, has a primitive set of values entirely opposed to that of the adult. The child is a defenseless little entity, without means of self-protection or self-assertion. His own body, his activities, and the functional activities of his organism are his only possessions. He has nothing else in the world. These also are the sole means of expression of his will, of his feelings. His environment contains giants, powerful personalities, mother and father, who more often than not in the early days fulfill his every wish and whim, but who later create an atmosphere which is in collision with the impulse of the child. Angry and annoyed by the superiors about him, how may he indicate his displeasure? Crying after a while is recognized to be futile. Sometimes it works, sometimes it does not.

From a very early age, the child learns of moral values in connection with its bodily functions. If its bowels move, mother or nurse smiles and says it is a good child. On the other hand, these godlike beings frown severely if the bowels do not operate, and he is a bad child. These are notions which, whilst apparently trivial, are deeply ingrained in us and survive unconsciously in the adult, as everyone acquainted with psychology knows.

Likewise the child learns that if the bowels move mother is satisfied and happy. When stasis occurs, the whole nursery is in a furor, and a very great deal of attention of different kinds is bestowed upon this kingly child. This being so, if the child feels neglected or annoyed or irritated with its parents—as so easily can happen—what more simple than that he should withhold his excreta, which clearly have been stamped with importance and great value? These valuable contents of his bowels are the sole means left of displaying his satisfaction with the external environment. These are his possessions, the actual withholding of which is employed to procure his own ends. The parents, worried and frightened by the possibility of serious illness resulting, bestow attention and concern upon him. Pleased and happy, he gives up his treasure. The movement not only gives him personal pleasure, but it is certainly indicative of an underlying sense of treasure, value, and personal possession. Thus gold receives, later on in life, some of this transferred effect. It is in direct association with this early primitive treasure of his infancy.

But what issues from the bowels has a superior symbolic significance merely to this. For one thing, the symbolic meaning is more important than the symbol—power and pleasure being the meaning here. And this is certainly what gold *does* represent. Moreover, the bowel itself is an involuntary muscle or viscera under the dominion of the old nervous system, the sympathetic. As such it represents the mode of activity of the basic factor of the psyche, the Unconscious. This underlies all human activity no matter of what kind. It is to this stratum of our psychic constitution that constantly we must turn for edification of obscure psychological problems.

Thus the freed consciousness which I have mentioned above must refer to one which has attempted to enlarge its own horizon by becoming aware of, or including within itself, as much as it can of the Unconscious and its continuous activity. In particular it so refers when the ego has passed through a rigorous discipline and training so that exalted it manifests its own innate divine nature. It is masculine and positive, as the Moon and Silver are feminine and passive. The Sun is Father of all, the giver of life and light, warmth and heat, the joy of all existence. Whereas the Moon reflects the light of the Sun, and is the mother who bears life or reflects it when once it has been radiated upon her. Astrologically, the Moon and Silver also refer in general terms to the instinctive and emotional background of man, that foundation of dynamic impulse upon which his consciousness rests, and from which it has emerged. Hence it is said "our Suns and Moons are in their nature living."[7] What else could they be, then, than living?

This idea is fundamental to all archaic systems of thought. Even in the Chinese text *The Secret of the Golden Flower* translated by Richard Wilhelm, we find a similar emphasis. There we find mention of the *Yang* and *Yin* principles, the two opposite principles inhering within Nature and consequently in man. For the laws of the cosmos, whatever their nature, are likewise existent and operative in the human psyche. In his Introduction to the text, Wilhelm writes: "*Yin* is shadow, therefore the north side of a mountain and the south side of a river (because during the day the position of the Sun makes the river appear dark from the south). *Yang* in its original form shows flying pennants, and, cor-

---

7. See page 35.

responding to the character *yin*, is the south side of a mountain and the north side of a river. Starting with the meaning of "light" and "dark," the principle was then expanded to all polar opposites, including the sexual. However, both *yin* and *yang* are only active in the realm of phenomena, and we have their common origin in an undivided unity, yang as the active principle appearing to condition, and yin as the passive principle seeming to be derived or conditioned. It is therefore quite clear that a metaphysical dualism is not at the bottom of these ideas. Less abstract than *yin* and *yang* are the concepts of the creative and receptive (*Ch'ien* and *K'un*) that originate in the Book of Changes *(I Ching)* and are symbolized by Heaven and Earth. Through the union of Heaven and Earth, and through the activity of the two primordial forces within this scene (an activity governed by the one primal law *Tao*) there develop the 'ten thousand things' that is, the outer world." [8]

This latter philosophical tenet of the undivided unity from which *yang* and *yin* have their origin and in which they are grounded is comparable to the alchemical Mercury. In point of fact, it is so defined in the several texts. From its homogeneity spring forth the opposites, the white and the red, the Sun and the Moon, Gold and Silver, "for these two are the world's eternal way." [9] The Chinese text itself defines the philosophical Mercury in a way that would not be unacceptable to the European alchemists. "Master Lu Tsu said: That which exists through itself is called Meaning (*Tao*). Meaning has neither name nor form. It is the one essence, the one primordial spirit. Essence and life cannot be seen. It is contained in the Light of Heaven. The Light of Heaven cannot be seen. It is contained in the two eyes. Today I will be your guide and will first reveal to you the secret of the Golden Flower of the Great *One*, and, starting from that, I will explain the rest in detail." [10]

---

8. Richard Wilhelm, trans., *The Secret of the Golden Flower: A Chinese Book of Life* (London: Kegan Paul, Trench, Trubner & Co., 1962), 12–13.

9. Charles Wilkins, trans., *The Bhagvat-Geeta, or Dialogues of Kreeshna and Arjoon* (Bangalore: Wesleyan Mission Press, 1846), 42. This text can be found at Google Books. (Originally published in London: C. Nourse, 1785.)

10. Wilhelm, 23.

The Golden Flower is the Chinese glyph for what in Europe has been termed the Stone of the Philosophers. Interestingly enough there is a set of mythological correspondences or associations in which the right eye is attributed to the Sun and the left eye to the Moon.

The triad of Mercury, Sun and Moon refer to the three major classifications of the psyche—a classification which also has been expressed as Mercury, Salt and Sulphur. Mercury is the fundamental consciousness principle itself, that which underlies every psychical activity. It is the very nature and substance of the thinking principle, the underlying Self, or, as one Buddhist Sutra puts it, "the essence of mind which is intrinsically pure." [11] Whilst the Sun and Moon respectively, as before defined, are two polarities or opposites functioning in the psyche, the rational thinking activity and the emotional and feeling activity.

Let us imagine a piece of string, at each end of which there is a knot. One knot let us call mind or consciousness, and the other knot the body and the feelings and emotions associated with the physical aspect and instinctual expression of life. The entire stretch of string between the two represents the fundamental stuff, as it were, of which both knots were made, the stuff of which consciousness itself is composed, the Mercury of the Wise, that subtle dynamic spiritual link existing between mind and body. It unites them firmly together, enabling the communications or impulses of the one to be impressed upon and conveyed to the other.

Moreover, this same dualism or polarity exists and repeats itself in every department or aspect of the psyche. The polarity of the mind expresses itself in a self-conscious thinking ego, some of which is conscious and some unconscious—and a much larger feeling and emo-

---

11. "Who would have thought," I said to the Patriarch, "that the Essence of Mind is intrinsically pure! Who would have thought that the Essence of Mind is intrinsically free from becoming or annihilation! Who would have thought that the Essence of Mind is intrinsically self-sufficient! Who would have thought that the Essence of Mind is intrinsically free from change! Who would have thought that all things are the manifestation of the Essence of Mind!" Knowing that I had realized the Essence of Mind, the Patriarch said, "For him who does not know his own mind there is no use learning Buddhism."—*The Platform Sutra of the Sixth Patriarch*, Huineng

tional and instinctual principle which likewise is dual in nature and operation. This medium, separating and binding together the polar functions of the psyche, is also the realm of memory, personal and racial, and of forgotten impression; the seat of enormous vitality and the life forces impressed with the stamp of an inconceivable antiquity. Since theorize we must here, because only psychological or interior mystical experience along the alchemical lines can give final proof, this is the sphere of what present-day psychologists consider to be that deep primitive level of intelligent being from which the superficial self with all its powers and faculties has gradually and laboriously emerged in the course of the evolutionary process.

In his essay *De Insomniis*, the Neo-Platonist Synesius makes an incursion into philosophy, contriving to bridge that chasm stretching between mind and matter. His attempted solution is the postulation of this principle or medium which he chooses to name "phantasia"[12] and which, in his estimation, makes the long sought-for bridge. He claims it belongs exclusively neither to mind nor matter, neither to intellect nor emotion, but mediates each. It is, in his own words, a "no man's land" obtaining between the unreasoning and reason, the bodiless and the body, and is a boundary common to both. Through it, the divine elements of mind and consciousness are brought into contact with those elements furthest removed from them—body, matter and instinct. He defines this bridge as that "perception of perceptions," and also as "the first body of the soul."[13] Here we have, basically anyway, the concept of a breath or pneumatic-body, the etheric or astral sheath of

---

12. "Aristotle sometimes recognizes as a distinct capacity, on par with perception and mind, imagination *(phantasia)* ... Although he does not discuss it at length, or even characterize it intrinsically in any detailed way, Aristotle does take pains to distinguish it from both perception and mind. In a brief discussion dedicated to imagination ... Aristotle identifies it as 'that in virtue of which an image occurs in us'... where this is evidently given a broad range of application to the activities involved in thoughts, dreams, and memories."—Christopher Shields, "Aristotle's Psychology," *Stanford Encyclopedia of Philosophy* (Spring 2011), ed. Edward N. Zalta, http://plato.stanford.edu/archives/spr2011/entries/aristotle-psychology.

13. Saint Synesius, *On Dreams*, translated by Augustine Fitzgerald. (See part 4 at www.livius.org/su-sz/synesius/synesius_dreams_04.html.) Also see Saint Synesius, *On Dreams*, translated by Isaac Myer, 6–13.

metaphysics which is the vehicle of the evolving self. He speaks of it as "lurking there in its fastness and directing the government of the living being as from a citadel, for about it Nature has constructed all the functions of the brain." And in *The True Book*, Synesius (for so let us conveniently name our unknown scribe) says: "If they are acquainted with the Medium, they shall find all things feasible and fortunate." [14]

Once having admitted the possibility of such an unseen medium existing in nature, both within and without, a further problem arises. How may we become aware of its presence? Here it is that alchemy is such an irritating problem to most who have made but a slight study of it. Actually no instructions are given. Not only are the texts vague in their definitions of that basic material with which we are to work, but they offer apparently no intelligible clue as to what means are to be employed to tap it and use it. Apart from the fact that most writers continually exhort the reader to prayer and meditation and frequent perusal of the classical texts, all appears dark and forbidding. It is more than puzzling.

On the other hand, there are some people who claim that this is precisely the major virtue of alchemy. It is their contention that the alchemical writers were men of ineffable religious experience. That is, their experience related to the spiritual aspects of the universe and man. And what they wrote therefore, obscure though it may seem to us, incorporates and embodies and expresses those experiences. Runs the argument accordingly, that by steeping oneself by meditation in their writings, by constant reflection on significant phrases, and introspection of a deep and penetrating kind, those writings by themselves and of themselves will awaken within the sincere reader, otherwise prepared by life, an echo, some dim formulation, an uneasy awakening of a similar spiritual experience.

How could this occur? What is the rationale of such a theory?

It is not far to seek, nor difficult to understand. We must recall to mind the psycho-analytical technique of free association. Understanding this, the clue is at hand. To ponder over ideas which convey

---

14. See page 32.

very little to the rational side of one may not conduce at first to deep understanding. But, by permitting the mind slowly to dwell upon enigmas, whether they be actual dreams thrown up by the psyche or the mysterious dream-like references of alchemy—both use the same archaic symbolic language—by allowing the mind freely to drift from words, cryptic phrases and ideas, there are formed association tracks in the mind. Other words link themselves in strange combinations to the original thought.

The idea of "cat" may, by association, bring about a vast concatenation of thoughts totally, at first sight, unrelated to our feline pet. It may evoke the thought of a mouse since, after all, cats do catch mice. Not too irrational an association. From that we could drift to traps, where mice are caught and practically guillotined. Cheese—cheese is used as the tasty bait whereby these mice are lured to their doom. Cheese—Switzerland, where an excellent cheese is made and exported over the face of the whole wide world. Switzerland, hotels, restaurants, sports, ice, and mountains. Mountains—this strikes on strange unfamiliar roots—and one pauses. In wonder one gazes at mountains—a little awe-stricken and mute before such eternal grandeur looming in the unconquerable heights. Even the most garrulous and superficial amongst us is no little impressed, even inspired by these majesties of nature. The mind flits from mountain to—well, did not Moses receive the law on Horeb? The psalmist, did he not declare that from the hills came his help from on high—and did not Jesus ascend the mountain to deliver his great sermon? And so on ... slowly following associations freely backwards, noting first of all the purely personal reactions arising in the mind, to be followed by more abstract and impersonal archetypes. If no inhibition develops to hinder the tracing backwards of the track, then yet others arise, and so forth. Finally a species of meditation has developed by means of which the mind enters into an immediate experience of that with which it deals. The process is entirely distinct from the clear-cut precise operations of the intellect and its ratiocinative processes. But since it does conduce to an increased understanding it possesses a very great virtue. It produces results, and as such it is most emphatically to be encouraged.

In modern times, because of our history and environment with its special social habits, we are become a people which has violated itself and frustrated its own nature. We have become over-conscious, top-heavy as it were, living too much and too often on the surface. It is a one-sided mode of life, an exaggeration of one particular psychic function at the expense of another. We have lost contact with the vital processes and dynamic cycles of nature. Life has become mechanized in most of its branches, and with it we too have become fixed. Our thinking is done for us by the newspapers. We feel as film-stars have taught us to feel and as we are dictated to by insidious suggestions from our politicians. Our work and occupations are sterile and fruitless of lasting or satisfying result. As a result we are cut off from our roots.

The danger is a typical one of over-civilization. One that has afflicted not only us moderns but the peoples of earlier and equally great civilizations. A wall becomes erected through habit in the mind itself. It eventually comes to act as an impenetrable partition between consciousness and that kinetic side of its nature which we name the Unconscious. A cleavage or duality is thus engendered in the individuality, and integrity and happiness are lost—a condition reflecting itself from the individual into the national order and life, and vice-versa.

Thus our age is sterile and uneasy and barbarous. That whole continents and nations may live in a perpetual state of fear of the outbreak of war—even in undeclared but none the less hideous states of war—sounds incredible. But this is the age. These things exist. This is our experience. Is not this barbarism?

None of us consciously desires such a state of affairs. Yet merely its presence indicates its nature as an expression of mass psychology. That is to say, it is an emanation of some part of ourselves of which individually we are not aware. And so it becomes projected outwards, to be seen not as the mote in our own eye, but the beam in our neighbor's. The Unconscious has become transformed into a dangerous entity individually because of abuse, repression, and lack of understanding. What wonder that collectively it has been transformed into a universally terror producing monster, a fearful destructive process the responsibility for which no one will shoulder.

Yet the responsibility is ours. Each one of us has this psychic stratum that we call the Unconscious. And that Unconscious is but a part of what has been named the Collective Unconscious. We are a part of it, and so are individually responsible for the state of the collective psychic sphere and its activity. Hence any technique enabling us, no matter how, to penetrate this hard and fast division set up in the psyche, to dissolve as with a sharp acid the false and arbitrary dualism which inhibits our living the deeper inner life of us, is supremely essential. Nothing could be more important for us all. Analytical Psychology is a modern technique for achieving this supreme height of self-understanding, and a very efficient one it is, too. By means of free association, deliberate fantasy and dream analysis, a way is opened up whereby the spontaneous irrational activities of the psyche may be understood and thereby assimilated into the conscious structure of the ego. With understanding comes insight that these inner spiritual activities are to be encouraged, since they are co-equal factors in the personality and constitute the vital creative root of our being.

We have then one instrument to hand whereby we may improve our understanding of the hermetic significance of *The True Book*. It is, I confess, one instrument only. Being a partitive system it gives a one-sided partial picture. But at the same time it does serve as an efficient means of coordinating our other spheres of knowledge, the sum total of which will enable us to bring this text, or at least parts of it, into the clear light of intellectual appreciation.

Let us take the contents of this work and subject them, not so much at first to rational criticism as to subjective digestion. What we must aim at is to let the book work upon us, to let it evoke from the dark within that which answers to it. With patience and cultivation, deep will answer to deep.

CHAPTER THREE
THE MYSTICAL EXPERIENCE

The psychological point of view is, as I have dilated above, most significant in suggesting a line of approach to the alchemical mystery. But apart from this theory, another great illumination is shed upon our present text and similar works by a study of comparative religious philosophy and mysticism. No matter to what religious literature we turn, or to what people we may go for our information on such topics, always do we find a complete agreement on fundamentals. Surface creeds and differentiations of formal ritual may differ. But at the foundation of every great religion is one identical thing—the basic mystical experience. Every system, from archaic times until today, bases itself on that single fact. Under certain conditions, different men and women, regardless of race or creed, have experienced a sudden exaltation to the heights—a momentous and incomparable experience. An obscuration of the ordinary human consciousness occurs, a sense at absolute freedom develops spontaneously, and an awareness arises, at first dimly and vaguely, of the ineffable nature of the experience. No longer human, the individual finds himself in sweet and intimate contact with, what, no doubt because of early training, he presumes to call divinity under one of its innumerable guises. So staggering is this experience always, that never at any time, in spite of the difficulty of clear definition or explanation, is there the least shred of doubt but that what has occurred is some

71

incomprehensible linking of the human soul with something larger, greater and finer—with God, the Oversoul, the Absolute, the Void.

Not only so, but these systems did not rest idly with the initial experience of any one individual. Scientifically they labored to evolve a method whereby any individual anxious to experience similar interior results could do so, provided he applied himself vigorously and patiently and sincerely to the practice of such a technique. Thus we have in India and Tibet even to this day, the various Yoga and Tantra systems. These we may safely say display a rare and fine knowledge of the human psyche and its mechanism such as has never been equaled. Early Christianity, culminating in Gnosticism, was shot through with all sorts of cults practicing analogous forms of spiritual culture. Magic, likewise is a similar though archaic technique which proceeded by a way of invocations and the exaltation of consciousness and, particularly, through an appeal both to the aesthetic sense and the imagination. Using the latter as its principal engine, consciousness could formulate to itself specialized images and mental forms of various kinds. Through these visualized formulations, links were created by which or through which the primitive archetypes of the Unconscious, if we wish to use psychological nomenclature, or a cosmic level of consciousness, could pour into the human soul.

Devotional exercises and prayer are yet further means, having a very wide following and appeal. Quiescence of mental function, relaxation of thought and feeling, and complete passivity of will, are still others that have found adherents and devotees at different times in the world's history. But all of them have in view the same experience, no matter by what name it is called, or the special terms used in describing the ineffability of that which makes its unheralded entry into the mind.

Our difficulty in appreciating methods such as these may be attributed to the fact that no longer do we Westerners inherit the feeling of them in our blood. Because of bias and prejudice and predilection, the Church in past times never openly encouraged these techniques, however widely they may have been privately pursued. It had come to rely exclusively on one or two favorite approaches, and absolutely refused to tolerate any individual who was sufficiently independent in spirit to apply himself to others. At all times the Church recommended prayer, devotional exercises and meditation of certain limited kinds. In fact, the Church considered devotion to be its greatest spiritual weapon; love of God and Christ as a means to attain the distant heights of glory. In itself, this weapon is certainly not to be despised. But the Church committed the supreme error in failing to recognize that what is one man's meat may well be another's poison. Not all are so constituted by nature as to be capable of great devotion. Some actually may be incapable of it. Nor is everybody intellectually fitted for these stupendous flights into the lofty and rarefied heights of metaphysics and philosophy. Likewise it is only an individual here and there who is capable of sustained and prolonged meditation, in its deepest implication of Yoga training. By this I am to be understood as defining Yoga as a rigorous mental discipline, in which the mind is turned in on itself so as to obtain a complete awareness and control of its own faculties, resulting in the arousal of various spiritual functions and powers normally latent within. In this sense, Yoga has many points of similarity with Magic. And it was these methods which the Church objected to principally. So it was that the knowledge of the psyche revealed by these technical processes became lost to European thought and culture.

Occasionally there must have arisen an individual here and there who had an intuitive knowledge of these things, or had received in the East some similar special training. Perhaps as so often happens, he had in some accidental way stumbled not only on this wonderful experience, but also on the technical methods whereby it might suitably be induced—or had in some other way sought to revive that knowledge. Such an individual we know historically was bitterly opposed and persecuted as dangerous and inimical to the faith. The tragic fate of the Albigensians, to name out of a large number but one particular group, is eloquent testimony to the horrible tactics of organized ecclesiasticism. In view of the fact that so-called occult disciples of the mind develop peculiar powers which in the popular mind are conceived of as "magical," and which in the religious mind are ascribed only to Christ and perhaps a few saints, it is again obvious why such persecutions occurred. In the opinion of the Church, Christ was a unique being. He was not, as is maintained by modern religious and ethical groups, a very highly evolved spiritual type comparable to Buddha or Krishna and similar individuals. He was the Son of God. As such, he was unique. He was alone in the entire history of the world. Consequently any person who claimed to develop, no matter by what mystical or other means, potencies of soul and spirit similar to those possessed and exercised by Christ, stood in direct competition as it were to the Church's claim. The Church has always preferred to ignore the claims of other religions, especially the claims of the various mystical and occult systems that such powers were not supernatural but quite normal to people who had pursued certain techniques and trainings.

One may not close this topic of the possible relation of alchemy to religion and religious experience without first making at least some reference to that aspect of Buddhism called Zen. To define Zen is, in one sense of the word, impossible. It does not readily lend itself, because of its peculiar nature, to definition. But if we examine it generally our insight may be so sharpened as to enable us to divine something of its meaning. By doing so we will thus have received an overwhelming illumination into the possible import of all alchemical writing.

"The Wisdom of Enlightenment," says the Sutra of Wei-lang, "is inherent in every one of us. It is because of the delusion under which our mind works that we fail to realize it ourselves, and that we have to seek the advice and guidance of the highly enlightened one before we can know our essence of mind. You should know that so far as Buddha-nature is concerned there is no difference between an enlightened man and an ignorant one. What makes the difference is that one realizes it, while the other is kept in ignorance of it."[1]

---

1. Christmas Humphreys, ed., *The Sutra of Wei Lang* (Shanghai: Yu Ching Press), 37. From "Chapter II: On Prajna" of the Platform Sutra of the Sixth Patriarch Hui Neng (Wei Lang).

Buddha

In a word, the basis of Zen is self-realization. The entire object of the peculiar Zen approach to life was to realize this pure essence of mind, the Buddha-nature so-called. At the outset I should like to add, by way of speculation, that if one translates the Alchemical Mercury by the Buddhist term "pure essence of mind" and then interprets alchemy closely along Zen lines, that translation of terminology becomes an event of supreme and momentous importance. It will give us another highly significant clue into what it was that the alchemists were desirous of achieving, and the nature of the transmutation they sought to produce.

What therefore is Zen? We know what Buddhism is—more or less. From this we would be led to suspect that Zen is but one of its several branches. This is quite true, as far as it goes. But Zen is more. It claims to be a special "transmission outside the scriptures, rising through and beyond words and letters, pointing directly to the mind-essence of man, a seeing into one's own nature and the attainment of enlightenment." [2]

The teaching of Gautama Buddha was spread in India five hundred years prior to the birth of Christ—a thousand years before Mohammed. Buddhist Scriptures were translated into Chinese by native and Indian translators, dynasty after dynasty, from the first century of our era. The essence of Buddhism, however, was carried from India to China in 520 A.D. by Bodhidharma, known generally as the first Zen patriarch. The wisdom of enlightenment perceived by the Buddha, and the inner experience of the silent-sitting Bodhidharma, was likewise inherited by his successor, and similarly handed down through many generations. It was thus that Buddhism entered and was nurtured and promulgated in China and Japan. Its aim was the realization of what Buddha himself realized—the emancipation and illumination of the mind.

Zen is an extra-canonical branch of Buddhism, relying upon no sacred scripture or text. Its *ultima thule* is experience. Its system and its teachers attempt to break through the inflexible strata of the mind by various techniques and artifices so that the student may, in one swift flash of enlightenment, realize his own inner core of wisdom. The core is there all the time. You and I, and everyone else in the world, possess this core of wisdom. In one sense, it is that prima materia which the alchemists claimed to be the most common thing in the whole world. But we neglect it because of lack of realization of its presence. If only we could divine it, realizing that deep within us behind the blind façade of conventional thinking, is the real self which we have never known, the whole face of life in consequence could be altered and enriched for us.

The following excerpts from a letter of Yengo (Yuan-wu in Chinese) may answer somewhat the question "What is Zen?"

> The great truth of Zen is possessed by everybody. Look into your own being and seek it not through others. Your own mind is above all forms, it is free and quiet and sufficient; it eternally

---

2. Daisetz Teitaro Suzuki, *Essays in Zen Buddhism* (New York: Rider and Co., 1949), 20.

stamps itself in your six senses and four elements. In its light all is absorbed.

Yengo continues:

Zen has nothing to do with letters, words or sutras. It only requests you to grasp the point directly, and therein to find your peaceful abode.

And finally:

Putting your simple faith in this, discipline yourself accordingly; let your body and mind be turned into an inanimate object of nature like a stone or a piece of wood; when a state of perfect motionlessness and unawareness is obtained all the signs of life will depart and also every trace of limitation will vanish. Not a single idea will disturb your consciousness, when lo! all of a sudden you will come to realize a light abounding in full gladness. It is like coming across a light in thick darkness; it is like receiving treasure in poverty. The four elements and the five aggregates are no more felt as burdens; so light, so easy, so free you are. Your very existence has been delivered from all limitations; you have become open, light, and transparent. You gain an illuminating insight into the very nature of things, which now appear to you as so many fairylike flowers having no graspable realities. Here is manifested the unsophisticated self which is the original face of your being; here is shown all bare the most beautiful landscape of your birthplace. There is but one straight passage open and unobstructed through and through. This is so when you surrender all—your body, your life, and all that belongs to your inmost self. This is where you gain peace, ease, nondoing, and inexpressible delight. All the sutras and sastras are no more than communications of this fact; all the sages, ancient as well as modern, have exhausted their ingenuity and imagination to no other purpose than to point the way to this. It is like unlocking the door to a treasury; when the entrance is once gained, every object coming into your view is yours, every opportunity that presents itself is available for your use; for are they not, however multitudinous, all possessions obtainable within the original being of yourself?[3]

---

3. Daisetz Teitaro Suzuki, *An Introduction to Zen Buddhism* (New York: Grove Press, 1963), 46.

Zen is based upon a fundamental philosophical fact. Logic and the ordinary processes of thought are unable by themselves to solve the riddle either of the universe or of oneself. Analytical Psychology in all its branches, has recently in the past several years shown us the validity of this assumption. For in many of the thought processes that we pursue, as we were wont to think, so abstractly and impersonally, we are guided not by the pure inevitable light of reason, but by personal idiosyncrasy and actual wish and whim. We may not be conscious of such a direction to our thought, but there it is, an unconscious motivation, coloring the very flower of our metaphysical effort.

Behind all its apparent trivialities and irrationalities that we shall soon uncover and examine, Zen asks us to acquire a new outlook upon life and ourselves. We may then see life as it really is, and obtain final satisfaction to our deepest needs. The new point of view to be adopted or cultivated is one which will strike right through the apparent duality of existence with its "A equals A" or "A equals not A." We shall realize that words by which we attempt to measure so much of life are but words and no more. Words have ceased to correspond with facts; we have become slaves to words. So we must part company with words and return to facts.

The following indicates with what contempt the Zen masters treated words in the way we normally use them. Yen, the national teacher of Ku-shan, when he was still a student monk, studied for many years under Hsueh-feng. One day, seeing that his student was ready for a mental revolution, the master took hold of him, and demanded roughly, "What is this?"

Yen was aroused as if from deep slumber and at once comprehended what it all meant. He simply lifted his arms and swung them to and fro. Feng said, "What does this mean?"

"No meaning whatever, sir," came quickly from the disciple.

To our great disappointment, despite the greatness of our philosophers and theologians, we have not been able to obtain peace of mind, perfect happiness, and a thorough understanding of life and the world. We have come to the end of our tether and there are no further steps to take which would lead us to a broader field of reality.

This is only too true of today, as it was of periods in past history. This is the beginning of Zen.

It argues that logic is one-sided, and that illogicality so-called, what Jung could call the irrational side of life, is in the last analysis not necessarily illogical. What is superficially irrational has after all its own order which is in correspondence with the true state of things. The irrational is not the chaotic—as will be testified to by anyone who has undergone some degree of psychological analysis or received the mystical experience. So far from this being true, life becomes more orderly, understandable and endurable through just such an acceptance of its irrational side.

When Shui-lao was trimming the wisteria, he asked his master Ma-tsu the question "What is the idea of the Patriarch's coming over here from the West?"

Ma-tsu replied, "Come up nearer and I will tell you."

As soon as Shui-lao approached, the master gave him a kick, knocking him completely over. This fall, however, says Prof. Suzuki, opened his mind at once to a state of *satori*. He rose with a hearty laugh, as if an event, most unexpected and most desired, had taken place.

Thus we find in Zen an insistence upon the apparently illogical. It is deliberately employed as a needed corrective to the inflexibility and sterility of most of our ordinary conscious thinking. Zen is a joyful and spontaneous emphasis of the irrational and much larger elements of ourselves. The result is a breaking up of the tyranny of mind. We will have realized how much we have been chained and imprisoned to solely false concepts of ourselves and the universe. At the same time it will be a spiritual emancipation, for then the psyche will no longer be divided against itself. Not only are we beings with a conscious thinking process but there is a process of another order altogether which is equally, if not more, important. And if this latter be not recognized, there is no peace, no happiness and no serenity.

By acquiring this intellectual freedom, the soul is in full possession of itself. Birth and death no longer torment it, for there are no such sharp divisions anywhere in nature—apparent though they seem. There is no dichotomy in consciousness. No Unconscious and

No Conscious. They are both aspects of the psyche without cleavage. There are only unknown recesses in our minds which lie beyond the threshold of the relatively constructed consciousness. "Beyond" is used only because it is the most convenient term to indicate their "position." Actually there is no "beyond," no "underneath," no "upon" in our consciousness. The mind is an indivisible unit which cannot be divided or torn into pieces or compartments. The phrase the "unknown recesses of the mind" is but a concession to our ordinary method of talking.

Whatever field of consciousness is known to us is generally filled with unqualified assumptions, dogmas, prejudices, and the results of unexamined crystallized mental habits. To get rid of these, to open the spring of living water within—which is necessary for arriving at the Zen experience known as *satori*—the Zen psychologists sometimes point to the presence of some hitherto inaccessible region in our minds. Though in reality there is no such region apart from our everyday consciousness, we talk of it as generally more easily comprehensible. When all hindrances to the ultimate truth are eliminated, we all realize that there are, after all, no such things as hidden recesses of mind, or even the truth of Zen or alchemy appearing as mysterious for so long. Alchemy and Zen run parallel one with another, and the truth of one system is the truth of the other.

But how does Zen work? Granted that the mind in its ordinary working is barren and sterile, what shall we do? How does Zen propose to break down the inflexible habits of thinking to reveal the bright clear mirror of the mind beneath? At the core of all Zen procedure is the *koan*—so extensively used and, like the spagyric riddles of our text, so little understood. The *koan* is neither a riddle nor a witty remark, however much it may seem to partake of both. It has, remarks Professor Suzuki in his *Introduction to Zen Buddhism*, a most definite objective, the arousing of doubt and pushing it to its furthest limits.[4] A statement built upon a logical basis is approachable through its rationality; whatever doubt or difficulty we may have had about it dissolves itself by

---

4. Suzuki, *An Introduction to Zen Buddhism,* 108.

pursuing the natural current of ideas. All rivers are sure to pour into the ocean; but the *koan* is an iron wall standing in the way and threatening to overcome one's every intellectual effort to pass ... You feel as if your march of thought had been suddenly cut short. You hesitate, you doubt, you are troubled and agitated, not knowing how to break through the wall which seems altogether impassable. When the climax is reached, your whole personality, your inmost will, your deepest nature, determined to bring the situation to an issue, throws itself with no thought of self or no self, of this or that, directly and unreservedly against the iron wall of the *koan*. This throwing your entire being against the *koan*, unexpectedly opens up an hitherto unknown region of the mind. Intellectually, this is the transcending of the limits of logical dualism, but at the same time it is a regeneration, the awakening of an inner sense which enables one to look into the actual working of things. For the first time, the meaning of the *koan* becomes clear and in the same way that one knows that ice is cold and freezing. The eye sees, the ear hears, to be sure, but it is the mind as a whole that has *satori;* it is an act of perception, no doubt, but it is a perception of the highest order ... The wall of *koan* once broken through and the intellectual obstructions well cleared off, you come back, so to speak, to your relatively-constructed consciousness.

Thus the *koan* is a sort of intellectual riddle which challenges the mind to overthrow itself by an introspection of far reaching implications. It is a riddle before which the mind bends as before a gale and is broken, producing a state which well might be compared to the alchemical corruption. The alchemical aphorisms are riddles of the same obscure order, for their writers constantly enjoin us to turn the mind upon itself. For example, Hermes in *The Golden Treatise* says, "My Son, whatsoever thou hearest, consider it rationally. For I hold thee not to be a fool. Lay hold, therefore of my instructions and meditate upon them, and so let thy heart be fitted, *as if thou wast thyself the author of that which I now teach.*" [5]

---

5. See "The Golden Treatise of Hermes" in Israel Regardie's *The Philosopher's Stone: Spiritual Alchemy, Psychology, and Ritual Magic* (Woodbury, MN: Llewellyn Publications, 2013), 46.

The type of riddle which we find in alchemy includes such statements as this. "Take the flying volatile and drown it flying, and divide
and separate it from its rust which yet holds it in death."[6] "Extract
from the ray its shadow and impurity by which the clouds hang over
it." "Return then, O my Son, the extinct coal to the water for thirty
days, as I shall note to thee."[7] And many another.

They are quite different in expression from those employed in Zen,
but I have no doubt the object is the same. Moreover, the effect is similar. For if one reflects upon the hermetic writings, one comes to feel as
though a knock-out blow has been administered to the mind. In the
ordinary terms of mind, these things are not understandable. We cannot come to terms with these mysteries, these riddles. They seem to belong to another order of being which we cannot reach. But we take the
riddle, make it part of ourselves, worry over it, and it creates a species
of mental crisis. We are taken to the edge of the abyss. Shall we retreat
or...? There is the gulf stretching in front of one. Shall one take the
chance of plunging?

The riddles used by the Zen masters are, as I have said, totally different in subject matter but not in essence. We are asked in Zen to consider that the clapping of two hands makes a noise—what would be
produced by one hand? Obviously, taken on its face value, it is nonsense
of the grossest kind—but it is unanswerable, and thus by its very irra-
tionality and irrelevancy produces the intellectual crisis so earnestly desired. Another is "What was your original face before you were born?"[8]

Questions were asked which likewise challenged the questioner's
very integrity and sanity almost. For instance, Nan-chuan was once
asked by Hyakulo, one of his fellow-monks, if there was anything he
dared not talk about to others. The master answered "Yes."

Whereupon the monk continued, "What then is this something
you do not talk about?"

The master's reply was "It is neither mind, nor Buddha, nor matter."

---

6. Ibid., 47.

7. Ibid.

8. Suzuki, *An Introduction to Zen Buddhism*, 104.

But the monk answered and said, "If so, you have already talked about it."

"I cannot do any better. What would you say?"

"I am not a great enlightened one," answered Hyakulo.

The master replied, "Well, I have already said too much about it."

Possibly one may think this is much ado about nothing. But before reaching this conclusion the advice of Hermes in *The Golden Treatise* is worthy of consideration. Put yourself in the place of the master, and by this identification, attempt to divine what he is endeavoring to achieve. If you do this, some degree of understanding will arise as to the object of this cross-talk which superficially is so meaningless. A friend of mine, when confronted by the questions and answers of Zen, said it reminded him of a childish game he used to play. He would ask a playmate:

"Do you know Mr. John Doe?"

The playmate of course could answer, "I don't think so. Who is he?"

"Who?" would enquire my friend, facetiously.

"Mr. John Doe."

"Never heard of him!"

Even this, so gleefully indulged in by children, is strictly speaking of the same irrational order as the Zen *koan* and *zazen*, and if carried to the same logical conclusion, no doubt would produce the same result.

Another of these irrational statements is expressed in a couplet:

Empty-handed I go, and behold the spade is in my hands; I walk on foot, and yet on the back of an ox I am riding.[9]

The method of application is best expressed by a Zen master himself. Tau-hui says, "Just steadily go on with your koan every moment of your life. If a thought arises, do not attempt to suppress it by conscious effort, only renew the attempt to keep the koan before the mind. Whether walking or sitting, let your attention be fixed upon it without interruption. When you begin to find it entirely devoid of flavor, the final moment is approaching; do not let it slip out of your grasp. When

---

9. Suzuki, *An Introduction to Zen Buddhism*, 58.

all of a sudden something flashes out in your mind, its light will illuminate the entire universe, and you will see the spiritual land of the Enlightened Ones fully revealed at the point of a single hair." [10]

Zen is thus a unique product of the Oriental mind. At least it has been so considered until recently. But I think if we analyze alchemical writing aright, we will see that its method is similar. Its uniqueness consists, so far as its practical aspect goes, in its methodical training of the mind in order to mature it to the state of satori. The mind may grow by itself even when left to nature to achieve her own ends. But man cannot always wait for her. He likes to meddle, for better or for worse. "Art perfects what nature began" is an alchemical aphorism, and it has application to the matter on hand. The position is similar to that taken by the advocate of the Eastern Yoga systems. It is true that all men eventually may obtain liberation and spiritual freedom. But the processes of Nature, whilst certain, are slow and ponderous. By the application of human intelligence and sympathetic skill, these natural processes may be considerably accelerated, and the development of spiritual evolution hastened. Thus both alchemy and Zen Buddhism are processes deliberately designed to further what Nature began and what Nature eventually may finish by herself. The advocates of both systems believe that, when certain stages of psychic development have been reached, it is possible to accelerate it enormously by judicious and careful training. The goal of that training is what the Zen Buddhists name *Satori*, and the alchemists call it the transmutation of lead or baser metals into gold.

Satori is the sudden flashing into consciousness of a new truth hitherto undreamed of. It is a sort of mental catastrophe taking place all at once after much piling up of matters intellectual and demonstrative. The piling reaches a limit of stability when the whole edifice tumbles madly to the ground, the putrefaction so often spoken of in alchemy. Suddenly, a new heaven is open to full survey. When the freezing point

10. Daisetz Teitaro Suzuki, *The Zen Koan as a Means of Attaining Enlightenment* (Rutland, VT: Charles E. Tuttle Co., Inc., 1994), 90–91. This work was originally published by Rider & Company in 1950, in *Essays in Zen Buddhism*, second series, edited by Christmas Humphreys.

is reached, water turns in an instant to ice. The liquid has suddenly turned into a solid body, and no more flows freely. *Satori* similarly comes upon a man unawares, when he feels that he has exhausted his whole being. Religiously, it is a new birth. Intellectually and psychologically, it is the acquiring of a new viewpoint which partakes of all levels of consciousness. The world now appears as if clothed in some resplendent garment into which everything fits by right of place.

In one sense Zen Buddhism has nothing to do with religion in the ordinary manner of thinking. Here we find nothing to do with the ordinary concepts of God, the soul, repentance, sin, and salvation. Rather we must assume that it is more akin to a psychology than a religion. It seeks to produce radical and far-reaching changes in the consciousness of its devotees, changes and transmutations induced within because of a sense of present inadequacy and insufficiency. The outlook upon life is somehow defective. Within there is no peace of mind, no stability and integrity. There is a warfare waged between different elements within the personality, and the crucial problem is somehow to solve that warfare, to bring quiet and peace to a troubled mind. Zen's method is so to aggravate that conflict until it reaches a peak when the intellect itself crumbles, unable any more to fight. It gives up—relaxing its efforts finally in the face of too formidable obstacles. And then takes place that miracle of the ages. It is as though there were an element within, latent and dormant throughout the ages, which is stirred to activity only by the aggravation of conflict and by the threat of possible spiritual extinction. Only when the mind has accepted itself and released its tension does this other dynamic element commence its operation, transmuting in an instant the entire personality and changing the whole outlook upon life.

I suggest that if alchemy is rigidly interpreted along such lines as these, as its own internal evidence seems definitely to suggest, we have more than a satisfactory clue as to its nature. Its mysteries are riddles deliberately invented so as to tax the reader's patience and activate the innate intelligence. The mind, rendered furious by these inexplicable obscurities, rams itself headlong into the stone wall of darkness, and in time sees itself defeated by the inevitable. This continued and persisted in, as the alchemists intended it should be, results in psychic relaxation and an unburdening of the soul, and the manifestation of new principles intrinsic to the personality.

For the Neo-Platonist of Synesius' day, the source of true knowledge was supposed to exist likewise not in the development of logical thought but in those ecstatic moments of ineffability when the soul became conjoined with the divine Being itself. The belief was held that when we seek to define God by intellectual definitions we confine him within the boundaries represented by our finite notions of what truth must be, and, therefore, degrade him. We attain to God, so held the Neo-Platonists, not by making our knowledge more complete, correcting what we know by a deeper and richer intellectual knowledge, but by giving up altogether our feeble attempt at comprehension. By relaxing the fibers of the mind, and allowing the distinct yet arbitrary conceptions of the intellect to fade away, we may enter into an immediate and ineffable identity of feeling. Centuries earlier, Plato had argued that to know God it was necessary to eliminate the sense and bodily life. The Neo-Platonists went much further. They said we must get rid of the intellect as well. The predominant tinge to the entire philosophy was that no intellectual process will bring us into that immediate vital contact with reality which is Deity. Rather, such a process is a hindrance. The ultimate method of religion as a practical scheme is not thought, but mystic contemplation and feeling, an unconditioned acceptance of the irrational element of life. This is the way to regeneration. And the final goal is that indefinable ecstasy in which the finite personality and thought and self-consciousness drop away, and the individual consciousness melts to a oneness with the Absolute wherein no trace of difference or separation abides.

This recognition of the side of immediate experience is also found, it must be admitted in all honesty, in Christianity in the doctrine of the Holy Spirit. In later Christian mysticism a direct Neo-Platonic influence continued—and still continues today. But at first the Church emphasized the fact of a single historical revelation in the past—that of Christ. Accordingly, the insistence upon the authority of a definite and final historical revelation in Palestine came more and more to be the orthodox body of Christianity. The mystical attempt to elevate the personal ego in the acquisition of a higher state of consciousness was considered dangerously lawless, and condemned as heresy. It was the Church view that no man by himself and by his own unaided efforts could attain divine illumination save by the grace and intervention of God. This view therefore expressly outlaws all human effort and aspiration in a mystical direction. For Providence, at a moment's notice, and to us in a wholly capricious way, could illuminate a clod. Sterile and uncreative as it is, such a conception permeates even alchemical literature. We find certain of the alchemists expressing the opinion that only by prayer and the grace of God could the knowledge of the secret Fire of the Wise be revealed. Others, nevertheless, stressed meditation and human effort as the means by which divine grace was obtained.

Because it was heresy to develop in a mystical direction, the alchemical jargon came into being. Or at least, shall we say it was adopted by those who had occult and mystical ideas to express. It was a convenient code already fully developed. For several reasons it became imperative to employ a medium for the expression not only of the religious or mystical experience, but to describe the technical means whereby such illuminations, and that which developed therefrom, could be induced. The hermetic writings were also means by which the alchemist wished to make himself known to his unknown brethren everywhere who had likewise done the same work and achieved the same results. He craved as only such a human being can crave the society of those with whom he could converse freely of those wonderful things—those with whom he could reside and travel without having to put a continual restraint upon his words and actions. Alchemical literature is one repetitive testimony to this end and to this obfuscation of motive, despite the fact that occasionally actual chemical formulae were used as a cloak. And despite the fact too that imposters and charlatans had employed impossible fraudulent receipts as a means of enhancing their own vile reputations, or to swindle the avaricious or unsuspecting of their worldly goods.

When examining this and similar texts, if the reader will bear such ideas in mind, I feel he will approach that which the unknown author had in his heart to express. As Synesius himself says: "Upon this ground was it that they were pleased to speak by figures, types, and analogies, that so they might not be understood but by such as are discreet, religious, and enlightened by (divine) Wisdom. All which, notwithstanding, they have left in their writings a certain method, way and rule, by the assistance whereof the wise man may comprehend whatever they have written most obscurely, and in time arrive at a knowledge of it." [11]

---

11. See page 32.

CHAPTER FOUR

THE GREAT WORK

If I may repeat my basic definition, the first Matter of the Alchemists was a certain virginal, pure or metaphysical substance, universal in its operations, pervading and vitalizing every living and chemical thing. In the *Golden Treatise* of Hermes Trismegistus, it is defined as: "In the caverns of the metals there is hidden the Stone that is venerable, splendid in color, a mind sublime. and an open sea ... Know that this matter I call the Stone; but it is also named the feminine of magnesia, or the hen, or the white spittle, or the volatile milk, the incombustible ash, in order that it may be hidden from the inept and ignorant, who are deficient in goodness and self-control; which I have nevertheless signified to the Wise by one only epithet, viz., the Philosopher's Stone." [1] It is this concept that answers to the spiritual principle affirmed by every religious scheme, the Oversoul, the Soul of the World, the One Life vivifying all things, the Light itself. It is commonplace that the mystical experience is also termed illumination because its major characteristic is a flooding of the mind and entire personality by an incomparable brilliance. No simile will describe its luster and incandescence. Sun and moon and stars fade away into utter blackness before its face—the light that was never seen on land or sea. And Synesius here says of the splendor which is "the force, the beginning

---

1. See "The Golden Treatise of Hermes" in Regardie's *The Philosopher's Stone: Spiritual Alchemy, Psychology, and Ritual Magic* (Woodbury, MN: Llewellyn Publications, 2013), 46.

and the end of the whole work" that it is "a clear Light, which sheds true goodness into every Soul that hath once tasted of it." [2]

Dormant within man, because obscured by his busy everyday but superficial consciousness, it passes unnoticed and unvalued. Thus the alchemists say their first material is uncommonly cheap. Hermes asserts "Our most precious stone cast forth upon the dunghill, being most dear, is made altogether vile." [3]

Whilst Thomas Vaughan, in a letter from the R. C., says: "This matter which for the crowd is vile, exceedingly contemptible and odious, yet not hateful but lovable and precious to the wise, beyond gems and tried gold. A lover itself of all, to all well-nigh an enemy, to be found everywhere, yet discovered scarcely by any, though it cries through the streets to all: Come to me all ye who seek and I will lead you in the true path. This is that only thing proclaimed by the true philosophers, that which overcometh all and is itself overcome by nothing, searching heart and body, penetrating whatsoever is stone and stiff, consolidating that which is weak, establishing resistance in the hard." [4]

No one notices or becomes aware of that within him which is most valuable. It requires to be mined from the depths, from the cavern of the metals which is man himself. The alchemical references to man as a mine, and to his different principles as metals or minerals, is by no means so utterly fantastic or absurd as at first sight may have seemed. Man, chemically *is* an aggregation of various minerals. His physical constitution consists of calcium, phosphorus, magnesium, iron, potassium, sulphur and so forth, in various proportions. In fact, his

---

2. See page 33.

3. See "The Golden Treatise of Hermes" in Regardie's *The Philosopher's Stone: Spiritual Alchemy, Psychology, and Ritual Magic* (Woodbury, MN: Llewellyn Publications, 2013), 50.

4. According to Vaughan, the Rosicrucian Frater who was the source of this letter went by the title of "Sapiens." See E. J. Langford Garstin, *Theurgy, or the Hermetic Practice: A Treatise on Spiritual Alchemy* (Berwick, ME: Nicolas-Hays, Inc., 2004), Chapter 10. (Originally published in London by Rider & Co., 1930.) Also see "Anima Magica Abscondita" published in Arthur Edward Waite, *The Magical Writings of Thomas Vaughan* (London: George Redway, 1888), 63.

wellbeing depends on a certain balance of these minerals being maintained. In a sense, then, man is, as the alchemists claimed, a mine. Deep within that mine is latent that first principle of consciousness which in itself is both the beginning of life and the goal of the Great Work.

This principle of life so obscurely defined is that which they call the Mercury of the Philosophers. That this cannot possibly refer to common quicksilver or hydrargyrum is persistently thrust home to us as we read their writings. "The name of Mercury doth only properly agree with that which is volatile."[5] "Mercury substance of all metals; it is as a water by reason of the homogeneity which it possesses with vegetables and animals and it receives the virtues of those things which adhere to it in decoction."[6] "If your *argent vive* has no life, it is not what they mean."[7] "The matter of our stone, mercury, is a commonly diffused subject, and though it is found with greater ease in some minerals, it may be discovered everywhere."[8] "The metals— especially the gold of the vulgar—are dead, but ours are living, full of spirit, and these wholly must be taken."[9] "Or what more shall I say," asks Morienus, discoursing with an Arabian monarch about the Stone. "The thing, O King, is extracted from thee, in the which mineral thou doest even exist; with thee it is found; by thee it is received;

---

5. From "The Hermetic Arcanum." See William W. Westcott, ed., *Collectanea Hermetica* (York Beach, ME: Weiser Books, 1998), 20. This important text was written in Latin by Jean d'Espagnet as "Enchiridion physicae restitutae" and published in Paris in 1623. It was translated into English by Elias Ashmole in 1650. The treatise was included in several alchemical compilations. See online text at www.alchemywebsite.com/harcanum.html. R. W. Councell attributes this phrase to Paracelsus. See "Section IV. The Mercury of the Philosophers," in Councell, *Apollogia Alchymiae: A Restatement of Alchemy* (London: 1925). Online text at www.alchemywebsite.com/counsell.html.

6. See "Section IV. The Mercury of the Philosophers," in Councell, *Apollogia Alchymiae: A Restatement of Alchemy*. This quote is attributed to Bernard Trevisan in his book on the "Transmutation of Metals." (See Edward Kelly, *The Stone of the Philosophers* (Hamburg: 1676), paragraph 48. Online text at www.levity.com /alchemy/kellystn.html.

7. See Councell, "Section IV. The Mercury of the Philosophers."

8. Ibid.

9. Ibid.

and when thou shalt have proved all by the love and delight in thee, it will increase, and thou wilt know that I have spoken an enduring truth." [10] "My Son," counsels Synesius, "it is necessary that thou work with the *Mercury of the Philosophers* and the Wise, which is not the *Vulgar*." [11]

Surely there can be no misunderstanding here? How could scholars have imagined that hydrargyrum was meant? Yet for centuries chemists have maintained obstinately; in the face of inviolable evidence and testimony otherwise, that alchemy sought a metallic transmutation, and that the philosophical Prima Materia was a metal.

For the purpose of this thesis, I define Mercury, this living quicksilver, as a species or type of consciousness, of life, of spiritual vitality. This we must discover in our own hearts, for until we do, so say the alchemists, we are hardly alive at all. "As soon as any discerns the intention of the Philosophers, from the seeming sense of the letter, the dark night of ignorance will fly away, and a glorious morning of light and knowledge will break forth." [12] Until this glorious morning of Light, a frequently encountered term for the mystical experience, does arise—until we have divined the presence of this interior light, we cannot proceed with the work. Once having become conscious of this "blessed nature" permeating us, and lying dormant within the inner heart waiting to be called upon, then all things are possible. Life then becomes transformed and hallowed. All things are realized to glow with their own inward light, and gold is seen in them and about them.

---

10. Quoted in Mary Anne Atwood, *A Suggestive Inquiry into the Hermetic Mystery, with a Dissertation on the More Celebrated of the Alchemical Philosophers Being an Attempt Towards the Recovery of the Ancient Experiment of Nature* (London: Trelawney Saunders, 1850), 153. (Online text at www.rexresearch.com/atwood /cont.htm.) See also *The Book of Morienus: Being the Revelations of Morienus to Khalid Ibn Yazid Ibn Mu'Awiyya, King of the Arabs of the Divine Secrets of the Magisterium and Accomplishment of the Alchemical Art* (Paris, 1559). (Online text at www.rexresearch.com/alchemy3/morienus.htm.)

11. See page 34.

12. William W. Westcott, ed., *Collectanea Hermetica, Vol. III: A Short Enquiry Concerning the Hermetic Art* (London Theosophical Publishing Society, 1894), 18.

Mercury

First of all, awareness of it must be widened, enhanced and heightened. It must be permitted freely to work its effect on us. We must become onlookers, objective spectators of and participants in the work of recreation, in the real sense of the word. For having divined the latent inner life, we can never turn back to forget it. At once, by that first second's perception of oneself, it has produced an ineradicable effect on the personality. Instantaneously we become aware of a contrast. On the one hand we see the petty human consciousness bound by apparently unbreakable bonds to a world of convention, insincerity, hypocrisy, and commercialism—a sham shadow of our own creation. On the other hand is the interior dawning of the Light itself, vision, life, and love. Forthwith conflicts begin to corrupt the ego. "As an acid eats into steel, as a cancer that utterly corrupts the body; so am I unto the spirit of man. I shall not rest until I have dissolved it all." [13] So has one poet expressed the effect of the Light upon the ego. The narrow restricted vision, hidebound and crystallized, undergoes a transformation. Eventually, new values form. A new attitude evolves to life. No hard and fast barrier is permitted to exist in consciousness to prevent the easy upwelling of this inner life. No opaque ideas are allowed to bar the translucence and illumination of the Light. But that is an ultimate stage. Meanwhile, until that takes place, there is fear and pain and sorrow.

All births, all great changes, are attended by pain. We are hurt at any vital change that occurs to us. Anxiety at once commences to corrode our spirit. We seek to erect barriers to change, forgetting that life itself is constantly changing. The universe is in a state of flux—and we with it too. Walls are erected around us to maintain the *status quo* and to defend what we falsely imagine to be our menaced integrity. But whilst the defense mechanism keeps off all intruders without, and shuts us up within all safe and sound, it also becomes the unconscious means of cutting us off from the swift moving current of life. Life moves and, because of our defenses, we do not move—become static and divorced from reality. The ego becomes swollen. The energy from the Unconscious levels becomes repressed, for the Unconscious is life and movement. Conflict is developed as the order of the day, and conflict spells tension. Tension and conflict are but the outcome of fear and anxiety. These prevent one from realizing the true nature of reality, thrusting one into a deluded world of one's own creation. And then, as the *Bhagavad Gita* says "from delusion is produced loss of the memory, from the loss of memory, loss of discrimination, and from loss of discrimination, loss of all!" [14] We have lost the knack of "sitting loose to life," as one clever psychological expositor has termed

---

13. Excerpt from *Liber Cordis Cincti Serpente*. See Aleister Crowley, *The Holy Books* (Dallas, TX: Sangreal Foundation, 1972), 55. Online text at http://hermetic.com /crowley/libers/lib65.html, 13–17.

14. See William Quan Judge's recension of the *Bhagavad Gita* (1890), "Chapter II: Devotion through Application to the Speculative Doctrines." Online text at www.theosociety.org/pasadena/gita/bg-eg-hp.htm.

it,[15] and letting life without hindrance work its changes and its effects upon us.

If we enjoy and ardently seek pleasure let us also realize that it is but a part of life. Pain and sorrow is the other half. Let us not be Hedonists, living our lives solely devoted to pleasure. Nor let us be Buddhists who assert that all is sorrow and productive of pain. If we would not lose the one, let us not try to exclude the other. Acceptance is the key towards the formulation of the only satisfactory world view for us. We have to accept the whole of life—life and the universe and its effects in all its branches, not merely one alone which appeals to us. It is presumption of the crudest kind to believe that we may escape from pain. On the other hand, with acceptance of the whole of life unconditionally, life transforms itself so that one functions on altogether a different level than that of pain and pleasure. The new birth or the development of a higher psychological attitude induced by the discovery of the Light is equally feared. Particularly is it feared because the old viewpoint is perceived for what it is. It is valueless and degrading, preventing spontaneity and creativeness in life. At the same time, moreover, no new or final vision has formulated itself clearly within the mind. It is difficult and hurtful to let go of the old and be content to wait patiently and see what happens as the new life comes to birth within. The future seems dark and unknown.

It is dark. But we must be patient and relax and wait. A child will become impatient and fretful, demanding tearfully that it must have what it wants when it wants it. The hysteric may do likewise, and develop all sorts of adverse psychic and physiological symptoms in consequence of what he deems to be his frustration. But the adult in the true sense of the word may not behave thus for he realizes that he cannot coerce nature. Nature can only be conquered by submission and acceptance of her laws. He must leave to life whatever it may wish to bring forth—and be calm and philosophical in his waiting. No crutch is to be found anywhere to lean upon. What is unknown and unseen

---

15. Geraldine Coster, *Yoga and Western Psychology* (London: Motilal Banarsidass, 1934).

is always feared. The child's psychology should have shown us that. Fear and anxiety induce this blackness within the ego. Such a blackness arising within the psyche is a recognized phenomenon, and by the alchemical authorities do we find it so named and described. It is an admirable correspondence with what in religious mystical literature is called the dark night of the soul.

In all the alchemical works do we read that the blackness is a significant stage of the Great Work. It is a necessary stage because it represents the corruption and putrefaction of the false inflexible ego sense itself preparatory to the complete upwelling of the archetypes of the Unconscious. Synesius affirms that "the blackness which appears is a sign of putrefaction. And the beginning of the dissolution is a sign of the conjunction of both natures." [16] Note the wording here—"the conjunction of both natures"—it is significant.

What the alchemists aimed at, apparently, was a primary dissolution of consciousness into its own root, the Unconscious. Nor was this all. Following this psychic immersion, the elements of consciousness re-form themselves on a new pattern, in such a way as to exist not as an opponent of the Light, but as an integral part of one single psychic entity, the vehicle and means of expression of the Light. This idea of the re-arrangement of the psychic pattern after the dissolution of its own constituents has been very concisely expressed by Aleister Crowley in these words: "There is an obvious condition which limits our proposed operations. This is that, as the formula of any work affects the extraction and visualization of the Truth from any 'First Matter,' the 'Stone' or 'Elixir' which results from our labors will be the pure and perfect Individual originally inherent in the substance chosen, and nothing else. The most skilful gardener cannot produce lilies from the wild rose; his roses will always be roses, however he have perfected the properties of his stock. There is here no contradiction with our previous thesis of the ultimate unity of all substance. It is true that Hobbs and Nobbs are both modifications of the Pleroma. Both vanish in the Pleroma when they attain Samadhi. But they are

---

16. See page 37.

not interchangeable to the extent that they are individual modifications: the initiate Hobbs is not the initiate Nobbs, any more than Hobbs the haberdasher is Nobbs of 'the nail and sarspan business as he got his money by.' Our skill in producing aniline dyes does not enable us to dispense with the original aniline, and use sugar instead. Thus the Alchemists said: 'to make gold you must take': their art was to bring each substance to the perfection of its own proper nature." [17]

After restoration to life following the immersion in the dynamic stream of Universal Life, consciousness becomes the *Lumen Vestimenti*, the golden robe of light and glory, the true Philosopher's Stone. In the *Tibetan Book of the Dead*, scholarly edited and introduced by Dr. Evans-Wentz, a similar view may be found. The passage I quote below is supposed to be uttered by the officiating lama who is conducting the deceased through different levels of consciousness after physical death. "Now thou art experiencing the Radiance of the Clear Light of Pure Reality. Recognize it … Thy present intellect, in real nature void, not formed into anything as regards characteristics or color, naturally void, is the very Reality, the All-Good … Thine own consciousness, shining void and inseparable from the Great Body of Radiance, hath no birth nor death and is the Immutable Light." [18]

But before the Stone can be concocted—that is before consciousness can achieve integration—the material of which it is constructed must be broken down to its own homogeneous base and dissolved. "Include, therefore, and conserve in that sea, the fire, and the heavenly Flyer," advises Hermes in the *Tractatus Aureus*, "to the latest moment of his exit." [19] The heavenly flyer is the volatile fantasy-creating consciousness of the ego. It is to be conserved or immersed in the Sea

---

17. Aleister Crowley, *Magick in Theory and Practice* (New York: Dover Publications, 1976), 187. Originally published in 1929.

18. Walter Y. Evans-Wentz, ed., *The Tibetan Book of the Dead* (London: Oxford University Press, 2000), xxxviii–xxxix. Originally published in 1927.

19. See "The Golden Treatise of Hermes" in Regardie's *The Philosopher's Stone: Spiritual Alchemy, Psychology, and Ritual Magic* (Woodbury, MN: Llewellyn Publications, 2013), 46.

of the Wise, the Unconscious, and "drowned," the baptism of the soul in God.

Immediately the ego, which has very definite precise limits and powers, comes into contact with the Unconscious, which is a wide delimited or universal stream of life of extremely greater potency in that it has behind it aeons of evolutionary development, it tends to disintegrate.

By the use of the words disintegration and corruption we can readily understand their meaning. Corruption is a chemical change involving a complete alteration of substance. And disintegration means a structural breaking down of a whole. If the ego by nature is definite, inflexible, crystallized and dogmatic in its expression as all of us are mostly agreed it is nowadays, then this process will bring about a diminution of that over-definiteness. Its absoluteness will be modified, its "cock-sureness" and over-certainty too. We could expect a relaxing of its inflexible and crystallized nature to a very marked degree. Actually if a very extensive and intensive degree of relaxation could be induced to include every department of the mind-body system, we would be near to achieving that ultimate goal of the alchemical philosophy. Such a disintegration or corruption is that which the alchemists anticipate and demand as the first stage of the Great Work. *The True Book* speaks of this blackness of dissolution or the consciously produced schizophrenia as "the dark mantle of the Stone," which is eloquent enough. Again, Synesius refers to it as "the sable robe, night, or the crow's-head."[20]

This latter phrase is one commonly employed by the alchemists. In fact, *The Golden Treatise* states that "what is born of the crow is the beginning of this art."[21] The crow or the raven—they are synonymously employed—is a black bird and, in the sense in which it is symbolically used of the alchemists, is like the vulture in that it is a bird of prey. It

---

20. See page 36.

21. See "The Golden Treatise of Hermes" in Regardie's *The Philosopher's Stone: Spiritual Alchemy, Psychology, and Ritual Magic* (Woodbury, MN: Llewellyn Publications, 2013), 53.

feeds upon the dead. Black is the color we associate with death, with fear, guilt and anxiety.

After its immersion in the wide expanse of the Collective Uncon-scious, the ego dies as it were, and becomes extinct. In psychology, the idea of the extent of the Unconscious has been variously portrayed. Commonest is the notion that if a large iceberg represents the entire self, the one-tenth visible above the waters refers to the surface rational consciousness, the ego: whilst the nine-tenths below the waters com-prise the activities of the Unconscious. Together they constitute one psyche, one unit, but for convenience' sake we consider them separately.

Hence when the ego is made extinct through immersion in the deeper and more vital levels of its own being, we may speak of it as being fed upon or swallowed by the Unconscious. Dark and black the Unconscious seems to be, because of its disintegrating or putrefying effect on the ego—a very telling symbol of death.

Immediately the disintegrating process is begun, however, a sec-ondary law in the psyche comes into operation. Were this process once begun and were it to continue indefinitely without check—as it does in psychosis where schizophrenia is purely a conscious resultant of internal conflict, and an unrestrained flight from reality into the world of phantasy—the end of the individual would be in sight. But because consciousness co-operates with the Unconscious in this psy-chic baptism, a reversal of motion operates automatically once a cer-tain degree of disintegration has been accomplished. After the psychic crisis subsides, the dualism inherent within the self tending always to schizophrenia is eliminated. The innate and hitherto concealed life or spirit builds up a new vehicle of consciousness through which it may function more adequately and satisfactorily than before. In Zen we have already seen a parallel of this. In the Chinese text of Wilhelm's already referred to, this is named the Golden Flower. The rationale is comparable to the course of certain somatic pathologies. The disease grows more and more acute and virulent, gradually reaching a crisis. Spontaneously it subsides, slowly, and without the need for further interference. So by the law of reversed effort, what Jung, after Heracleitus, has termed *enantiodromia*, the life of the psyche instead of becoming extinguished, passes over into its opposite and is self-sustained, seeking life in an entirely new direction.

The process involved, the use of the word *enantiodromia* sounds a little terrifying, does it not? In reality however, this lengthy word only indicates something you long have been familiar with. In order to give a theoretical instance of its application in another sphere which may assist the understanding and also provide a definition, let me briefly delineate a simple observation in physics.

Heat we are told causes expansion. Expansion and the consequent diffusion of heat leads to loss of heat. Cooling sets in, bringing about a state of contraction. Contraction generates heat, and heat gives rise to expansion—and so the same cycle begins again. In other words, one extreme in nature, by a slow and gradual process passes directly over into its antithesis.

This is *enantiodromia*, the law of conversion into opposites. Possibly you are more familiar with it under its old guise of the pendulum and its swing from one side to another.

Abnormal psychology gives us a first rate example of it in manic depression. Here the patient sinks slowly into the most horrible depression, a melancholia in which he is utterly inert and miserable. This is succeeded by a bout of elation and light-headedness which would make the pleasure and joy of a normal person appear like a three-year old weeping because his favorite toy was broken.

Manic depression is almost a perfect parallel from a psychopathic viewpoint to our present social and spiritual state. We rise and we fall in spite of ourselves—and a glance over history will show how one condition is inevitably succeeded by that which is its reverse. Only self-knowledge can end this involuntary swing, an awareness of the motives and forces operating in the background of our lives.

I may point out that St. Paul stands as an excellent example of the enantiodromiatic principle. As a Jew, Saul was decidedly antagonistic to the development of the new faith of Christianity. He was a confirmed opponent of it, a fanatic. Because of his hatred he was determined to do all he could to stamp out the new faith. Fanaticism we well know is born of secret doubt. If there are doubts hidden in your own soul, and in fear you will not permit yourself to face them, they find a necessary outlet in the form of a fanatical and extreme attitude towards life. This is a well-observed psychological phenomenon. A sudden and unexpected conversion changed Saul from an unbeliever to a believer, Paul. From an opponent contorted with hate, he became the greatest proponent of Christianity.

Although the actual incidence of a conversion—that is, a right about face, a switch around of the outlook upon life—often seems sudden and totally unexpected, yet we know that nothing in nature happens suddenly. There must have been a long period of preparation beforehand. It is only when such preparation is completed that the new view manifests itself violently. The conversion itself would coincide with the arrival of the pendulum at its opposite point. Prior to reaching that point, it had slowly been swinging over—from hate, in the case of St. Paul, to love itself.

Speaking of St. Paul's conversion on the way to Damascus and the blindness that afflicted him, Dr. Jung remarks that psychogenetic blindness is readily explainable. He regards it as a symptom of a psychological unwillingness to see and understand and realize something that has been made incompatible with the conscious attitude. This was obviously the case with St. Paul. His unwillingness as a Jew to see what virtue might lie in Christianity corresponds with his fanatical resistance to it. This resistance was never wholly extinguished, as his epistles evince. But because of this irrational attitude, he laid himself open to *enantiodromia*—the conversion of his religious viewpoint into something diametrically opposed to it.

To take another example. The so-called Middle Ages were a period characterized by an extreme belief in things of mind and spirit, as opposed to the materialistic feeling and belief that prevailed in the late Roman Empire. Nowadays we are not dogmatically to assume that such a belief was unreasoning and blind. On the contrary, there were then many men whose minds may well have rivalled those of present day thinkers. They were well trained in the processes of logic and philosophical speculation. The opinions of these few became mirrored in the general credulity and ignorance of the masses, exactly as nowadays is the case.

When the historical peak of belief was reached, gradually the pendulum began its backward movement—*enantiodromia* had operated. Instead of believing in spirit and spiritual things, today the masses profess a belief in matter and economics. Their belief is just as irrational and extreme as it was in former times for they fail to realize the factor of mass psychology, which is that factor producing economic and social conditions.

Matter and spirit and economics are psychological concepts designed to better our understanding of the inscrutable things of life and the universe. Mankind sees but the symbol without in the least divining what is concealed behind. Excellent minds have led the masses into this cul-de-sac, men who sought a deeper knowledge of nature through empirical and scientific methods. Their investigations and the conclusions they reached have been irrationally and conveniently accepted by men at large who thus have become irreligious and materialistically inclined. But the pendulum will swing back. *Enantiodromia* will once again operate, and without a doubt mankind in the near future will once again believe in spirit and mind and things of the higher life.

However, I am not really concerned just now with these matters of belief. These are matters for theologian and philosopher—not for the psychologist. What concerns me now is *enantiodromia* and its operation. It brings about radical changes in points of view covering long, long periods of time. This phenomenon can be observed in other than historical movement and individual lives. The substance of literature likewise offers eloquent testimony as to its operation. At certain periods literature is specious. It exhibits artificiality and falsity, and does not depict life save through the purblind eyes of prejudice and misanthropy. Puritanism and moral brittleness pervade its every word. Lively healthy literatures follow, writing which does exhibit the pulsing, vibrant core of human life. It deals with aspiration and nobility and purpose, caring naught for an artificial morality foisted unnaturally upon a passionate dynamic people. The tide turns. Again the pendulum swings back. A puritan spirit breathes coldly upon us as an automatic reaction against humanity and freedom. Once more mankind is swallowed up by the unconscious movement of forces operating unknown to itself within the depths of its own collective sphere.

To analyze the idea a little more closely, it would seem that to swing from one extreme to its opposite, the latter must be present within the heart at least as seed, as potentiality, as possibility. The mere fact of Saul's great hatred of the early Christians demonstrates at once the presence of his abiding love for the religion of "Christ crucified and resurrected."

A Chinese aphorism has it that when Yang is at its height Yin is born. Yang and Yin are, as I have indicated on a former page, the two opposites enunciated by Chinese Taoism. They are light and darkness, heat and cold, life and death—and all the other opposites that we daily experience. The aphorism would seem to indicate that light, upon reaching its maximum brilliance, slowly passes into its decline. At the very attainment of its zenith, darkness is conceived as a possibility and as an eventual goal of the pendulum swing. When an empire reaches the height of its imperial achievement and conquest, *enantiodromia* has already commenced its operation. Decline, decay, and corruption have set in.

The moral of the story as a mentor of mine would have said, is that if you are an extremist in anything you do, (…)[22] beware! More likely than not as time goes on you will become just that which you have abhorred and detested. The youthful communist becomes the aged conservative and reactionary. The boy who has hated his father for his domineering traits and unemotionalism becomes, by process of

---

22. Regardie had included a couple of additional words here. Unfortunately the original text has disintegrated to a point where it is no longer possible to determine what was written. However, Regardie's meaning is fairly clear.

unconscious identification, a man indistinguishable in the eyes of the world from his father before him.

Beware of uncontrolled expression of any extreme emotion. The time may come when the law of your own psyche may operate to your discomfiture to convert your expression into its antithesis. It is, however, only unconsciousness that permits the unbridled operation of this law. If you were really aware of yourself, your emotions and the motives that propelled you into activity, at once your behavior would be subject to some degree of correction, criticism and modification. In this event, your own self-knowledge would have overcome the operation of *enantiodromia*. What wonder the Greeks lauded the oracle "Man know thyself!"[23]

A knowledge of this law should go far towards shaping a more satisfactory attitude towards life. It is not what happens to us externally that is important or most significant. How we react to stimuli and how we feel about them—these are the important things. Your love eventually may turn to hate. Your elation may die, giving place to melancholy and gloom. All the things you loathe and despise may, in time, change and yield pleasure and happiness. These are inevitable. But to know yourself and to realize that this law of conversion into opposites works unceasingly within your own psyche day in and day out, should help you considerably in adapting yourself more effectually to life itself.

Presumably the materialism and license of our age—since these are expressions of the Collective Unconscious—will convert itself hereafter into an age of adherence to things of the spirit. Not only so, but reading the signs of the times and watching the backward swing of the pendulum, the near future will be characterized by an almost puritanical code of ethics.

Capitalism may be replaced by socialism—or something which serves as a pendulum opposite to its extreme. The present economic

---

23. The exact origin of the Ancient Greek aphorism *gnōthi seauton* (γνῶθι σεαυτόν), or "Know Thyself," is a subject for debate. It is often attributed to the Oracle at Delphi as well as to Socrates and other sages.

depression[24] will be followed by a wave of prosperity. That prosperity will in turn be followed by a depression. But before *enantiodromia* can operate the very depths of the depression have to be reached. We must taste of the very lowest dregs of despair and bitterness and horror before the pendulum can begin its slow swing over to the other side of economic security and stability.

This can be asserted with a certain degree of emphasis. For economics are not simply external events. They represent subjective psychological values. Why do I say this? Does it seem strange to associate the economic fluctuation with interior psychic events? It may seem incredible at first to one not familiar with the significance of modern psychology, but this is a conclusion that daily is borne in upon the practitioner. A patient of mine—a Wall Street operator—in discussing his occupation, remarked incidentally, almost with reflection, that the stock market was the life-blood of the nation. This being too good an opportunity to be missed, I asked him to consider the significance of this remark in our usual manner. That is to transfer it from the purely objective level onto the subjective plane. By this, I mean to imply that any objective fact has an inward significance to the patient. The mother, for example, in a dream, means not only the objective mother, but is a symbol of the emotional and spiritual side of the patient, his Unconscious. Sex, translated into libido, likewise is a general term and field of activity symbolizing the creative side of the psyche. Likewise the phrase "the life-blood of the nation" may be interpreted as an objective symbol of an inward psychological principle or fact. So I asked my patient what was the life-blood of the individual—the individual being the ultimate root pattern of the nation. And after some few seconds of deliberation, he expressed the belief that the emotional life was the life-blood of the individual.

Without emotional expression, the individual was as good as dead. Repression was the killing process. And he came to associate his own condition of penury and financial embarrassment and lack of commercial success which he so ardently desired with just such a repression of

---

24. Regardie was referring to the Great Depression.

his emotional nature. Thus in his mind and power were direct symbols of emotion and libido.

In so far as we are not fully conscious of ourselves, our potentialities, and what we really think and feel, there will be always aspects of ourselves of which we will remain unconscious. Because of this unconsciousness, they cannot be recognized as facets of ourselves. And if not perceived as ourselves, these forces of our own being are solely as objective happenings, mysterious and uncontrollable. Yet they are only the externalizations or the projections objectively of what exists within our own minds. Thus the fluctuations and unconscious pendulum swingings within the psychic deeps that occur unknown to ourselves are projected on to the external world as the working out of economic and business laws and events.

One day perhaps we may decide to awaken and attempt this achievement of self-consciousness as an integrated nation in order to perfect out economic and spiritual lives. When a higher degree of racial awareness has been achieved, we shall become aware of the operation of *enantiodromia* within. We can then decide to do something about polarizing ourselves between the opposites—regardless of their specific nature. With such an awareness, we will find ourselves able to modify the pendulum swing and, because of our understanding, overcome the operation of *enantiodromia*. Until we do this however, we shall forever be subject to the swing from one painful extreme to the other—to our own eternal detriment.

To return to our text, however, the conjunction of the two polarities of the psyche through this reversal and change of attitude is a goal envisaged both by psychological analysis and by the alchemical or spagyric art. What is born of this interior death is evidently the beginning of the Great Work, the reformulation of the Son, the king-born, which is a resurrected consciousness. It is this which is also the aim of every religion and mystical system which has arisen since the dawn of time. It is this ideal of inner integrity which is expressed by Socrates in the passage at the conclusion of the *Phaedrus:* "Beloved Pan, and all ye gods who haunt this place, give me beauty in the inward soul, and *may the outward and inward man be at one.* May I reckon the wise to be the wealthy, and may I have such a quantity of gold as none but the temperate can carry. Anything more? That prayer, I think, is enough for me."[25]

25. Benjamin Jowett, *The Dialogues of Plato, Translated into English, with Analyses And Introductions* (London: Oxford University Press, 1871), 489.

CHAPTER FIVE

THE SECRET FIRE

W here the major difficulty always arises in the consideration of alchemy is in connection with practical tactics. How may this change be induced in consciousness? This is indeed a problem. It is by now evident that we must labor to produce some intensification or widening of the horizon of the mind. As to how this is to be accomplished, apart from our hazard that free association may be useful, is not elucidated by the text with any degree of clarity. In one place we are advised to decoct the water of the Wise "gently by little and little." [1] It cautions us to "have great care at the beginning" not to burn "its Flowers and its vivacity, and make not too much haste to come to an end of thy work." In that section entitled *The First Operation, Sublimation*, we read that the First Matter or the Hyle, must be "put into its vessel" and then we must "make it hot in its place, well-prepared, with temperate heat." [2] Elsewhere, Synesius advises us that to "extract the soul, or the spirit, or the body, is nothing else than the abovesaid calcinations, in regard they signify the operation of Venus. It is therefore through the fire of the extraction of the soul that the spirit comes forth gently, understand me." [3] Possibly these cryptic instructions may convey but little. Analyzed however in terms of the material culled

1. See page 33.
2. See page 36.
3. See page 34.

from an examination of comparative religion and in the light of modern psychotherapeutic processes, we can I feel certain arrive at some knowledge of the technique proposed.

The first and momentous problem is the interpretation of the decocting or cooking process required. The expressions of fire and heat are consistent throughout all hermetic writing. And always we find Sulphur mentioned in connection with this Secret Fire. Like all the other alchemical terms, Sulphur is ambiguously and allegorically defined. *The Golden Tract* in *The Hermetic Museum* defines it as "nothing but mature mercury."[4] That is to say, by the above mode of interpretation, a well-developed, mature, and concentrated mind. Elsewhere we find such definitions of Sulphur as: "The fat of the mercurial wind joined to the scum of the red sea."[5] "Our fire is the true sulphur of Gold."[6] Raymond Lully asserts: "When we say that the Stone is generated by fire, men neither see, neither do they believe there is any other fire but the common fire, nor any other Sulphur and Mercury but the common Sulphur and Mercury[7] ... If thou shalt work with too strong a fire, the propriety of our spirit, which is indifferent as yet to life or death, will separate itself from the body, and the soul will depart to the region of her own sphere."

While Thomas Vaughan writes illuminatingly in *Lumen de Lumine:* "It is—as they describe it—moist and invisible. Hence they have called it the horse's belly or horse dung—a moist heat but no fire that

4. Arthur Edward Waite, *The Hermetic Museum: Containing Twenty-Two Most Celebrated Chemical Tracts* (York Beach, ME: Samuel Weiser, 1991), 19. Originally published in 1893. Text online at www.sacred-texts.com/alc/hm1/hm104.htm.

5. R. W. Councell, *Apollogia Alchymiae: A Restatement of Alchemy* (London, 1925). See "Section V. Sulphur and Salt." Text online at www.alchemywebsite.com/counsell.html. The quote is attributed to Nicolas Flamel.

6. Eirenaeus Philalethes, *Ripley Revived: or An Exposition upon Sir George Ripley's Hermetico-Poetical Works* (London: T. Ratcliff and N. Thompson, 1677). Online text is at www.rexresearch.com/riplrevv/riplyrevv.htm. Also quoted in E. J. Langford Garstin, *The Secret Fire: An Alchemical Study* (London, 1932), chapter IX.

7. Raymond Lully, quoted in A. E. Waite, *The Works of Thomas Vaughan: Eugenius Philalethes* (London: Theosophical Publishing House, 1919), 283–284. Also see Atwood, 126.

is visible."[8] And in his *Aula Lucis* he adds: "Our fire then is a natural fire; it is vaporous, subtle, and piercing, it is that which works all in all, if we look on physical digestions; nor is there anything in the world that answers to the stomach and performs the effects thereof but this one thing. It is a substance of propriety solar and therefore sulphureous. It is prepared, as the philosophers tell us, from the old dragon, and in plain terms, it is the fume of Mercury—not crude but cocted."[9]

At least two possible renditions are here open to us. First of all, we often speak of the fiery penetrative quality of the mind on any problem, we obtain our solution. A burning up of that problem is a colloquial description of the result. Such colloquialisms are so true in fact that they have been universally adopted by mankind and have passed into current speech. Possibly, the instrument involved in producing the first effects of the work is a species of free association or meditation. The mind must be turned in on to itself. Consciousness must be heightened and cocted or cooked.

What do we mean by cooking? Let us imagine that we have a psychological patient in the consulting room reclining on the divan, and we ask him to associate on this term. Varied ideas are brought up. First of all there will arise a distinct sexual association. We have to face this—regardless of how unpleasant it may seem to some people. It has to be faced calmly and accepted in all its implications.

Cooking is a term often used to indicate coitus, and the act of instigating fertilization. The vernacular is full of vulgar expressions centering about copulation and cooking. However vulgar and offensive they are, there is information of great value for us here. The vernacular is of the same type of expression as is dream language, and the language of mythology and alchemy. Hence colloquial expressions tell a very great deal to those who will look for them. But to learn that cooking represents sexual intercourse does not help us very much

---

8. A. E. Waite, *The Works of Thomas Vaughan: Eugenius Philalethes* (London: Theosophical Publishing House, 1919), 280.

9. Ibid., 324.

where alchemy is concerned. It may be an interesting fact, but after all it is not particularly useful.

Transferring the basic idea to the subjective level of interpretation, we see it may pertain to an attempt to render the mind fertile and pregnant. Coitus is an affair between male and female animals and humans. In terms of consciousness then, the mind becomes fertile or pregnant because of the dynamic action within itself of its own positive and negative elements, the male and female latent within itself. It refers to the union of consciousness with its own *anima* or feminine side.

Not only so, but cooking as applied to food is an art having for its object the preparation of that food for human consumption. The emphasis is on preparation. It is a preparation by which apparently unpalatable or crude or uninteresting items of food are transformed by culinary skill into delicious and delectable viands consumed for our pleasure and welfare.

So also consciousness by skill and art is to be prepared—transformed from its former crude entity into a divine center of light and power. It must be prepared so that the contents of the "essence of mind which is intrinsically pure," the underlying basis of consciousness normally latent, may arise to the surface.

Since writing the above passage, there recently came my way an interesting confirmation of this piece of speculation. In one of the current popular monthly journals, I came across an article on popular psychology by Robert R. Updegraff, dealing with the conscious use of the so-called Subconscious mind. Updegraff expressed the idea that the process of thinking is strangely akin to the process of cooking. He goes on to say: "Although direct heat is ordinarily used, many dishes are better after long, slow cooking. To permit this, some ranges have fireless ovens in which the cooking is completed with retained heat." [10]

"The subconscious mind is a fireless cooker into which we can put our problems to finish the cooking on what might be called 'retained

---

10. Robert R. Updegraff, "The Conscious Use of the Subconscious Mind," *Reader's Digest* 33, no. 198 (October 1938). Condensed from *Forbes* (September 15, 1938).

thought.' To do all of our mental cooking with our conscious minds is to burn mental energy wastefully, and at high cost to our nervous systems ... The cooking process must first be started by focusing our minds on this material long and intently enough to get it thoroughly heated with our best conscious thinking." [11]

Failing contact with this inner revitalizing source of life, consciousness becomes sterile due to the terrible and prodigal waste of mental energy needlessly. Because of the death of vitality that it receives, and because of repressed psychic material harbored in the Unconscious where, owing to the dynamic quality of the latter, it develops explosive tendencies, the ego tends towards disintegration. It does so because it is also separated from its own stem and root.

It is to be understood that this species of involuntary disintegration is entirely different from that which the alchemists labor to produce. In the one case it is unconscious and automatic—a psychotic development. In the other it is deliberately induced with conscious intent. And being consciously induced, it occurs with a knowledge of the laws that govern the psyche, thus eliminating undue danger and tension. To prevent tension and psychic explosion is the obvious reason why the mind's root or essence must be found, laid bare, understood, and cultivated into open expression and manifestation.

Sulphur is thus the dynamic vital side of the Self, its spirit considered not so much in terms of any aspect of consciousness or mind as of energy and activity. It is the libido, the power and active side of the psyche, the energy which must be released from the primordial deeps. Without the activated cooperation of this libido, which is the secret alchemical fire, nothing can be done to reduce the Stone, the egoic consciousness, to its divine Water in order to produce the first solution. Nor, without this fire, can the ego be coagulated into the re-formed personality, the precious jewel of mythology, with its transformed sense of values.

It is well known that, in the beginning, meditation exercises are fatiguing. And at first also, before students become aware of their own

---

11. Ibid.

limitations and capabilities, they strain entirely too much. So great an effort to restrain the mind to a consideration of only one idea is wearying. The brain is unaccustomed, despite the advantages of a good education, to such acute strain and effort, and there is a high mortality rate, so to say, amongst the brain cells. It is always insisted upon by all the authorities that meditation should commence easily and slowly, without too strenuous a forcing, otherwise severe damage is done to both brain and mind. It is as though too keen a heat burned up the cells. Hence the admonition of all the texts. Let the heat be gentle and temperate at first. If it is otherwise then the flower of consciousness, the intellect and the powers of reason, developed by nature after long evolutionary effort, may become destroyed or, at any rate, impaired. These are precisely those faculties to be retained as being the very flower and summit, so far, of the evolutionary process. As concentration is obtained and one-pointedness develops through persistent effort and training, the libido or vital stress normally resident in the Unconscious is activated, welling up to the surface to heat or stir up the contents of the mind.

This gave Geber reason to say, to quote our text, that all perfection is sublimation. So far as psycho-therapy is concerned, Georg Groddeck the very eminent German psychologist, has said, that in reality we are not ultimately concerned in bringing up memories from the Unconscious. This is the impression most people have of analysis, but this is false. What we are concerned with primarily is the elimination of resistance. This is certainly true, and experience corroborates Groddeck's impression. For what occurs when resistances have been eliminated? Simply that libido rises from the depths of the Unconscious and floods or illuminates the higher aspects of the psyche. Thus, this would be tantamount to a real sublimation—a subliming of the libido from the lowest levels of being to those of a higher self-consciousness plane. An exaltation of every mental faculty then follows as the mental horizon becomes exceedingly enlarged, if only because a large field of memory hitherto cut off is made once more accessible to the ego. Conflicts latent in consciousness become resolved because the libido flow is drained away from them into the open sphere of egoic control, and. mental tensions are eased and eliminated.

The heating produces, as its first resultant, what the alchemists were prone to term "putrefaction." Putrefaction is simply chemical change. They imply by this but little more than a breaking down of sterile and inflexible mental habits, and the onset of an intellectual change of viewpoint, a transformation of nature. Because of this psychic change, a breaking up of the stereotyped and habit-bound and crystallized ego-consciousness is induced by the activation of the dynamic content of the Unconscious. A new point of view, with all that such a change implies, comes to birth. It is an attempt towards a transvaluation of all life's values.

Not only, however, is there demanded a heightening of the intellectual faculties by means of meditative processes—a pronouncedly one-sided change, but the other parts of man's nature are to be exercised. The emotional and feeling constituents of the psyche must be stimulated considerably. Emphatically the text states that the various alchemical operations signify the operation of Venus. We find frequent mention elsewhere of the doves of Venus. In another text we are counselled to bathe the Son in the bath of the innocents with Venus, the bride.

Venus is the goddess of Nature, at once the mind conjures up images of woods and forests, of fields and meadows, of flowers and plants, and all green things. Green somehow for us indicates Nature in all her implications. In *Splendor Solis*, Salomon Trismosin, a 16th Century alchemist has said that the Philosopher's Stone is produced by "the Greening and Growing Nature." [12] Hali, another alchemist of a much earlier date, says that "This Stone rises in growing greening things." [13] These expressions are very significant and worth pondering over. Growing and greening things can only imply Nature itself, who like the wise and lovely artist that she is, bedecks herself in gowns and lacework of the

---

12. *Splendor Solis: Alchemical Treatises of Salomon Trismosin, Adept and Teacher of Paracelsus* (London: Kegan Paul, Trench, Trubner & Co., Ltd.), 17. Original manuscript dates from 1582. See www.rexresearch.com/splsol/trismosin.htm.

13. Ibid.

loveliest greens. Due to long and pleasant associations, Nature for us is Green, and both may be symbolized by Venus.

From the study of mythology it is also admissible to apply a psychological interpretation to its content. We may identify the various Gods and Goddesses of myth and legend with principles or primordial archetypes of instinct inhering within the human psyche. And we know from her behavior in such myths that to the Greeks Venus represented the faculties of love and feeling and emotion. She is what Jung would call a typical *anima* figure. When such a figure occurs in a man's dream or fantasy, or artistic creation, which one and all emerge from the Unconscious creative depths of the psyche, we would interpret it along general lines as being a dramatic projection of his emotional and feeling nature, his feminine self. Some psychologists identify it with the object of the primordial incest complex—the mother imago.

Moreover, emotional faculties such as these often have a fiery significance colloquially. How often do we not speak of the fire of love, for example? Poets have always employed such eloquent expressions as "fiery ardor," "unquenchable flames of desire," "the white heat of passion" and many other similar phrases. Hence we may gather that the emotional fire, so far from being neglected or suppressed, must be employed in conjunction with the intellectual fire. The latter would be sterile and meaningless were it not dynamized and sustained by the passion and force of the emotions. These two psychic functions or aspects of the psyche considered together, obviously refer to the engine or means to be employed in the production of the changes already described.

Venus

From the psychological point of view, therapeutic analysis is an intellectual survey of the emotional life tending towards an ultimate acceptance of both intellectuality and emotion. That is, both sides of human nature are to be considered as opposite but necessary constituents of the psyche, the play of polarities so imperative to the maintenance of life itself. When such an acceptance occurs, at once there is a vast increase in the individual's power and vitality—quite apart from the sense of freedom from inner problems which results and the renewed ability to handle life more decisively and efficiently. It seems that a denial of any one phase of life or any rejection of a particular function of the psyche causes the vital flow, the libido, to return inward upon itself, to lie unused in the depths of the unconscious. It is unable to flow outwards to objects and people of the external world, or to penetrate the normal activities of the personality. As soon, however, as a philosophical corrective is employed, and life is really accepted as actually it is—and not as the fantasy that we fondly would like it to be—then the flow of life and spirit is enhanced.

The idea of acceptance is a fundamental psychological concept. Not only psychological, but I may add religious too. For at the bottom of religious philosophy it is assumed that the universe and man is the creation of a perfect God. Consequently everything that exists must exist for a special purpose and have its own proper place. The more unconditionally that mankind accepts that scheme the more it will tend to accept the creation of God. Obviously the happier it will be.

Actually this is psychologically valid, however much one may be inclined to spurn the religious point of view. The neurotic is one who cannot accept either his environment or himself. He is forced to repress one side of himself or to flee from a certain aspect of life. As a result he is in a state of severe conflict—which is to say in a state in which happiness is conspicuous by its absence. To overcome this sad state of affairs, the individual must learn to see that before any changes can be engineered in the environment, he has to accept it as actually it is. The order of his life must be an unconditional acceptance of reality in its widest sense. There must be no aspect or phase of life which he seeks to reject because of fear, a pseudo-idealism or a false spiritual philosophy. Nothing in life is ugly. All fits into a scheme.

This idea was excellently borne out by a dream of a patient of mine. I had been endeavoring to make this individual realize that he would never be happy until he accepted himself and the environment in which he found himself. For some while it seemed that we were making little or no progress. He was stubborn, displaying a high degree of resistance. Then one day he brought along this dream:

"I am stopping in somewhere for breakfast. A woman is sitting at another table, ready to serve the food. I ask her what there is, and she shows me a dish of macaroni. I do not care much for the stuff—but tell her to give me some. When my plate is before me I see that it is filled with turkey—much more than I can eat."

It requires no psychologist to divine the meaning of this dream. It is even unnecessary to analyze each individual symbol, though to do so does yield interesting and significant material. But the most obvious meaning of the dream was so significant so far as the immediate analysis was concerned, that spontaneously my patient saw the idea. The effect that it had upon him was tremendous. He accepted himself and his work instead of attempting to run away from it as he had been conniving to do in all sorts of ways for the past thirty years. Strange to say he found himself supremely happy in that task. It did not seem duty or work to go to his professional office every day; it had been transformed into sheer pleasure.

The meaning is transparent. With acceptance there is a rare and beautiful transformation of life. It is an inner attitude towards life which is worth cultivating, for then one finds oneself working with and cooperating with Nature instead of opposing her. To oppose her is a thankless task, one bound to eventuate in disaster. But to attempt to cooperate in every conceivable way with her is to find that one lives life, that behind one there comes as a support the whole of the inertia of the universe. Where in such a case could there be sadness, unhappiness or failure?

The one major, though elementary, phenomenon of any meditative process is the considerable increase of vitality that it appears to foster. As the art is mastered and as meditation deepens and becomes more profound, tremendous streams of power and vitality are made conscious. So tremendous are these streams as almost to appear incredible. In the Hindu systems such a power is termed Kundalini-shakti. A fascinating and intricate technique for the stimulation and arousing of this power has been developed in the East. The Gnostic literature of the early Christian era terms it the Speirema, and in Hebrew Qabalistic literature it appears under the guise of the Serpent. It is termed the Dragon in alchemical works, it being frequently portrayed with wings, or devouring its own tail. Symbolically, such a power is supposed to reside at the base of the spine—a surrogate symbol of the Unconscious depths, physiologically portrayed—whence as meditation proceeds it ascends to the brain. On its passage upwards to the cerebral centers, it awakens dormant intellectual and spiritual faculties, whilst its arrival at the brain coincides with illumination and religious exaltation of a very high order. In Egyptian vignettes, and on some of the God-forms of the ancient Egyptians, we often find a little serpent or Uraeus, perched as it were on the forehead between the eyes. Whilst above the head on these forms is often shown the Solar disc, representing that they are Light and Light-bestowers.

In a remarkably erudite piece of research, *The Apocalypse Unsealed* by James M. Pryse, gives a definition of Kundalini which bears quoting in this connection: "Semi-latent within this pneumatic ovum is the paraclete, the light of the Logos which in energizing becomes what may be described as living, conscious electricity, of incredible voltage and hardly comparable to the form of electricity known to the physicist. This is the 'good serpent' of ancient symbology; and, taken with the pneumatic ovum, it was also represented in the familiar symbol of the egg and the serpent. It is called in the Sanskrit writings *Kundalini*, the annular or ringform force, and in the Greek *speirema*, the serpent coil. It is this force which, in the telestic work, or cycle of initiation, weaves from the primal substance of the auric ovum upon the ideal form or archetype it contains, and conforming thereto, the immortal Augoeides, or solar body *(soma heliakon)*, so-called because in its visible appearance it is self-luminous like the sun, and has a golden radiance."[14]

In Tibet, the Knowledge of this inner force and the means of its stimulation, has led in several curious directions. One of the most interesting and significant to our present enquiry is the so-called Psychic Heat. Consider the climate of this land. A plateau, it is considerably over 10,000 feet above sea level—in some places about 18,000 feet. The entire country is covered in winter with ice and snow. Climatic conditions must be very rigorous and severe. Yet, despite this, we know that anchorites and monks live on these snow-capped

---

14. James M. Pryse, *The Apocalypse Unsealed: Being an Esoteric Interpretation of the Initiation of Iôannês* (New York: 1910), 11–12.

heights clad only in a single cotton gown. In some instances they have been seen naked. How are they able to survive these frigid conditions of such intense severity, especially when the meals partaken by them are so very meager and sparse?

We know they follow a special system of mental and psychic training whereby, through the powers of the inturned mind and the visualizing faculty, the latent serpent power is aroused into full and dynamic activity. Special forms of breathing likewise constitute an integral part of this training. It is common experience even in our climate that several minutes of deep and full breathing will, because of the increased oxygenization of the blood, produce copious perspiration and a marked sense of warmth. How much more marked would this not become with a more perfectly developed technique? The Tibetan monks and lamas have carried this idea a great deal further than ever we have deemed to be possible. The following is a quotation from Mme. Alexandra David-Neel's work *With Mystics and Magicians in Tibet*, dealing with just such a technique: "The novice must begin his training each day before dawn, and finish the special exercises relating to *tumo* (the psychic heat) before sunrise… Various breathing drills are first performed which aim at clearing the passage of the air in the nostrils. Then pride, anger, hatred, covetousness, sloth, stupidity, are mentally rejected with the rhythmic breathing out. All blessings from saintly beings, the Buddha's spirit, the five wisdoms, all that is good and lofty in the world are attracted and assimilated while drawing in the breath. Now, composing oneself for a while one dismisses all cares and cogitations."[15] Then several exercises are followed, in which letters and mystic forms are formulated in certain parts of the body. "The exercise goes on, through ten stages, but one must understand that there exist no pause between them. The different subjective visions, as well as the sensations which accompany them, succeed each other in a series of gradual modifications. Inhalations, retentions of the breath and expirations continue rhythmically, and a mystic formula is continually repeated. The mind must remain

---

15. Originally published in Paris, 1929. First English edition, 1932. See Alexandra David-Néel, *Magic and Mystery in Tibet* (New York: Dover Publications, 1971), 220.

perfectly concentrated and one-pointed on the vision of the fire and the sensation of warmth which ensues ... Sometimes a kind of examination concludes the training of the *tumo* students. Upon a frosty night, those who think themselves capable of victoriously enduring the test are led to the shore of a river or a lake. If all the streams are frozen in the region, a hole is made in the ice. A moonlight night, with a hard wind blowing, is chosen. Such nights are not rare in Tibet during the winter months. The neophytes sit on the ground, cross-legged and naked. Sheets are dipped in the icy water, each man wraps himself in one of them and must dry it on his body. As soon as the sheet has become dry, it is again dipped in the water and placed on the novice's body to be dried as before. The operation goes on in that way until daybreak. Then he who has dried the largest number of sheets is acknowledged the winner of the competition. It is said that some dry as many as forty sheets in one night." [16]

The above obtains corroboration from Dr. Evans-Wentz who has written with understanding and erudition on these matters in his scholarly work *Tibetan Yoga and Secret Doctrines*, published by the Oxford University Press. [17]

All this material is not needlessly quoted. It casts a very valuable light on the nature of the alchemical secret fire. It gives us some notion of what it was that the alchemists sought to perform. That they had any intention of developing the so-called psychic heat, it hardly behooves me to deny. Such a feat was not necessary here. Climatic conditions in Europe had not rendered this imperative to their spiritual welfare. But that they were deeply interested in the kundalini or the libido or its equivalents, and the spiritual phenomena that followed upon its arousal, there can be no manner of doubt. The caution that they employed in their writings and the enigmatical nature of the obscurities and cryptic passages in which they delighted became transparent once given the necessary key. Even the fear of personal

---

16. Ibid., 222–227.

17. Walter Y. Evans-Wentz, ed., *Tibetan Yoga and Secret Doctrines* (London: Oxford University Press, 1978), 158–159. (Originally published in 1935.)

persecution assumes second place in the light of the above. Fear of abuse and the personal danger to an unwise practitioner are far more telling and significant reasons. However, they have interspersed clues, innumerable clues of an eloquent nature, in their writings. *The True Book of the Learned Synesius* is a splendid case in point, showing the motives and direction of the alchemical practice.

CHAPTER SIX

MAGNETISM, VISUALIZATION, AND HEALING

Ihave dilated thus far regarding Sulphur and the Secret Fire because always the problem has assumed such outstanding proportions that if we can throw some ray of light on it we will have illuminated the entire nature of the spagyric art. Apart from the foregoing
interpretations along psychological and meditative lines, then, there
is yet a third line of enquiry which may yield us significant material
in connection with this mystery. In a former work, *The Philosopher's
Stone*, I devoted a great deal of space to a more or less lengthy consideration of the historical antecedents of hypnotism. For centuries prior
to the discoveries of physicians such as Braid and Bernheim, a form
of therapy was practiced in Europe based upon the supposed transmission of a vital flaw from operator to subject or patient. Mesmer,
who was the 18th Century exponent of this technique with which
his name has subsequently become associated, was but one of many
who had employed it. He was very largely responsible for bringing its
ideology once more before the attention of the scientific world. That
the latter completely rejected his claims and theories is of very little
credit to that world, or of very little concern to our present enquiry.
Modern research has achieved much in demonstrating the validity of
certain of his ideas. Principal amongst these is the fact that emanations of a subtle magnetic kind do issue forth from a human frame. I
refer the interested reader to Dr. Bernard Hollander's *Hypnotism and*

Self Hypnotism,[1] a very able work where these debatable doctrines are quite fully discussed.

Now it is the hypothesis of a quite recent expositor of the alchemical mystery that for an explanation of the Secret Fire of the Wise we must look to the mesmeric art. It is claimed that the transmission of vital power is a valid and tangible activity—one that not only can be demonstrated but can be taught and mastered by any individual of average intelligence and vitality. Personally I can substantiate this claim. Study and experience with this power over a number of years have enabled me to develop a technique, startling in its simplicity, precisely to this end. My little book *The Art of True Healing*[2] delineates a therapeutic method based upon just such an internal stimulation of vital currents.

The theory is based upon the empirical fact that any faculty grows by repeated use. Not only so but that power increases its potency and efficiency through utilization. Hence, argue the proponents of this hypothesis, repeated efforts to transmit this magnetic power by an effort of will, aided by manual passes, from one person to another will eventually stimulate to an inconceivable extent the quantity of such a force. Nor is this all. For if the subject be stimulated to assume on occasion the active role of operator and project his own power backwards on the former operator, who for the time being acts as a passive recipient, a vast increase in magnetism is affected. In a word, if power be thrown from A to B, and then back from B to A, the whole process being repeated frequently over a long period of time, the unconscious depths of both experimenters become considerably activated, freeing very considerably the libido currents in both parties. This is a matter of common experimental work, and need not be taken as a dogmatic statement.

---

1. Bernard Hollander, *Methods and Uses of Hypnosis and Self-Hypnosis* (London: George Allen & Unwin Ltd., 1928). See e-book at www.pnl-nlp.org/courses/ebooks/book_model/METHODS%20AND%20USES%20OF%20HYPNOSIS%20AND%20SELF-HYPNOSIS.

2. See appendix I.

What confronts us now is the possible psychological effect of such a transmission. We have several analogies available to assist us. The first I have already discussed. That is to say that certain simple breathing exercises produce an astonishing degree of internal heat and vitality within the space of a very few minutes. This can be developed with time and practice, in the direction of the Tibetan *tumo*, the production of the psychic heat to withstand the force of the elements. It may also be developed into a psycho-spiritual technique for the arousing of what the Hindus call the kundalini, the serpent power, the coiled up or latent libido, stored in the base of the spine. As this serpent uncoils and rises, moving slowly towards the brain, various states of heightened consciousness are revealed, culminating in a species of kinetic illumination as the brain is enlivened.

I have suggested elsewhere that there is indeed a similarity between the effects of *Pranayama,* the breathing exercises developed by the Orientals with a view to awakening the serpent power, and the willed mesmeric transmission of vital power. In the one case, the technique is adapted to the Easterner who has time at his disposal and possesses patience as an integral part of his psychological constitution. The second method is an intentional development for the Westerner who is endowed with but little patience, and because of the economic conditions in which he has been placed, has but little more time.

According to the oriental theory, vitality or *prana* or spirit exists all around us, we being bathed in it as a fish in the sea. Consequently the breathing exercises undertaken are so many efforts to open the personality to the ever-present surrounding ocean of power, so that the practitioner becomes a species of sponge absorbing the life about him. When saturation point is reached, the power becomes kinetic and exerts an influence upon the human sponge which has absorbed it. To master this technique thoroughly, so that concentration of the mind is induced and illumination floods the mind, requires months and perhaps years of daily practice. This manifestly, for the average Occidental, required by circumstance to attend to family and business matters, is quite impossible. The technique as such cannot be transported here nor adopted by the European with impunity.

On the other hand, through the concerted use of imagination and will, without any special or complex breathing exercises, the individual may open himself very considerably to an astonishing influx of power from all about him, augmenting his own store of power. Then the prana latent in one individual may be communicated, in some small measure at least, to a second. When so transmitted, inasmuch as power awakens or tends to produce power, it awakens a response in the psyche of the subject. The response elicited is a very slight increase of the subject's own vitality, as though the power, penetrating the body-mind system, awakened the libido dormant in the psychic deeps. When this slight increase of libido or prana, as well we may define it, is returned on a later occasion to the former operator, a similar reaction is induced. Eventually a very high potential or voltage is produced which must resemble the kinetic quality of Kundalini awakened by pranayama and the psychic states that the latter produces.

The results achieved by psychotherapeutic or analytical methods in individual cases where a freed libido has resulted, present a useful analogy. In the first place a marked sense of freedom from endopsychic problems and perplexities is the immediate outcome. Furthermore the hard and fast barriers erected between the different constituents of the psyche become broken down, and an integrity of consciousness is achieved. In short, the usual psychological results are obtained.

What concerns me in this enquiry is whether or not such a mesmeric or hypnotic freeing of libido would correspond in any way with the preliminary dissolution which the alchemists posit as the first stage of their work. We know already that one of the stages of freeing libido by the psychotherapeutic methods is distinctly unsettling. The girders or hinges of the mind become loosened. The old complexes, broken up as the ego perceives their falsity as practical solutions or adaptations to life and their inadequacy to every-day problems, dissipate themselves as autonomous constellations of idea and feeling in the psyche. But prior to the full development of a mature adult point of view there is no little suffering and emotional disturbance entailed. The psyche is obliged to adapt itself to a species of self-immersion. It gives up its formerly accepted standards. It sacrifices itself. "Whoso loseth his life shall find it." The ego dies in a mystical death. In a sense this must correspond to the alchemical dissolution we are considering.

As the libido tends towards an untrammeled freedom of expression by means of the so-called "work of the hands" or the "manual work," which cryptic expressions we may quite reasonably associate with the mesmeric transmission of prana, consciousness undergoes the change we spoke of. When the saturation point, so to speak, is reached in the beginning, a trance state is produced. The patient is plunged into a condition in which the ordinary every-day faculties of the ego undergo an eclipse. The focus of attention seems now shifted altogether to another level, with new memories and new points of view. The body becomes relaxed and released from muscular tensions. Slow and deep is the breathing and the pulse drops several beats to an even measured pace. The facial expression alters, becoming immobile and peaceful, whilst quite often an appearance even of ecstasy makes itself apparent. It is as though consciousness were transported out of itself into a higher and nobler sphere, where no longer its equanimity is perturbed and unduly disturbed by the petty problems of the objective world. In this highly concentrated state, suggestions may easily be implanted into the fertile mind of the subject. Not only so, but various abnormal or unusual faculties make their appearance. Clairvoyance, telepathy and community of sense and emotion are phenomena which have been observed to occur by careful and trained scientific investigators.

Possibly you may be one of those who mock at this sort of statement and decry the fact that such statements can be made. All I ask here is an honest approach and a willingness to recognize and accept such facts wherever they may be found. However one may regard hypnotism, the fact remains that hypnotic therapy and psychical research is as valid and as verifiable a body of knowledge as any other science. This statement I challenge any critic to refute or deny—honestly, decently, and intelligently. A host of scientific men, of extraordinary intellectual caliber and scientific patience and inventiveness, from Sir William Crookes to Dr. Hereward Carrington of the American Psychical Institute of the present day, including Professor William James and Sir Oliver Lodge, and a host of other celebrities, have contributed a mass of verified evidence which serves as the basis for my statements and assumptions.

When finally the subject is permitted to return to his normal self, he usually retains but little awareness of this deeper level of consciousness, nor of what has transpired during the trance state. But with training and practice and repeated suggestion this difficulty may readily be overcome. The result is that the two poles of consciousness may be united and integrated and the horizon of the ego considerably enlarged. By these means we achieve what is the goal of all mystical and occult and even psychological systems—making conscious that which formerly was unconscious. It is to widen the scope of consciousness which is the end of these many systems.

In alternating the roles of operator and subject, and the states of trance and willed projection of magnetism, a rounded development of the psyche is secured. The dangers, though slight, and usually very much exaggerated in the lay mind, both of passivity and the aggressiveness of the power complex, are thus avoided. And the effect of the vast increase of power playing on consciousness is incalculable. It is soon bound to dispel the neurotic cleavage within the personality, and to destroy the crystallization induced through the undue domination of habit, custom, and hypocritical convention. We have here, it is contended, a most suggestive interpretation to these alchemical cryptograms, as we may term them, and an explanation of the many obscure references and technical terms.

Closely allied to this hypothesis there is another scheme which, from personal experience, has been more than useful in assisting me to come to a better understanding of alchemical processes.

The cornerstone of my professional practice, so to say, rests upon the art of relaxation. I have always assumed it to be imperative to any patient that I may have that he learn how to relax every muscle and fiber at will. We are all familiar with mechanical and chemical methods of producing a state of relaxation. A warm bath, a hot drink, a nightcap, massage, a soft springy bed—all of these tend to induce a relaxing of the almost constant tension to which most of us are subject. The chiropractors, likewise, have devised an excellent mechanical method of relaxation by means of basic pressures upon sensitive points of the ilium and sacrum which are the points of origin and insertion of the powerful spinal muscles. As a result of these pressures, the musculature about the spine is automatically released from contraction. But none of these are, finally, of much practical and lasting avail to the average individual. He is unable to induce relaxation at the very moment when he wants it without resorting to the aid of another person or thing.

A relaxation that is *true*, in the deepest sense of the word, is one that must be self-induced. One must be able at any moment—whether riding in the car or subway, sitting in the chair in one's office, or enjoying a play in the theatre—deliberately to let go of muscular and nervous tension, and let the body fade into oblivion.

This, you may add, is certainly a desirable state—but is it one that is readily attainable? It is, and very easily so. At first one may require the assistance of a second person in order to have one's own unconscious somatic tension called to one's attention. Afterwards, however, one realizes oneself to be more of a master in one's own household, and that therefore the body may be made to respond to one's wish and will. The basic technique has been ably delineated by Annie Payson Call in her excellent treatise *Power Through Repose*.[3] In that work she has entered into the intricacies of relaxation development, and explained for what reasons she considers it to be so necessary. In the main, I am in complete agreement with her.

But I should like to see the system outlined by her developed still further, extended into another realm. What do I mean by this? First of all, we have to realize that the energy we use up in organic functioning is obtained, when all is said and done, from the food that we consume. It may not be generally realized that the specific amount of energy required to run the different parts of the body has already been

---

3. Annie Payson Call, *Power Through Repose* (Boston: Little, Brown, and Co., 1891). Available through Google Books.

experimentally verified and measured. For example, we find that L. Jean Bogert, Instructor in Experimental Medicine at Yale University, has asserted that "Metabolism is a term used to cover those chemical changes in the tissues by means of which the body gets energy out of food or tissue material. *Only about one fourth of this energy needed for the internal work of the body goes for the activities of the various organs, while the greater part is used for life processes in the cells and for maintaining the tone of the muscles which, waking or sleeping, are never completely relaxed.*" [4] (The italics are mine).

A certain amount of this energy goes to maintain the various physiological functions of the body—dealing with excretion, secretion, reparation, reproduction, transmission of motor and sensory impulses, nutrition, growth and heat production in certain quite definite amounts. A larger amount goes into maintaining muscular tension which, as Bogert observes, is never completely relaxed. The greater part of this energy is totally wasted in maintaining muscular tensions which are completely unnecessary in every way. The abdominal and cervical muscles of the average individual are not only in a constant state of contraction, but he is actually *unable* to release that tension when he wishes to do so. Thigh and leg muscles are similar cases in point. Tensions become habitual, and habits soon become unconscious.

The object of the art of relaxation is so to train the individual that he may withdraw the energy continually pouring along the nerve channels into these muscles and organs, thus achieving a state of rest. I may say that most individuals upon achieving this for the first time, sink swiftly into a state of heavy sleep. Later, as they become more habituated to this new state of bodily freedom, they remain wide awake and alert even although their bodies are completely still and the normal channels of nervous expenditure in abeyance.

Skill in the art is achieved principally through consciousness. The theory is that by becoming aware of the tensions present in the body

---

4. L. Jean Bogert, *Dietetics Simplified: The Use of Foods in Health and Disease* (New York: The Macmillan Company, 1940), 11–12.

it is possible to relieve that tension. In order so to become aware, it is necessary to have a second person present to raise and drop one's arms and legs. The limbs are deliberately and slowly raised in order to make one aware of the stiffness that is normally afflicting them. Having become conscious of these stiff places—principally neck, abdomen, hips and thighs, one may alone use one's imagination as the principal means of achieving the desired condition of perfect rest.

There are two principal techniques requiring the application of the imagination. One calls for the visualization of the musculature, the other of the blood-system. Both are very simple.

While I do not wish to make this a handbook on the art of relaxation, nevertheless it is urgent to make a sufficiently full statement to render my conclusions clear and logical. Lying flat on his back, one attempts to visualize the muscles in different parts of the body to look like the loose strands of a skein of wool. Obtain a skein of ordinary darning wool, and dangle it in the air. This will give you the best impression of the result to be envisaged. Then, beginning with the feet, imagine the muscles of the tarsus and ankle being composed solely of several skeins of wool, with each strand perfectly free and loose, without tautness or stiffness of any kind. In a few seconds, possibly a couple of minutes, a distinct sensation may be experienced of warmth and tingling, accompanied by a perceptible relaxing of parts. Here is no suggestion or hallucination. It is an experience as real as that of reading this book. Extend the same idea to the calf, thighs, different sections of the trunk, neck and head. Ease is obtained in a very short while, and a relaxation develops which is perfectly startling in the pleasure and feeling of newly won freedom that unexpectedly it evokes.

The second method likewise uses of the imagination, but demands the visualizing of the various organs of the body being saturated by blood. We know from general pathology that where there is congestion of blood, there is heat; this heat causes relaxation of tissue. It is a well-authenticated physiological principle moreover, that to think of any part of the body is to produce an increased flow of blood. We have only to think of food, and there is an increased flow of blood to the stomach with an accelerated secretion from the glands supplying the gastro-intestinal tract. Let a stray thought of sexual indulgence or eroticism cross the mind, and at once a marked vascular stimulation of the genitalia develops. If an individual not used to compliments be made aware of the beauty of her face and form, very soon the phenomenon of blushing may be observed. These common facts being quite well known, we may apply them practically by quiet reflection upon our viscera and musculature to the end that there will be increased vascularization and enervation accompanied by relaxation. Hence we proceed by visualizing the brain first of all. Soon there is sensation there. One becomes aware of the brain as a fact of personal experience. This realization is to be succeeded by imagining that blood flows downwards from that brain to eyes, nose, ears and mouth. Continue with the rest of the body in this way until the tips of the toes have been concentrated upon and thus vascularized. The state of relaxation that then ensues is very marked, and can be tested instrumentally. Blood pressure shows a decided fall; pulse rate and temperature likewise have been noted to respond.

The practical value of all this so far as our thesis here is concerned is very simple. If a very tense person begins to apply such a relaxation technique to withdraw from the body this energy that otherwise would have been prodigally wasted, what happens to this energy? Prior to relaxation, this nervous energy was enervating nerves, muscles, arteries, veins and organs. But now a very large part—naturally not all, since the physiological functions still require to be fulfilled—has been withdrawn, eliminating this constant tension. Where has it gone?

Clearly there can be but one answer. It has sought another level of expression. Energy is energy, regardless of what plane it happens to manifest upon. If prevented or debarred from expression at one level of life, it will seek manifestation on another. Moreover, let us remember that energy is life, and life is creative. "Life and more life" is the motto of living creatures. And an abundance of life and vitality is the typical characteristic of genius, no matter whether he be religious, scientific, or artistic.

Dammed up at one level, the physical level in this case, the energy regresses inwards to the psychological or spiritual level. Here it vitalizes the mind. Being creative as I have suggested, this pent-up energy instigates a process of regeneration or re-creation of the entire personality. Slowly but surely it commences to circulate in its own psychic sphere, awakening the dormant archetypal images of the deepest strata of the Unconscious, eliminating emotional and intellectual inflexibility, widening the sphere of conscious awareness, and stimulating the latent intuitive and creative powers that are within every individual.

That such a process *could* occur at all, is a fact that is widely accepted. However, the rationale or the simplicity of it has, I believe, but rarely been realized. The alchemists did realize some such fact. Their entire speculations, for let us call them such for the time being, confirm the hypothesis that this vital energy in regressing to deeper psychological levels, transforms itself into a creative fire. The secret fire of the alchemists is none other than that prodigious energy which daily we handle, employ and, to our sorrow, waste. It is our own life. The cooking or decoction of which they so frequently and ambiguously speak has various points of resemblance to what occurs in this relaxation technique. Energy, in being released from its habitual task of tensing muscles and viscera, turns inwards upon the mind and "cooks" it. A vitalization of consciousness then occurs. There is a conversion of the elements, to use the archaic language. Moreover, because of this vitalization, the whole mental outlook upon life is changed, and there is a transformation of the mind.

Let it also be noted that this transformation or conversion or "turning about" of the mind is the crucial experience of all religious systems—whether we consider Christianity, Buddhism or Taoism, or any of the major religions of the world. For example in one of the most interesting of the Mahayana Buddhist texts, the *Lankavatara Sutra*, we read "the cessation of the discriminating mind can not take place until there has been a 'turning about' in the deepest seat of consciousness. The mental habit of looking outward by the discriminating mind upon all external objective world must be given up, and a new habit of realizing Truth within the intuitive mind by becoming one with Truth itself must be established."[5]

In his Commentary to *The Secret of the Golden Flower*, Jung also has a few very pertinent remarks to make in confirmation, I believe, of my hypothesis. Discussing the mystical experience always accompanied by the subjective phenomenon of light, he remarks:

"I know a few individuals who are familiar with this phenomenon from personal experience. As far as I have ever been able to understand it, the phenomenon seems to have to do with an acute condition of consciousness as intensive as it is abstract, a 'detached' consciousness which, as Hildegarde pertinently remarks, brings up to consciousness regions of psychic events ordinarily covered with darkness. *The fact that in connection with this, the general bodily sensations disappear, shows that their specific energy has been withdrawn from them, and has apparently gone toward heightening the clearness of consciousness.*"[6]

The mystical experience, whether we call it *Samadhi* with the Hindus, or *Satori* with the Zen Buddhists, or Union with God as supposed by the Christian mystics, is almost always accompanied by such a withdrawal of energy from bodily function. I suggest that we can reverse the process. Withdraw energy from the body, and thus heighten consciousness. It is my contention that this, in one sense at any rate, is the alchemical supposition. It is at the root of the whole of alchemical procedure. Sublimation is simply another word for it. Energy is withdrawn from somatic processes and is sublimed to an inward spiritual state. Energy produces energy. And energy is life and creativity. The outcome can only be transformation and transmutation.

---

5. See Dwight Goddard, *A Buddhist Bible* (1932). Online text at www.sacred-texts .com/bud/bb ("The Lankavatara Sutra: Chapter V: The Mind System").

6. Richard Wilhelm, trans., *The Secret of the Golden Flower: A Chinese Book of Life* (London: Kegan Paul, Trench, Trubner & Co., Ltd., 1931), 104.

This, I again contend, is the archaic alchemical theory which is amply corroborated by psychological practice in its widest and highest application. An examination of several alchemical treatises in the light of this particular hypothesis is bound to prove very illuminating.

CHAPTER SEVEN

ALCHEMICAL SYMBOLISM
AND THE AURA

Before terminating this suggestive inquiry into alchemical myster-ies, one final set of symbols remains to be touched upon. Certain of the more didactic treatises, in the course of their lengthy ramblings through open gates and flower gardens and fairy palaces, refer to animals, birds, and other wild beasts. The illustrations accompanying some of these texts depict lions, crows, eagles, pelicans, dragons and serpents. From the analytical experience that has been garnered during the past thirty years, it has become possible to make an attempt in the direction of interpretation. We now know that these animals, whether they be painted by man or whether they appear spontaneously in dream or fantastic creation, have reference to the libido, the vital spirit in man. Animals, to mankind, have always appeared to be creatures whose behavior is unmodified and unrestrained by considerations of duty, morality, or herd-consciousness. They represent moreover crude energy, power in an undifferentiated, undomesticated and uncontrolled state. What symbol then, could be mere eloquent for the unconscious in man, than that subtle dynamic energy which motivates its life?

Whilst the libido—the sulphur, or the secret fire, lies dormant in the deepest, most concealed levels of the Unconscious, the tendency of the psyche is to portray that condition as a dragon or serpent.

There is a fundamental psychological law upon which we here have to reflect. If you are not altogether conscious of the dynamic interior principles within, their activity must appear to come from a source other than yourself. In a word, from without, from your environment, and from the people in that environment. Hence, if within your own being there is a vast store of energy of enormous potential, what is happening to it? Unrecognizing it, you are unable to use it. But it itself is active continually. The experiments in hypnotism and psychical research will have indicated to the reader something of its tremendous power and capacity. Its effect upon us includes all those strange and mysterious events in our personal lives which we are not able to explain and which perturb us so deeply. Unused, it remains in a crude and undeveloped or undomesticated state. Its level is that of primitive men or beasts of a bygone era. Thus it represents itself in our dreams as fantastic primitive beasts, horrible slimy creatures that awaken us out of the deepest slumber. Small wonder the snake is little loved by man—quite apart from its poisonous and venomous ways. We have unconsciously invested it with enormous affect. It has become the symbol for us of our animal past and of its descendant—the animal lying within. But we have to remember that the latter seems obviously dangerous only when unrecognized and unused. In mythology this beast has always been susceptible of innumerable interpretations. "More subtle than any beast of the field," as Genesis puts it, the serpent was symbolical of divine wisdom. In fact, in the Grecian myths, the serpent was sacred to Athena, the goddess of wisdom, more than a hint as to the true nature of the beast. The fact always that this animal was capable of shedding its skin, and still surviving, came to symbolize to the ancients that rebirth and resurrection were somehow associated with it. Moreover it occurs quite frequently in dreams as a phallic or generative symbol—the spermatozoon being directly suggested, indicating its relationship with or expression through the sexual instinct. But the serpent is capable of interpretation not only in sexual terms but also as representative of power and creative energy; of time and eternity when it is represented as a circular shape with its tail being swallowed by its mouth; of life, immortality and regeneration. It is also of interest that in primitive religions, the

Sun and the Moon gods were figured not only as a lion and lioness, bull and cow, etc., but also as a male and female serpent. In alchemy it is more often used as a generative symbol, as a symbol of the power that is capable of regenerating the individual and manufacturing the philosopher's stone.

As the libido awakens, either through the psychotherapeutic methods, or by meditation, or by the magnetic technique, it becomes volatile. That is to say, it commences to penetrate the various levels of the psyche, infiltrating consciousness as well as the bodily system. A new sense of power and vitality is felt dynamizing the entire activity of man. Then the myth or dream-making faculty depicts this active state of the libido as an eagle or winged dragon or a winged lion. As with the progress of time, it becomes more volatile and more manifest to consciousness, other symbols are used—such as a winged ruby-blood, or a phoenix feeding her young with her own life-blood, or a serpent bearing a crown, and many another.

Winged Dragon Eating Its Own Tail

Each of these symbols is more than expressive. Each one could be taken as a topic for meditation, or as the stimulus idea for free-association. By so doing they would, by stimulating association tracks in the mind, awaken those archetypal co-relatives in consciousness corresponding to themselves. Just think of the wealth of symbolism involved in the idea of a phoenix feeding her young. Each of us is that phoenix, and each is the litter of young ones. We each have to kill ourselves in order that the newly developing centers of life within may grow. The childhood state has to perish in order that the adult may grow therefrom. This is a new world—an exciting and thrilling world of vital symbolism—to enter.

Colors likewise are variously employed to convey the extent of awakening and the degree of vitality achieved. One of the most significant of the combinations of color and animals in alchemical writing is the Green Lion. It sometimes is asserted that the stage symbolized by such a figure is quite as important as the preliminary dissolution and the blackness of corruption. As the libido or the vital spirit stirs in the psychic deeps, no matter through what agency, it is often depicted in the authentic texts as such a Lion. The lion is an undomesticated animal, vigorous, large, swift and active, fierce and dangerous. Its color is given as green, because symbolically it is the color of unripeness, of immaturity, as well as of expectancy and hope of further growth. A greenhorn is one who is crude and naive, simple and unsophisticated. Green, as we have previously suggested, is the color of Nature. But it is the color of Nature only in the dayspring of her youthful existence just after the Sun begins his journey northwards once more, and warmth and life returns to her loved ones. Actually the symbol depicts a half-way house, as it were, of the libido shortly after awakening from its long drawn out sleep and prior to the achievement of its final goal of maturity. One alchemist writer, the Vicar of Malden, quoted by Elias Ashmole in the *Theatrum Chemicum*, says:

> *It's because of the transcendent force*
> *It hath; and for the rawness of its source,*
> *Of which the lyke is nowhere to be seene,*
> *That yt of us is named the Lyon Greene. 1*

---

1. From "Hunting the Greene Lyon" in Mary Anne Atwood's *A Suggestive Inquiry into the Hermetic Mystery, with a Dissertation on the More Celebrated of the Alchemical Philosophers Being an Attempt Towards the Recovery of the Ancient Experiment of Nature* (London: Trelawney Saunders, 1850), 316. Online at www .rexresearch.com/atwood/cont.htm.

The employment of colors proceeds much further than the example given above. The use is a curious one, permeating the whole of the literature. Our text employs quite frequently a well-defined color scheme, and similar ones may be found elsewhere. In the *Tractatus Aureus*, Hermes gives instructions with regard to color, and in one place observes the following: "Extract from the ray its shadow and impurity, by which the clouds hang over it, defile and keep away the light."[2]

One of the early things the novice in meditation experiences when he closes his eyes is the obscureness of inner vision. That is he perceives only an indeterminate mistiness within his head, the clouds and impurity of which Hermes speaks. As time goes on, the darkness seems to deepen and become blacker and more profound. Actually there is no such deepening of gloom at all. It is only his increase in self-awareness that makes the student conscious of the darkness and heaviness that had hitherto clouded his mind, of the shadow and impurity which conceal the ray from his sight. With continued effort the darkness and the cloud lift. He becomes aware of an increasing airiness and luminosity in the brain, as though a light—the candle of vision—burned within the skull, permeating the whole sphere of sensation.

So far as psychological analysis goes the effect upon the patient is equally definite. Whereas for most of us dreams are our experience in "another world," a dream world which is vague and hazy, a marked clarity and definiteness begin to appear after some weeks or months of psychological work. No longer is the dream indistinct and grey in color. The whole experience becomes invested with color and perspective and vivid reality with the firm realization that the nightly adventure in the empyrean is as "real" as any experience of normal waking consciousness. And more so, for it becomes the dominant of that consciousness, producing effects in the outer objective world, and evolving an effectual and satisfactory line of life. This too, is a result of the activation of the

---

2. See "The Golden Treatise of Hermes" in Regardie's *The Philosopher's Stone: Spiritual Alchemy, Psychology, and Ritual Magic* (Woodbury, MN: Llewellyn Publications, 2013), 47.

contents of the mind by the libido. In mediaeval legends such an activation of libido from fixation in outworn unconscious complexes, is depicted as the aura, or the halo that blazes up as a great flame from the roof of the hut in which a saint is lying in a state of ecstasy. In the faces of holy men, mankind has always seen the sun of this power, the fullness of light. In the Old Testament, this magical force shines in the burning bush. It appears in the Acts of the Apostles, in the pouring forth of the Holy Ghost from heaven in the form of tongues of flame.

A warning is not out of place here. These mediaeval statements regarding the holy flame about the body are not to be construed only in a symbolical sense. I grant the validity of symbolism. In fact I use it very largely and extensively myself. But I go further, expressing a fundamental belief in the actual experience of such a flame. There are drawings in various of the alchemical writings which show flames and fire ascending the legs. How shall we construe this? Shall we say that this is symbolism only? Let us remember that the legs are symbols of the Unconscious itself, that on which we actually stand in a psychic sense. It supports us, and it stands under all our conscious intellectual and psychic activity. The fire is the libido ascending from the deeps into the conscious levels of the psyche. Well, it is good symbolism. But we could be more literal about it—even as the alchemists were.

The libido is the fire; the prima materia, the first stuff of life, present everywhere in this world of ours. It has to be assimilated by being drawn into the human body via the soles of the feet. In a large number of texts, whether European alchemical or Oriental texts, we find it said that one must learn to breathe through the feet. In the feet, the libido, drawn up by means of the breath and by means of the disciplined mind, creates heat, the effect of which is so crucial in the spagyric art.

But to find the libido manifesting within the brain as color and as light requires time and much effort. And the injunction of our text is particularly appropriate in that it cautions the novice to "have great care at the beginning that thou burn not its Flowers and its vivacity, and make not too much haste to come to an end of thy work." [3]

The result of eliminating the shadow and impurity from the ray, so that the Light may illuminate the mind, is that alterations occur in the colors of what must for convenience sake be termed the aura. This is not merely a legendary appearance, but, briefly, is the magnetic or electrical field surrounding each individual. Its extent and texture depends entirely upon the state of mind of the person, his moods, and his health. This idea is not altogether without confirmation in recent years. Some years ago, Dr. Walter J. Kilner, late electrician to St. Thomas's Hospital, London, published a book entitled *The Human Atmosphere*. In this book he claimed to have demonstrated the presence of the aura by means of certain chemical slides or screens by means of which anyone could see the aura surrounding the body, after a little experimentation. His theory was that, although the unaided human eye cannot see the aura because it lay just beyond the visible spectrum, it can nevertheless be brought into visibility by means of his dicyanin screens, which render the eye susceptible to the wave-lengths composing the aura. Dr. Kilner himself believed these to lie in the ultraviolet end of the spectrum.

He came to believe that the aura, or the emanation from the body, has three distinct portions. A dark line or band, about a quarter of an inch wide, surrounded and was adjacent to the body. Around this was a misty, semiluminous strip, known as the inner aura, radiating outwards to a distance of possibly several inches from all parts of the body. The outer aura, commencing at the distal edge of the inner aura, extended outward into space for several more inches, and appeared to blend with the inner aura where the two merged into one another.

---

3. See page 34.

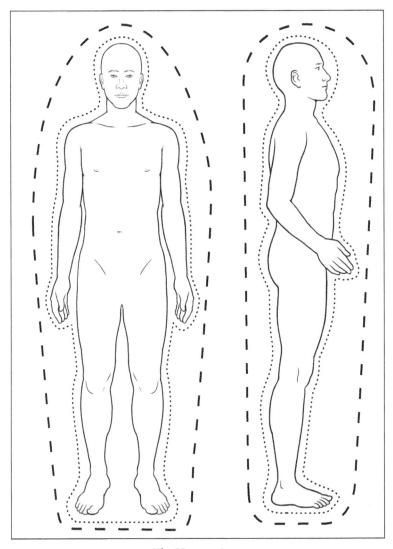

The Human Aura

Kilner himself believed that "there cannot be the least doubt of the reality of the existence of an aura enveloping a human being, and this will in a short time be universally accepted now that it can be made visible to nearly every person having normal eyesight... Ninety five percent of people with normal eyesight can see the aura...At first sight the cloudlike appearance might suggest that the aura was some form of vapor. This is highly improbable...the most probable interpretation of the aura that at present can be given is that it is the outcome of a force emanation from the body which (like all forces) is invisible, but becomes perceptible through its action...If the aura be the outcome of a physical force proceeding from the body and acting on the surrounding medium, it would appear that external forces would influence it...When the poles of a horseshoe magnet, after the removal of the armature, are held from six to eight inches away from the body of a healthy person, the observer will almost immediately be able to distinguish an increase of brilliancy of the aura at the part of the body nearest the poles, and simultaneously the base projected from the poles of the magnet will become more conspicuous. This will in a few seconds concentrate into a single streak or ray joining the body and the magnet, and will have the same width as the poles, including the space between them...When, instead of a horseshoe, one pole of a bar-magnet is held a short distance from the body of a patient, a corresponding display will be produced, only less obvious. As far as has yet been ascertained, neither pole of a magnet exerts a greater influence over the aura than the other. Consequently it is conjectured, that the aura is equally acted-upon by both poles of the magnet, and therefore, as far as magnetism is concerned, the aura does not possess any polarity. The mutual attraction of two auras belonging to different people is more intense than that between a magnet and the aura...An electric brush held near the patient causes the aura to increase in size..."[4]

Colors, we know from practical experience, have different effects on different people, as though in themselves they were tangible entities. The alchemistic doctrine is that perfection in the art alters this personal sphere so that it glows with, at first a golden color, changing finally to deep red or purple. It is this sphere of metallic hue which

---

4. Walter J. Kilner, *The Human Atmosphere: or the Aura Made Visible by the Aid of Chemical Screens* (New York: Rebman Co., 1911), 84–101. Online text at www .sacred-texts.com/eso/tha.

they called the Philosopher's Stone, in that it represented to their imagination as well as vision, some more than precious gem.

According to the text, the rubification is the final stage of perfection, prior to projecting the Stone upon other metals. It calls it the *"true Hyle* of the Philosophers, the bloody stone, the purple-red Coral, the precious Ruby, red Mercury, and the red Tincture." Now Hopkins, whose chemical theory has previously been mentioned, propounds a question with regard to this change of color. "Was this final stage," he asks, "so honorable because metal coloring and dyeing began in the same shop, so that the royal purple and the ios[5] of gold made possible the highest attainment of each in brilliancy of color?"[6] Apparently the suggestion involved in the question does not wholly convince him. For immediately he adds: "The analogy is attractive but does not seem sufficient."[7] Far from sufficient, I should like to add; it does not even begin to correspond to the facts.

Apart from the probability of observation and spiritual experience whereby the alchemists had perceived and noted keenly the interior changes in the psyche and its ethereal vesture, it is evident that throughout all nature red and purple are the colors of ripeness. Shortly after spring when the Sun wends his way northwards, bringing warmth and light to the wintery land, nature robes herself in a green colored mantle. It is her first manifestation of life. In it is implied the promise of further growth; of expectancy, of hope that ripeness will follow. This is succeeded, if we observe fruits and other vegetation, by a yellowy color, marking a definite stage of growth—of vegetable adolescence, as it were. Red follows as symptomatic of its growth to maturity and full stature. And as it deepens to purple, rich and bright, so does its maturity become more and more evident and pronounced. Thus the colors referred to by the alchemists have a reference and valid correspondence to a series of natural processes. And just as they

---

5. Iosis.

6. Arthur John Hopkins, *Alchemy, Child of Greek Philosophy* (New York: Columbia University Press, 1934), 98. Online version at http://babel.hathitrust.org/cgi/pt?id=ucl.b4566948.

7. Ibid.

claimed that the laws of nature are reflected within the sphere of man, so the color processes are recapitulated in the magnetic auric sphere as the Great Work of transformation and transmutation is undertaken.

CHAPTER EIGHT
IN CONCLUSION

I have given a brief sketch of certain of the more fundamental theories and general principles of alchemy. Now I wish to summarize the analysis so far made in ordinary and not alchemical language, in order to clarify and simplify the issue. It is necessary to do this because the question may arise as to the value of such investigations. From the scientific point of view such a query is baseless and needless. All forms of knowledge, no matter what they are, are fit subjects for research and enquiry. It is a case of knowledge for knowledge's sake.

On the other hand there is personal value here. If integrity is achievable by such means, is it not a valuable technique? A unity of one's own psychic structure may be encompassed, and this is no light gain. Especially if you ponder upon the fact that such spiritual unity of being is an age-old quest, and that for countless centuries it has been sought by countless myriads of people. Psychology is an invaluable modern agent to this end, but I think the ancients and especially the alchemical writers, can easily illuminate modern therapy. It expands our idea of the aim and purpose of our work.

We find that, though highly obscure, the Art propounds the view that secreted within that most common and cheap of all materials, human nature, is a certain precious substance. Invariably have the alchemists considered it as the root of consciousness as well as of objective things, that metalline mercurial radix which is the divine Light

151

itself, the radiation of which are to be cocted into the Philosopher's Stone. This inner root, when permitted openly to operate, is the intuited criterion of all values. From within ourselves must we mine this spiritual gold which eventually transmutes the dross of the external world.

But to discover this Mercury of the Wise is no simple matter. The assimilation of the Unconscious by consciousness is a process beset by all sorts of difficulties. For one thing completely false ideas of ourselves block our perception of the existence of the Unconscious. For another, erroneous religious and conventional education which has prevailed from our early infancy, has given us an erroneous and untrue conception of life. This combination leads us to place an overemphasis upon our conscious egos. An exaggerated evaluation of our intellectual thinking selves results, without so much as a vague trace of recognition of any deeper spiritual element. Failure of recognition naturally implies a failure of culture. If this deeper element of the psyche be not realized as existent, then it is evident that no technical means can be devised whereby either it may be harnessed and its power utilized, or by which the vast extent of its content of memory and inspiration may be allied to the normal self.

Ignorance is thus the first curse and it is this that must be overcome. It is the same old formulation. Within us is the light of life. We will not or cannot easily realize it. Therefore we project it outside and search fruitlessly for this light of our barren lives. In all places and at all times men have sought a god, a saving grace, somewhere in the universe—anywhere so long as we might not look within. Outside preferably. We have to learn to realize the intrinsic and final value of the Unconscious—as an inward potentiality that is capable of considerable development and elucidation. Something like bringing Christ to birth within our souls, or seeking Buddha within at the apex of the mind.

Writes Jung in his commentary to Wilhelm's *The Secret of the Golden Flower*, "The more powerful and independent consciousness becomes, and with it the conscious will, the more is the unconscious forced into the background. When this happens it becomes easily possible for the conscious structures to be detached from the unconscious images. Gaining thus in freedom, they break the chains of mere instinctiveness, and finally arrive at a state that is deprived of, or contrary to instinct. Consciousness thus torn from its roots and no longer able to appeal to the authority of the primordial images, possesses a Promethean freedom, it is true, but it also partakes of the nature of a *godless hybria*.[1] It soars above the earth, even above mankind, but the danger of capsizing is there, not for every individual, to be sure, but collectively for the weak members of such a society, who again Promethean-like, are bound by the unconscious to the Caucasus."[2]

How true becomes the Biblical verse "Where there is no vision, the people perish."[3] That people whose life excludes the dynamic quality of the unconscious, and who are cut off from their own vital roots, obviously are doomed to disaster. The outstanding feature of our own era is such a one-sided evaluation of life, an over-emphasis of intellectual values at the expense of the Unconscious and all that it implies. The irrational is rigorously excluded from consideration until finally, in a mad explosive burst of national barbarism and individual neurosis it forces itself upon our attention. As always is the case, when one psychic function is exaggerated to the detriment of the other, or is violently repressed, such a repressed or exaggerated faculty gains in power and fury. *Enantiodromia* must then begin its operation—and we are utterly powerless. Whilst air is left in a free and diffused state very little use may be made of it because it has but little kinetic power. Immediately, however, when it is gathered and limited and confined, its compression imparts great power to its content. Thus also, the mere fact that one phase of life is neglected, attention being devoted to its polarity, invests it at once with terrific potency by the very reason of its repression and damming up. Given no outlet in normal wholesome channels the bottled-up content of the psyche seeks a forced outlet in illicit and unwelcome ways.

---

1. Or "hubris."

2. Richard Wilhelm, *The Secret of the Golden Flower: A Chinese Book of Life* (London: Kegan Paul, Trench, Trubner & Co., 1962), 85.

3. Proverbs 29:18.

It is so easy to realize this principle in the tenor of our present lives. Wherever we turn today, mankind seems gripped by some nameless and unknown terror, dominating all men's minds unbeknown to themselves. Only its effect is known and realized, terror and fear. It is activating anxiety and terror of the unknown within them stirring the old undomesticated beast within into new and furious life. Its only result can be the destruction of mankind—almost like the end of a patient disintegrating with psychosis and dementia. Yet—in one sense it is all of our own making.

We are, as Jung has so accurately observed, chained like Prometheus to the Caucasus. As men we wished anciently to evolve. To evolve, the animal dynamic side had to be suppressed, to be forgotten—or so it seemed to us. We have evolved—somewhat. And, it results that the animal after all controls us. It would have been easier to have taken the animal with us—to have trained it, to have domesticated it by kindness and education so that it could be acclimatized to modern social life. We ought to have realized it was *our* animal—part of ourselves, inseparable from us, and therefore *must* be cultivated and retained within the psychic sphere of our awareness. There would have been no chaining to the Caucasus then. For the animal might have shown that it had a totally unsuspected side—a spiritual side. After all, religious experience, artistic and scientific inspiration, emanate from it.

We must remember that in the psychic depths, in that primitive archaic aspect of the personality we term the Unconscious, is resident the entire psychic force of the self, the libido. Since the Unconscious is that level of awareness which functioned in the distant and now faded periods of archaic evolution, it is directly associated and connected with the dynamic springs of life, somatic, intellectual and spiritual also.

Or, if we wish to take a philosophic religious view of the matter, in God or the Absolute is all life and all power. Without his life, existence in the phenomenal sense cannot be. The phenomenal world, anyway, by the Neo-Platonic hypothesis, is a falling away from supreme reality into unreality and negation. The intellectual denial of reality, therefore, would constitute an even further descent into the unreality of negation, a decadence of the human spirit, an increase of positive evil.

On the other hand, even the intellectual conviction that human life is grounded implicitly in divinity and partakes of the divine Light is sufficient to create a compelling link between the human soul and God, and to flood that soul with the Light and abundant energy.

The forces resident in the Unconscious charge and dynamize whatever material is forcibly repressed out of consciousness into its dark forbidding area and given no legitimate vent or outlet. Consequently such material gathers force, eventually becoming highly explosive and dangerous. The effect of such an explosive force seeking an outlet must be disastrous for the individual. This idea is paralleled by Jehovah in the Bible threatening his people with famine, disaster, and an appalling end if they forget him and no longer worship him. In this sense, Jehovah is the personified representation of paternal archetypal images of the Unconscious. Here we have the rationale of compulsive behavior and physical and mental disorders over which the individual has absolutely no control. In this theory too, is implicit an explanation of irrational fears and impulses which no amount of logical argument succeeds finally in dispelling or eliminating.

The one-sided exaggeration of the conscious outlook forms no inconsiderable part of the practice of nerve-specialists and psychiatrists and psychoanalysts of today, psychological practitioners who have arisen precisely because of such an exaggeration. Our time is one which over-values the conscious will. Not that one wishes to detract in the very least from the high moral value of conscious endeavor and ambition. On the contrary, in alchemical literature will and intellect are termed the Flower of Mind, as being the culmination of the evolutionary processes. Consciousness and will should not be depreciated but should be considered as the greatest cultural and progressive achievement of humanity. But of what use is an outlook upon life which destroys humanity? What value has a morality which soars in the clouds but yet which hinders free growth and expression? Morality, never let it be forgotten, was designed or invented to enable us to domesticate our instincts and thus enable us to live amicably with our fellows. Unfortunately, from something invented for our convenience, it has become elevated into an absolute. It rules over our lives with a rod of iron. We are slaves to its fantastically absurd domination. As Jung has so eloquently remarked, "The bringing of will and capacity into harmony seems to me to be something more than normality. Morality *a tout prix*—a sign of barbarism—oftentimes wisdom is better." [4]

It was such a wisdom that the alchemists sought. In fact, one alchemical expositor has defined the Art as "*The* philosophy; the seeking out of the *Sophia* in the mind." [5] The alchemists had recognized the fundamental polarity duality of consciousness and the tendency induced by life itself towards over-exaggeration of polar functions. This exaggeration they sought to remedy. Integrity, the joining of the polarities within consciousness by the development of a new point of view, the saving jewel of myth and fairy tale, that stone which would transmute all that was base into the purest gleaming gold, was the prize above all to which they aspired. How else could they discover the goddess of wisdom save through integrating themselves? How else could gold be made save through the discovery of gold in themselves? In what other way could the approach to the precincts of the Temple of Philosophy be found except insofar as the path made itself clear within their own minds?

The consciousness of primitive man expressed the one pole—domination by the Unconscious, signifying an unyielding and rigid rulership by the old stern gods, the primitive archetypes of the Unconscious. As evolution proceeded with consciousness becoming more developed and civilized, another factor tended to operate. Life became increasingly more difficult and complex in cultured communities as awareness arose of the conflict set up by the primitive instinctual side of man's nature. Consequently, repression and conflict were engendered in the psyche. In order to live communally without arousing the ire and dis-

---

4. See Jung's commentary on Richard Wilhelm's *The Secret of the Golden Flower: A Chinese Book of Life* (London: Kegan Paul, Trench, Trubner & Co., 1962), 86.

5. Mary Anne Atwood, *A Suggestive Inquiry into the Hermetic Mystery, with a Dissertation on the More Celebrated of the Alchemical Philosophers Being an Attempt Towards the Recovery of the Ancient Experiment of Nature* (London: Trelawney Saunders, 1850), 597.

approval as well as the ostracism of the herd, the primitive impulses had violently to be restrained—and occasionally to accomplish this, the personality was outraged. In reality, such an attitude which refuses to recognize the instincts is no solution to psychic problems at all. It is precisely this suppression which, in the long run, results in frustration and sterility. It is just as much a one-sided partial expression of the psyche as is that of primitive man who, theoretically speaking, indulged his impulses without restraint and thereby outraged his moral sense.

What is necessary, then, is a changed point of view. A new outlook upon life must be evolved which is all-inclusive of, and reconcile the legitimacy of both these psychic tendencies. It must be willing to accept, take cognizance of dualistic expressions. There must be no hegemony of power against power. Both consciousness and the instinctual side of the psyche are equal parts of and are comprised within the Self. Both demand a reasonable amount of fulfilment. Thus a higher, and an infinitely more civilized attitude towards life is requisite, approaching more nearly to wisdom than either of the others. Through this viewpoint the libido finds a wholesome outlet. Life is to be seen as a whole. Seen thus, if must be accepted as actually it is. There is, as Synesius says practically at the opening of our text, the red tincture and there is the white tincture, the male and the female, the positive and the negative, which were created together with the universe itself. Both are integral parts of the world system. Why therefore struggle against the scheme of things? Far wiser to accept. Then the whole man is to be seen, not as an assemblage of separate warring parts, but as a single homogeneous psychic system. Such a point of view makes for progress and real evolution. The unconditional acceptance of both psychic functions ends the internecine warfare that had been raging. At once there is rendered possible a state of inner tranquility and security. In turn, this inner peace reveals a wide vista, showing the true nature of life. Nor is this all, for the new viewpoint and the attained integrity permit the entry into the mind of other levels of consciousness, the existence of which had never been discovered because of conflict and neurotic compulsion. In the Hindu Yogi systems, the view is held that until one has experienced *Samadhi*, the mystical illumination of the mind, no true perception of the universe, no real understanding of life is possible.

I am a psychologist with only a minimum of free time. Like most people I have neither the time nor the inclination to waste my energies on futile inquiries. We are obliged to be practical people working in a practical world. But because we are practical and sensible we are sometimes *forced* against what appears to be better judgment into directions which, though seemingly barren and fruitless of result at first, ultimately yield a most bountiful harvest. Alchemy has been such to me. I would never have imagined it to be possible. My patients pay my fees certainly not for me to talk in platitudes to them. Lots of people will do that for nothing. But what these patients want and need is someone to advise and assist them out of their present psychological difficulties into a fuller, richer and more satisfactory life. They require aid in understanding themselves. In other words, to help transmute their valueless lead into that treasure so desired and desirable—gold.

Just stop for a moment to reflect upon what this means. And before coming to some conclusion, first read the following dream narrated to me by a patient of mine. I should add, by way of warning, that he has absolutely no knowledge of alchemy in any way, shape or form. He has never heard of it other than accidently in terms derived from his chemistry course in high school. And I had never mentioned it at all to him. Here is the dream:

"There is some kind of delightful park, in which are all kinds of animals and birds. They seem to be thoroughly domesticated. They are returning, after having been afield all day. I notice one strange bird particularly. A few of us are up on a high place looking down on the ground. A bright colored snake appears. It rears up, apparently ready to strike. We fear it will go for someone. A white vapor issues from its mouth. We suppose it is venom, but it reaches no one. There is a strong smell of ammonia, however."

No doubt this will at first give you the impression of being quite pointless—insignificant as most dreams are. You cannot be blamed for feeling as you do. However, many researchers have come to feel that dreams cannot possibly be meaningless. Whatever issues from the human mind must possess significance. The significance in many cases may not be at all profound. It may be paltry, trite, pathetic, humorous, or elementary. But some measure of significance it must have. And after a great deal of enquiry and investigation along certain quite distinct lines, it has been quite definitely proven that dreams have meaning. In fact, they tell us a great deal about the dreamer and his life.

It appears as though the dream is a dynamic effort on the part of some other deeper part of our make-up to give us some information about ourselves. The dream is an attempt to "get wise" to ourselves, projected into normal consciousness by the Unconscious. Its action seems compensatory to our conscious upon life. You have all seen a man who has a short leg with a twisted pelvis and a rotated or curved spine. The twisted pelvis and the curvature are what are known as mechanical compensations developed to maintain equilibrium. He may not have been conscious of the healing or equilibrating process as it gradually occurred, but it took place none the less outside of his conscious knowledge. If one of your kidneys is not functioning up to par, the other kidney will take over, slightly enlarging itself, perhaps, in order to do the work of both. This too is a compensation. Similarly the dream is a compensatory activity—I say compensating rather than contrasting, advisedly—set up to maintain psychic and mental equilibrium. It prevents intellectual one-sidedness in the same way that the twisted pelvis and curved spine prevent an actual physical one-sidedness.

In other words, the dream is to keep you straight. Whenever you are going off the rails in any direction, you will find, should you observe yourself closely enough, that somehow your dreams will move off in the other direction. It is an activity so designed as to give us a superior understanding of ourselves.

You feel inferior in the business and social world? Your dreams will be grand, eloquent, making you feel superior. Is life ugly and offensive, wounding you to your very soul? The dream corrects the situation by placing you for the time being in a world of gentle beauty, exquisite and lovely, even ecstatic and elevating. Love has disappointed you? During sleep, Don Juan will have absolutely nothing on you. There the ladies will fall right and left for your irresistible charm.

One simply cannot live with inferiority, nor with ugliness, if these qualities strike too deeply into the soul—nor with failure of any kind and disappointment. Life cannot sustain itself under these blows. They are terrible defeats before which you bow the head in shame. If these exist, you might just as well die. And you might die too, were it not for the compensating factor latent within your own mind. It shows you by contrast the other side of the picture, to teach you the relativity of the whole of life. If the one is true, the other may be also. Neither one is absolute or fixed for you. In this way, a balance is struck. Equilibrium is maintained, and you are prevented from blowing your brains out, slowly pining away, or from going more than a little bit crazy.

Freud has called this adjusting process wish-fulfilment. It means briefly that whatever it is that lies concealed within you as a wish or as a desire, and life thwarts you in its expression or gratification, finds its outlet in the act of dreaming. If you feel inferior, your wish is to succeed and be superior. Love—we all desire success and efficiency here. And most of us wish for lovely surroundings and a beautiful environment. Without a doubt this is true. Examine your dreams in the light of your everyday life and you will see how perfectly correct it is.

But this is only one half of the picture. Wish-fulfilment does not by a long shot begin to answer things. I have come to think, because clinical experience has led me to this conclusion, that the compensatory function in dreams actually represents something capable of being brought into manifestation in everyday life. I am not to be construed as saying that the literal fantastic terms of the dream represent realities. Dreams are full of grotesqueries. But if you can summarize the *meaning* implicit in these fantasies, and recognize them as the attempt on the part of a deeper wiser element in your own heart to your environment, you will have embarked upon a road work out your problems in a way satisfactory to you and of such high adventure as will make the old blood-and-thunders seem cheap and commonplace. The dream is always an attempt at release, at therapy, at self-revelation.

You will then discover, as I have been impelled, something of the real meaning of alchemy. And all the worthless dross of your existence—valueless and insignificant, will slowly transmute itself into something that surpasses all value and worth.

The dream of patient is something of the sort. It is an unconscious attempt to heal and equilibrate his own personality so that it could deal more adequately and satisfactorily with life. He is always afraid of events long before they materialize. Therefore life is always a continuous cycle of trouble and difficulty of his own anticipation, and he is constantly nervous, tense and jittery. By the end of a day he is practically in a state of nervous exhaustion. So much so that his professional life—he is a teacher of mathematics—is in jeopardy, and he is unhappy and unsuccessful. At least, this was true before he came for treatment. This dream occurred about half way through his analysis. I have selected this one because it presents a number of interesting and salutary symbols.

It may surprise you a little perhaps when I remark that beside me at this moment is an old alchemical treatise in which there are colored pictures and symbols which are almost exact replicas of those employed in the dream. This book speaks of strange gardens and parks with all sorts of queer beasts and birds. In these parks are hills and mountains where grow plants that never were seen in any botanical garden. Snakes are shown in this book, snakes rearing their heads, devouring a fellow, and some bearing golden crowns. Strange to say, the writer speaks of ammonia and magnesia; and all sorts of other metals and chemicals are thrown together cheek by jowl in description.

What is to be the due in our search for interpretation? How shall we analyze this dream? Analyze it we must, for we have declared that the dream has significance. There are at least two possibilities. Both yield equally interesting and valuable material.

One is Freud's approach, the other is Jung's. Both handle and interpret similar material. But how their final analyses differ! Freud interprets mythological material, arguing that ancient myths and legends indicate that mankind was heir to exactly the same inner sexual conflicts and endopsychic inadequacies that we experience today. Psychologically, mankind has changed but little. The fundamental parental conflict and its effect upon the developing ego attempting to come to terms with its sexuality—these are the themes of myth.

Jung likewise admits, but he proceeds a little further. He believes that myths were evolved as an expression of a purposive function of the mind. Not only did they express conflict and inward turmoil, but somehow for the maker of the myth they indicated a way out, a means of release. Not an escape, but a solution. This is not all; for he believes as I have already indicated at length, that latent within the cells of the brain is a stratum of consciousness in which lie dormant just such symbols as occur in myth, legend, early religious experiences and alchemical writing. We have in us at the base of our minds at this very moment an entirely new world—the Prima Materia of the Alchemists. It only awaits investigation and further discovery. And it explains why mankind's solutions of its own problems have always been alike; they express themselves in the basic pattern that we have carried over from the past.

If we accept the idea that the myth represented some kind of unconscious psychological solution to mental problems, a solution that was presented as an automatic compensatory activity of the psyche, we can at least divine something of what is implicit in the dream of my patient. Somehow his Unconscious—for so we may term this phase of himself of which he was not even aware—was attempting to solve the problems confronting him. Under the stimulus of psychological analysis, it was attempting to present a solution by way of the dream. Why it should present such a key under the guise of alchemical symbolism is hard to divine. All we can say is why not? Mankind's attempts to achieve salvation or integrity, insofar as they belong to the past, have become a part of our inherited Unconscious make-up. As we ourselves seek to integrate or transmute ourselves, so unconsciously we draw upon—or express ourselves in ways similar to those latent in—the deeper strata of our own souls. Alchemical symbolism, when understood, is just as eloquent as any other symbolism—and very much more to the point.

I do not wish to interpret this dream fully for that would take up too much space and time. All I wish to do is briefly to call attention to salient points and leave them to the reader to elaborate in his own way.

Nicolas Flamel, an alchemist of the sixteenth century in France, wrote of what he called the *pratum* or meadow, where there were hills, caverns, trees and plants and animals.[6] Another alchemical writer, Thomas Vaughan, the brother of Henry Vaughan the poet, has provided us with something of an interpretation of this *pratum* which he says is the garden of ideas, the rendezvous of all spirits.[7] In a word, he is endeavoring to make use of a pictorial expression to convey some idea of the Unconscious—a mystical place or psychical region which is foreign to our normal rational concepts. It is an "other world"—the other concealed side of our own consciousness where there is life and activity, albeit of a different kind to that with which we are familiar.

Animals, briefly, represent psychologically that part of us which is animal and brutal, the instincts. An animal is a perfectly good symbol of that which in us harks back thousands, even millions, of years to primitive evolutionary eras. It represents the instinctual energy striving for expression through us. It is this which is named libido—desire, instinct, psychical energy. There are many animals in this garden—many streams or currents of vitality and life within. Note that my patient seems to feel that all his animals are domesticated. That is to say that the instincts have made their adaption to the civilized social order, and are no longer at war with it.

The high place is, most suggestively, an elevation from which you can see all around you. Remember in what reverence the biblical scribes held hills and mountains. You may recall that Moses ascended Mount Horeb to obtain the law. The Psalmist declared that his eyes were lifted towards the hills whence he expected the help of God. And Christ, to

---

6. Atwood, 235.

7. Ibid.

deliver his sermon, went up upon the mount. If the meadow represents the unconscious level of our life, the hillock must represent some divine height in that psychic stratum, some portion which is struggling up-wards towards the light of day, towards a summit by means of which a clearer vista of life may be viewed. From this vantage point life could be dealt with more adequately. All of which indicates some inward peak of soul when, in drawn upon itself, the psyche gathers its forces to *prepare* for some great achievement, for some great move to save itself.

Below, in the dream, there appeared a snake. Again we are confront-ed with a peculiarly apt symbol, common both to alchemical and to psychoanalytical writing. In the Freudian system, the snake or serpent usually indicates libido interpreted solely in a sexual way. It represents a repressed sexuality, sexual desire and longing, even the genitals them-selves. But we may extend this considerably to give it an added and full-er meaning. In Genesis, the serpent who tempted Eve somehow repre-sents the forbidden knowledge of good and evil, in some way associated with sex for afterwards both she and Adam became ashamed of their nakedness and covered themselves up. Alchemically it represents the possibility of transformation, sublimation, and regeneration. It is wis-dom and power exalted to the heights—power becomes immortality. In some ancient religions, certain Gods were represented as serpents. The Gods, we know, are primitive power concepts, symbols of creative energy. Thus we have amplified some little the significance of the snake in the patient's dream.

That the dreamer should fear the snake is indicative of the source of his trouble. He is afraid of himself and his own instincts, which fear he projects outside of himself, transforming it into a fear of his profes-sion, of people, of life. But the dream hints that he should not fear. He is perfectly safe. And so far from the snake being dangerous, the psyche indicates otherwise. It draws upon that collective mythologi-cal symbolism which anciently also the alchemists used.

What issues from the snake's mouth? A white vapor smelling of ammonia. What strange metaphors this dreamer is using! Yet they tell him a great deal if only he would listen. His associations to ammonia were principally that it was used for cleaning purposes, for cleaning bathroom installations and tubs. And since all the symbols in a dream refer to the dreamer himself, this ammonia and its pungent cleansing properties issue from that of which he is afraid, his own basic self. In a great many alchemical writings we find it said that the First Matter from which the invaluable Philosopher's Stone is to be formed, is a white vapor, a silvery humid cloud, *the Sal Ammoniac of the Wise,* magnesia, or some other poisonous venom.

Strange, is it not? We might almost assume that the dreamer's real self is stating that fear is superfluous. Not only so but that from that part of himself which he fears something invaluable may be formed as a sublimate. If only the dreamer would recognize and *accept* himself entirely, casting out all fear and anxiety, a new process of regeneration and transformation might gradually develop within him. Almost, by inference, it says the Philosopher's Stone might be formed—a stone that is of untold price, a perfect gem with power to transmute. And the personality which hitherto had been so valueless, so impotent and sterile, just like cheap common lead, could undergo a transmuting process to become creative, valuable with an enormous potential for subsequent achievement.

Thus my psychological work has forced me to investigate a subject which seemed at first to be forbidding and quite incapable of yielding anything of value so far as my professional life was concerned. Certainly it would seem that alchemy would be the last subject on earth to investigate. Yet my patient's dream is full of naught but alchemical symbolism. By my study of it, apart from purely personal benefit which has been considerable, I have been able to assist him, if only a little, in his interior growth, enabling him to be bold and fearless in his attempt to adapt himself successfully to the external world. Because of alchemy, he thus may succeed and conquer. Had I not been obliged to turn to this dark page in the obscure history of intellectual and spiritual development, my patient might have encountered another frustration in the long series which life has afforded him. Instead of being able to assist him, my ignorance would have left him high and dry with his own inadequacies and neurotic problems. Now however, thanks to the suggestion which Alchemy made me, he has been able to see himself in a new creative and spiritual light, to overcome his own inner conflicts, and to strive with all his might towards achievement.

The elimination of the conflict, the clearing away of the animal dross and refuse from the mind, transmuting the mind spontaneously, is the one goal that the alchemists aspired towards. For, if we translate, their terminology, until the psyche is integrated by a conversion of the elements of its own being, producing a "conjunction of both natures,"[8] its house ceasing to be divided against itself, the true nature and purpose of life cannot be divined. Nor can the nature of the spiritual forces playing upon both the universe and upon man be realized. The dead weight of outlived idea, unnecessary addiction to habit and convention, these of necessity must be removed from the mind's sphere, so that when the individual acts it is with the whole individuality, with spontaneity, and with creative effort. The sphere of the mind's perceptions must be extended to an extensive knowledge of itself, so that true self-consciousness in the fullest and widest sense of the term is attained. Tranquilized and cleansed, then the hitherto dormant aspects of the psyche may awaken and grow. As the supreme and most important definition of Synesius asserts, in the discovery and manufacture of the Stone, we add nothing but only remove the superfluities.

As the superfluities are cleared away, and the nature of the alchemical gold within is revealed, that "essence of mind which is intrinsically pure," so is the Philosopher's Stone concocted. Consciousness is realized to be comparable to some more than valuable gem—a redeeming stone of untold price. It is a stone which imparts value to whatsoever is brought into contact with it, enlightening it and transmuting it to its own divine nature and integrity.

---

8. See page 37.

THE ART OF TRUE HEALING

A Treatise on the Mechanism of Prayer, and the
Operation of the Law of Attraction in Nature

By Israel Regardie

Within every man and woman is a force which directs and controls the entire course of life. Properly used, it can heal every affliction and ailment to which mankind is heir. Every single religion affirms this fact. All forms of mental or spiritual healing, no matter under what name they travel, promise the same thing. Even psychoanalysis employs this power, though indirectly. For the critical insight and understanding which it brings to bear upon the psyche releases tensions of various kinds, and through this release the healing power latent within and natural to the human system operates more freely. Each of these systems undertakes to teach its devotees technical methods of thinking or contemplation or prayer such as will, according to the *a priori* terms of their own philosophies, renew their bodies and transform their whole environment. None or few of them, however, actually fulfil in a complete way the promise made at the outset. There seems but little understanding of the practical means whereby the spiritual forces underlying the universe and permeating the entire nature of man may be utilized and directed towards the creation of a new heaven and a new earth. Naturally, without universal cooperation, such an ideal is impossible for all mankind. Nevertheless, each one for himself may commence the task of reconstruction.

How, then, is the crucial question, are we to become aware of this force? What are its nature and properties? What is the mechanism whereby we can use it?

As I have said before, different systems have evolved widely differing processes by which the student might divine the presence of such a power. Meditation, prayer, invocation, emotional exaltation, and demands made at random upon the universe or the Universal Mind, have been a few of such methods. In the last resort, if we ignore petty details of a trivial nature, all have this in common. By turning the fiery penetrating power of the mind inwards upon itself, and exalting the emotional system to a certain pitch, we may become aware of previously unsuspected currents of force. Currents, moreover, almost electric in their interior sensation, healing and integrating in their effect.

It is the willed use of such a force that is capable of bringing health to body and mind. When directed it acts magnet-like. By this I mean that it attracts to whomsoever employs these methods just those necessities of life, material or spiritual, that he urgently requires or which are needed for his further evolution.

Fundamentally, the underlying idea of the mental healing systems is this. In the ambient atmosphere surrounding us and pervading the structure of each minute body-cell is a spiritual force. This force is omnipresent and infinite. It is present in the most infinitesimal object as it is in the most proportion-staggering nebula or island universe. It is this force which is life itself. Nothing in the vast expanse of space is dead. Everything pulsates with vibrant life. Even the ultra-microscopic particles of the atom are alive; in fact the electron is a crystallization of its electric power.

This life force being infinite it follows that man must be saturated—permeated through and through with spiritual force. It constitutes his higher self, it is his link with godhead, it is God in man. Every molecule in his physical system must be soaked with its dynamic energy. Each cell in the body contains it in its plenitude. Thus we are brought face to face with the enormous problem underlying all disease, the enigmatical problem of nervous depletion.

What is fatigue? How *can* there be depletion if vitality and cosmic currents of force daily pour through man, simply saturating his mind and body with its power? Primarily, it is because he offers resistance to its flow through him that he becomes tired and ill, the conflict finally culminating in death. How is puny man able to defy the universe? Nay more, offer resistance and opposition to the very force which underlies, and continually evolves in, the universe? The complacency and confusion of his mental outlook, the moral cowardice by which he was reared, and his false perception of the nature of life—these are the causes of resistance to the inward flow of the spirit. That this is unconscious is no logical obstacle to the force of this argument, as all the depth psychologies have demonstrated. What man is really aware of all the involuntary processes going on within him? Who is conscious of the intricate mechanism of his mental processes, of that by which his food is assimilated and digested, of the circulation of his blood, of the arterial distribution of nourishment to every bodily organ? All these are purely involuntary processes. To a large degree also are his resistances to life. Man has surrounded himself with a crystallized shell of prejudices and ill-conceived fantasies, a shell which affords no entrance to light of life without.

What wonder he ails? What wonder he is so ill and impotent, helpless and poor? Why should there be surprise that the average individual is so unable adequately to deal with life?

The first step towards freedom and health is a conscious realization of the vast spiritual reservoir in which we live and move and have our being. Repeated intellectual effort to make this part and parcel of one's mental outlook upon life automatically breaks down or dissolves something of the hard inflexible shell of the mind. And then life and spirit pour abundantly. Health spontaneously arises, and a new life begins as the point of view undergoes this radical change. Moreover, it would appear that the environment attracts just those people who can help in various ways, and precisely those amenities of life that had been longed for.

The second step lies in a slightly different direction. Regulated breathing—quite a simple process. Its necessity follows from the following postulate. If life is all about one, all-penetrant and all pervasive, what more reasonable than that the very air we breathe from one moment to another should be highly charged with vitality? Our breathing processes we then regulate accordingly. We contemplate that life is the active principle in the atmosphere. During the practice of this rhythmical breathing at fixed periods of the day, there should be no strenuous forcing of the mind, no overtaxing of the will. All effort must be gentle and easy; then skill is obtained. We let the breath flow in while mentally counting very slowly—one, two, three, four, five. Then we exhale counting the same beat. It is fundamental and important that the initial rhythm begun, whether it be a five or ten beats count or any other convenient one, should be maintained. For it is the very rhythm itself which is responsible for the easy absorption of vitality from without, and the acceleration of the divine power within.

Immutable rhythm is everywhere manifest in the universe. It is a machine whose parts move and are governed in accordance with the cyclic laws. Look at the sun, the stars, and the planets. All move with comparable grace, with a rhythm in their inexorable times. It is mankind which has wandered, in its ignorance and self-complacency, far from the divine cycles of things. We have interfered with the rhythmic process inhering in nature. And how sadly have we not paid for it!

Therefore in attempting to attune ourselves once more to the intelligent spiritual power functioning through nature's mechanism, we attempt, not blindly to copy, but intelligently to adopt her methods. Make, therefore, the breathing rhythmical at certain fixed times of the day when there is little likelihood of disturbance. Cultivate above all the art of relaxation. Learn to address each tensed muscle from toe to head as you lie flat on your back in bed. Tell it deliberately to loosen its tension and cease from its unconscious contracture. Think of the blood in response to your command flowing copiously to each organ, carrying life and nourishment everywhere, producing a state of glowing radiant health. Only after these preliminary processes have been accomplished should you begin your rhythmic breathing, slowly and without haste. Gradually as the mind accustoms itself to the idea, the lungs will take up the rhythm. In a few minutes it will have become automatic. The whole process becomes extremely simple and pleasurable.

It would be impossible to overestimate its importance or efficacy. As the lungs take up the rhythm, automatically inhaling and exhaling to a measured beat, so do they communicate it and gradually extend it to all the surrounding cells and tissue. Just as a stone thrown into a pond sends out widely expanding ripples and concentric circles of motion, so does the motion of the lungs. In a few minutes, the whole body is vibrating in unison with their movement. Every cell seems to vibrate sympathetically. And very soon, the whole organism comes to feel as if it were an inexhaustible storage battery of power.

Simple as it is, the exercise is not to be despised. It is upon the mastery of this very easy technique that the rest of this system stands. Master it first. Make sure that you can completely relax and produce the rhythmic breath in a few seconds.

§

I now approach an idea fundamental and highly significant. It is the inability to realize or thoroughly to have grasped its importance which really underlies the frequently observed failure of many mental culture and spiritual healing systems. Just as in the physical body are specialized organs for the performance of specialized functions, so in the mental and spiritual nature exist corresponding centers and organs. Exactly as the teeth, the stomach, liver and intestines are so many mechanisms evolved and devised by nature for the digestion and assimilation of food, so are there similar centers in the other constituents of man's nature. The mouth receives food. Likewise there is an apparatus for rejecting waste effete products. In the psychic nature also are focal centers for the absorption of spiritual power from the universe without. Others render its distribution and circulation possible. The dynamic energy and power entering man from without is not uniform or alike in vibratory rate. It may be of too high a voltage, so to say, readily to be endured by him. Within, therefore, is a certain psychic apparatus whereby indiscriminate cosmic currents of energy may be assimilated and digested, their voltage thus becoming adjusted to the human level. The process of becoming aware of this psychic apparatus, and using the energy it generates, is an integral part of this healing system. It is my contention that prayer and contemplative methods unconsciously employ these inner centers. Hence we would be wiser and far more efficient deliberately to employ for our own ends this spiritual power and the centers it flows through. Let us call these latter, for the moment, psycho-spiritual organs, of which there are five major ones. Since name them we must, inasmuch as the human mind loves to classify and tabulate things, let me give them the most non-committal and non-compromising titles imaginable. For convenience's sake, the first we may name Spirit, the second Air, the succeeding ones being called Fire, Water and Earth.

To illustrate the concept, I reproduce here a simple diagram. It shows the position and location of the centers. Not for one moment do I wish to be understood as stating that these centers are physical in nature and position. They exist in a subtler spiritual or psychic part of man's nature. We may even consider them, not as realities themselves, but as symbols of realities, great, redeeming and saving symbols. Under certain conditions we may become aware of them in very much the same way as we may become aware of different organs in our physical bodies. We often speak of reason as being situated in the head, referring emotion to the heart and instinct to the belly. Similarly, there exists a natural correspondence between these centers and various parts of the body.

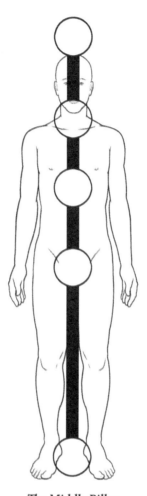

The Middle Pillar

It is axiomatic to this system that there are three principal engines or means whereby we may become aware of the centers to awaken them from their dormant state so that they may function properly within. Thought, color, and sound are the three means. The mind must concentrate itself on the assumed position of these centers one by one. Then certain names which are to be considered as vibratory rates must be intoned and vibrated. Finally, each center is to be visualized as having a particular color and shape. The combination of these three agencies gradually awakens the centers from their latency.[1] Slowly they become stimulated into functioning each according to its own nature, pouring forth a stream of highly spiritualized energy and power into the body and mind. When ultimately their operation becomes habitual and stabilized, the spiritual power they generate may be directed by will to heal various ailments and diseases both of a psychological and physical nature. It can also be communicated by mere laying of hands to another person. Simply by thinking fixedly and with intent, the energy moreover can be communicated from mind to mind telepathically or transmitted through space to another person miles away—objects in space affording no interruption or obstacle to its passage.

First of all the position of the centers as shown diagrammatically must be memorized. They are to be stimulated into activity either while sitting upright or whilst lying down flat on the back in a perfectly relaxed state. The hands may be folded in the lap, or else, with fingers interlocked, be permitted to rest loosely below the solar plexus. Calmness should be induced, and several minutes should be devoted to rhythmic breathing, until a gentle ripple is sensed playing over the diaphragm.

Then imagine above the coronal region of the head a ball or sphere of brilliant white light. Do not *force* the imagination to visualize the light sphere. To force would only result in the development of neuromuscular tension, and this would defeat our end. Let it be done quietly and easily. If the mind wanders, wait a moment or two and gently lead it back. At the same time vibrate or intone the word *Eheieh*. This word should be pronounced *eh-heh-yeh*. After a few days of practice it will become quite easy to imagine the name vibrating above the head in the so-called Spirit center. This is the indwelling or overshadowing divinity in each of us, the basic spiritual self which we can all draw upon. *Eheieh* means literally "I AM," and this center represents the I AM consciousness within. The effect of thus mentally directing the

---

1. The method presented in the following pages is the "Exercise of the Middle Pillar," a Golden Dawn technique that Regardie effectively made his own. It was described at length in his book *The Middle Pillar.* (See *The Middle Pillar: The Balance Between Mind and Magic.*)

vibration is to awaken the center to dynamic activity. At once it begins to vibrate and rotate, and light and energy are felt to emanate downwards upon and into the personality. Enormous charges of spiritual power make their way into the brain, and the entire body feels suffused with vitality and life. Even the finger-tips and toes react to the awakening of the coronal sphere by a faint pricking sensation at first being felt. The name should be intoned during the first few weeks of practice in a moderately audible and sonorous tone of voice. As skill is acquired, then the vibration may be practiced in silence, the name being imagined and mentally placed in the center. If the mind tends to wander, the frequent repetition of the vibration will be found a great help to concentration.

Having let the mind rest here for some five minutes, when it will be seen to glow and scintillate, imagine that it emits a white shaft downwards through the skull and brain, stopping at the throat. Here it expands to form a second ball of light, which should include a large part of the face, up to and including the eyebrows. If the larynx is conceived to be the center of the sphere, then the distance from it to the cervical vertebrae at the back of the neck will be approximately the radius. Naturally this dimension will vary with different people. A similar technique should be pursued with this sphere, which we name the Air center, as obtained with the previous one. It should be strongly and vividly formulated as a scintillating sphere of brilliant white light, shining and glowing from within. The name to be vibrated is *YHVH Elohim 2*—pronounced as *Yod Heh Vav Heh Eh-loh-heem.*

A word or two may not be amiss at this point with regard to the names. In reality they are names ascribed in various parts of the Old Testament to God. The variety and variation of these names are attributed to different divine functions. When acting in a certain manner, He is described by the biblical scribes by one name. When doing

---

2. In many of Regardie's early texts, he used the name *Jehovah* rather than the more correct *YHVH*. Jehovah was a Latinized version of the Hebrew godname YHVH, the Tetragrammaton or "four-lettered name." Most Golden Dawn magicians prefer to use YHVH (Yod-Heh-Vav-Heh) rather than Jehovah. For the purposes of this text, we have changed all instances of Jehovah to YHVH.

something else, another name more appropriate to His action is used. The system I am describing now has its roots in mystical tradition. Its ancient innovators were men of exalted religious aspirations and genius. It is only to be expected that a religious bias was projected by them into this scientific psychological system. But it must be explained that for our present-day purposes no religious connotation is implied by my use of these biblical divine names. Anyone can use them without subscribing in the least to my religious views—whether he be a Jew, Christian, Hindu, Buddhist or atheist. It is a purely empirical system which is successful despite the skepticism or faith of the operator. We today may consider these sacred names in an entirely different and practical light. They are keynotes of different constituents of man's nature, doorways to so many levels of that part of the psyche of which normally we are unconscious. They are vibratory rates or symbolic signatures of the psychophysical centers we are describing. Their use as vibratory keynotes awakens into activity the centers with which their rate is in sympathy, conveying to our consciousness some recognition of the several levels of the unconscious spiritual side of our personalities. Hence the actual religious significance does not concern us. Nor their literal translation.

To refer back to the Air center in the throat, let the vibratory sounds be intoned a number of times, until its existence is recognized and clearly defined as a sensory experience. There is no mistaking the sensation of its awakening. About the same length of time should be spent formulating it and the succeeding centers as was devoted to the contemplation of the coronal sphere. This period having elapsed, let it thrust downward from itself with the aid of imagination a shaft of light.

Descending to the region of the solar plexus, just beneath the sternum or breast-bone, the shaft expands once again to form a third sphere. This is the position of the Fire center. The allocation of fire to this center is particularly appropriate, for the heart is notoriously associated with the emotional nature, with love and the higher feelings. How often do we not speak of ardent passion, and the flame of love, and so forth? The diameter of this ambient cardiac sphere should be such as to extend from the front of the body to the back. Here vibrate the name *YHVH Eloah ve-Daath*, as *Yod-Heh-Vav-Heh Eh-loh-ah ve-Dah-ath*. Take care that the intonation vibrates well within the formulated white sphere. If this is done, at once a radiation of warmth will be felt to emanate from the center, gently stimulating all the parts and organs about it.

Since the mind functions in and through the body, being co-extensive with it, the mental and emotional faculties likewise become stimulated by the dynamic flow of energy from the centers. The hard and fast barrier erected between consciousness and the Unconscious, a partition which impedes our free expression and hinders spiritual development, slowly becomes dissolved. As time goes on, and the practice continues, it disappears completely and the personality gradually achieves integration and wholeness. Thus health spreads to every function of mind and body and happiness ensues as a permanent blessing.

Continue the shaft downwards from the solar plexus to the pelvic region, the region of the generative organs. Here, too, a radiant sphere is to be visualized approximately of the same dimensions as the higher one. Here also is a name to be intoned so as to produce a rapid vibration in the cells and molecules of the tissue in that region. *Shaddai El Chai* is to be pronounced *Shah-dye El Chi* (the *ch* is guttural as in "loch"). The mind must be permitted to dwell on the imaginative formulation for some minutes, visualizing the sphere as of a white brilliance. And each time the mind wanders from such a brilliance, as at the beginning it is bound to do, let it gently be coaxed back by repeated and powerful vibrations of the name.

It may be feared that this practice could awaken or stimulate sexual feeling and emotion unnecessarily. In those in whom a sexual conflict is raging such an apprehension is just and legitimate. Actually, however, the fear is groundless. For the contemplation of the Water center as a sphere of white light connected by a shaft to the higher and more spiritual centers acts rather in a more sedative way. And in point of fact sexual stimulation can be removed, not by ignorant and short-sighted repression, but by the circulation of such energies through the system by means of this practice. A thoroughgoing and far-reaching process of sublimation, alchemical almost in effect, may thus be insti-gated.

The final step is once more to visualize the shaft descending from the reproductive sphere, moving downwards through the thighs and legs until it strikes the feet. There it expands from a point approximately beneath the ankle, and forms a fifth sphere. We have named this one the Earth center. Let the mind formulate here exactly as before a bril-liant dazzling sphere of the same size as the others. Vibrate the name *Adonai ha-Aretz* as *Ah-doh-nye hah-Ah-retz*. Several minutes having been utilized in awakening this center by fixed and steady thought and by repeated vibration of the name, pause for a short while.

Then try to visualize clearly the entire shaft of silvery light, stud-ded as it were with five gorgeous diamonds of incomparable bril-liance, stretching from the crown of the head to the soles of the feet. But a few minutes will suffice to give reality to this concept, bringing about a vivid realization of the powerful forces which, playing upon the personality, are eventually assimilated into the psycho-physical system after their transformation and passage through the imagina-tive centers. The combination of rhythmic breathing with the willed visualization of the descent of power through the light shaft or Mid-dle Pillar, as it is also called, produces by far the best results.

As skill and familiarity are acquired in the formulation of the cen-ters, an addition to the technique may be made. Earlier I remarked that color was a very important consideration where this technique was concerned. Each center has a different color attribution,[3] though it is wisest for a long period of time to refrain from using any other color than white. To the Spirit or coronal center the color white is at-tributed. It is the color of purity, spirit, divinity, and so on. It repre-sents, not so much a human constituent, but a universal and cosmic

---

3. The Hermetic Order of the Golden Dawn developed a system of color cor-respondence known as the Four Color Scales, which were used to correlate the color attributions of various elemental, astrological, and sephirotic energies on the Qabalistic Tree of Life. Of these color scales, the most important are the King Scale (the positive, masculine, outgoing force) and the Queen Scale (the negative, feminine, and receptive force). King Scale or positive colors can be used for send-ing out energy; Queen Scale or negative colors can be used for receiving energy.

principle overshadowing the whole of mankind. As we descend the shaft, however, the colors change. Lavender is attributed to the Air or throat center,[4] and it represents particularly the mental faculties, human consciousness as such.

To the Fire center, red is an obvious association requiring no further comment. Blue is the color referred to the Water center; it is the color of peace, calmness and tranquility, concealing enormous strength and virility. In other words, its peace is the peace of strength and power rather than the inertia of mere weakness. Finally, the color referred to the lowest center of Earth is russet, the rich deep color of the earth itself, the foundation upon which we rest.

From this very brief and concise summary it will be seen that each of these centers has a species of affinity or sympathy with a different spiritual constituent. One center is peculiarly sympathetic to or is associated with the emotions and feelings, whilst another has definitely an intellectual bias. Hence it follows logically, and experience demonstrates this fact, that their equilibrated activity and stimulation evokes a sympathetic reaction from every part of man's nature. And where disease manifesting in the body is directly due to some psychic maladjustment or infirmity, then the activity of the appropriate center must be affected somehow in a deleterious way. Its stimulation by sound and color, tends to stimulate the corresponding psychic principle and thus to disperse the maladjustment. Sooner or later a reaction is induced physically in the disappearance of the disease, and the consequent building up of new cells and tissue—the appearance of health itself.

§

We approach a further and important stage in the development of the Middle Pillar technique. Having brought power and spiritual energy

---

4. Yellow would normally be the positive color associated with the element of Air. Lavender is the positive color associated with *Daath*, or the throat center. The remainder of the colors given in the following paragraph are the positive colors of the elements.

into the system by means of the psycho-spiritual centers, how best are we to use it? That is to say, use it in such a way that every single cell, every atom, and every organ becomes stimulated and vitalized by that dynamic stream?

To begin with, we throw the mind upwards to the coronal sphere again, imagining it to be in a state of extreme activity. That is, it revolves rapidly, absorbing spiritual energy from space about it, transforming it in such a way that it becomes available for immediate use in any human activity. Imagine then that such transformed energy flows, stream-like, down the left side of the head, down the left side of the trunk and the left leg. While the current is descending the breath should slowly be exhaled to a convenient rhythm. With the slow inhalation of the breath, imagine that the vital current passes from the sole of the left foot to the right foot, and gradually ascends the right side of the body. In this way it returns to the source from which it issued, the coronal center, the human source of all energy and vitality, a closed electrical circuit thus being established. Naturally this circulation is visualized as persisting within the body rather than as travelling around the periphery of the physical shape. It is, so to say, an interior psychic circulation rather than a purely physical one.

Let this circulation, once firmly established by the mind, flow evenly to the rhythm of the breath for some seconds so that the circuit has been traversed about half a dozen times. Then repeat it in a slightly different direction. Visualize the vital flow as moving from the coronal center above the head down the front of the face and body. After having turned backwards under the soles of the feet, it ascends at the back in a fairly wide belt of vibrating energy. This, likewise, should accompany the inhalation and exhalation of breath, and should also be persisted in for about six complete circuits.

The general effect of these two movements will be to establish in and about the physical form an ovoid shape of swiftly circulating substance and power. Since the spiritual energy dealt with by this technique is extremely dynamic and kinetic, it radiates in every direction, spreading outwards to an appreciable distance. It is this radiation which forms, colors and informs the ovoid sphere of sensation which is not conterminous with the shape or dimension of the physical frame. General perception and experience has it that the sphere of luminosity and magnetism extends outwards to a distance more or less identical with the length of the outstretched arm. And it is within this aura, as we may call it, that the physical man exists rather like a kernel within a nut. Circulating the force admitted into the system by the former mental exercises is tantamount to charging it to a considerable degree in every department of its nature with life and energy. Naturally this is bound to exert a considerable influence, so far as general health is concerned, upon the enclosed "kernel" within.

The final method of circulation rather resembles the action of a fountain. Just as water is forced or drawn up through a pipe until it jets up above, falling in a spray on all sides, so does the power directed by this last circulation. Throw the mind downwards to the Earth center, imagining it to be the culmination of all the others, the receptacle of all power, the storehouse and terminal of the incoming vital force. Then imagine that this power ascends, or is drawn upwards by the magnetic attraction of the Spirit center above the crown of the head. The power ascends the shaft until it violently surges overhead with a marvelous fountainous display and falls down within the confines of the ovoid aura. When it has descended it is again gathered together and concentrated in the Earth center preparatory to being pushed up the shaft again. As before, the fountain circulation should accompany a definite rhythm of inhalation and exhalation. By these means, the healing force is distributed to every part of the body. No single atom or cell in any organ or limb is omitted from the influence of its healing regenerative power.

The circulation completed, the mind may be permitted to dwell quietly on the idea of the sphere of light, spiritual and healing in quality, surrounding the entire body. The visualization should be made as vivid and as powerful as possible. The sensation following the partial or complete formulation of the aura in the manner described is so marked and definite as to be quite unmistakable. In the first place it is marked by an extreme sense of calmness and vitality and poise, as though the mind was placid and still while the body, completely at rest in a state of relaxation, was in all its parts thoroughly charged and permeated by the vibrant current of life. The skin over all the body will throw up symptoms, caused by the intensification of life within, of a gentle pricking and warmth. The eyes become clear and bright, the skin takes on a fresh healthy glow, and every faculty, mental, emotional, and physical, becomes enhanced to a considerable degree.

This is the moment when, should there be any functional disturbances in any organ or limb, the attention should be directed and focused on that part. The result of this focus of attention directs a flow of energy over and above the general equilibrium just established. The diseased organ becomes bathed in a sea of light and power. Diseased tissue and diseased cells, under the stimulus of such power, become broken down and ejected from the personal sphere. The revitalized blood-stream is then able to send to that spot new nourishment and new life so that new tissue, fiber, cells, etc., can easily be built up. In this way, health is restored by the persistent concentration there of the divine power. Carried on for a few days in the case of superficial ailments, and for weeks in the event of chronic and severe troubles, all symptoms may successfully be banished without others coming to take their place. There is no suppression of symptoms. Elimination is the result of these methods. Even psychogenic eruptions may thus be cured. For the currents of force arise from the deepest strata of the Unconscious, where these neuroses have their origin and where they lock up nervous energy, preventing spontaneous and free expression of the psyche. The upwelling of the libido, as the vital force is called in psychological circles, dissolves the crystallizations and barriers which divide the various strata of psychic function.

Where organic disease is the problem to be attacked, the procedure to be followed is slightly different.[5] In this instance a considerably stronger current of force is required such as will dissolve the lesion and be sufficient to set in motion those arterial activities to construct new tissue and cellular structure. To fulfil these conditions in an ideal sense

---

5. As Regardie stressed later, anyone suffering from disease should be under the care of a competent physician.

a second person may be requisite so that his vitality added to that of the sufferer may overcome the condition. A useful technique which my experience has discovered supremely successful, and which any student can adopt, is first of all to relax completely every tissue throughout the body before attempting the Middle Pillar technique. The patient is placed in a highly relaxed state, one in which every neuromuscular tension has been tested and called to the attention of the patient. Consciousness is then able to eliminate tension and induce a relaxed state of that muscle or limb. I have found a useful preliminary in the practice of massage, with deep kneadings and effleurage, for in this way an enhanced circulation of the blood and lymph is produced—which from the physiological point of view is half the battle won. A suitable degree of relaxation obtained, the patient's feet are crossed over the ankles and his fingers interlaced to rest lightly over the solar plexus. The operator or healer then seats himself on the right side of the person should the patient be right-handed—vice versa for a left-handed patient. Placing his right hand gently on the solar plexus under the patient's intertwined hands and his left hand on the patient's head, at once a form of *rapport* is established. Within a few minutes a free circulation of magnetism and vitality is set up, readily discernible both by patient and healer.

The patient's attitude should be one of absolute receptivity to the incoming force—automatic, should he have unwavering confidence and faith in the operator's integrity and ability. Silence and quiet should be maintained for a short while, following which the operator silently performs the practice of the Middle Pillar, still maintaining his physical contact with the patient. His awakened spiritual centers act on the patient by sympathy. A similar awakening is introduced within the patient's sphere, and his centers eventually begin to operate and throw an equilibrated stream of energy into his system. Even when the operator does not vibrate the divine name audibly, the power flowing through his fingers sets up an activity which will surely produce some degree of healing activity within the patient. His psycho-spiritual centers are sympathetically stirred into the active assimilation and projection of force so that, without any conscious effort on his part, his sphere is invaded by the divine power of healing and life. When the operator arrives at the circulation stage, he so employs his inner visualizing faculty, a veritable magical power indeed, that the augmented currents of energy flow not only through his own sphere but through that of his patient. The nature of this *rapport* now begins to undergo a subtle change. Whereas formerly there existed close sympathy and a harmonious frame of mind, mutually held, during and after the circulations there is an actual union and interblending of the two energy fields. They unite to form a single continuous sphere as the interchange and transference of vital energy proceed. Thus the operator, or his unconscious psyche or spiritual self, is able to divine exactly what potential his projected current should be, and precisely to where it should be directed.

A number of these treatments incorporating the cooperation and training of the patient in the use of mental methods should suffice to produce a cure.[6] Occasionally, since fanaticism above all is to be eschewed, medical and manipulative methods may usefully be combined with the mental methods described to facilitate and hasten the cure.

§

Quite apart from therapy, there are other uses of the Middle Pillar technique.[7] In this place I shall not deal with that aspect of it which concerns spiritual development, though the method is supremely efficient here. I have dealt with this subject elsewhere at some considerable length.

It may be for various reasons that certain necessities of life, either physical or spiritual, have been denied one—with a consequent cramping effect on character and the onset of a sense of frustration. The latter always has a depressing and inhibitory effect on the human

---

6. Or rather, as Regardie indicated later, these methods should certainly go far in alleviating the original condition.

7. In addition to healing, Regardie stressed that the Exercise of the Middle Pillar was suitable for application to a host of other problems, whether it be a problem of poverty, character development, social or marital difficulties, etc.

mind, producing indecision, inefficiency and inferiority. There is no real necessity why there should be any undue frustration and inhibition in our lives. A certain amount is no doubt inevitable. So long as we remain human it is quite certain that in some measure we are likely to be thwarted in our efforts fully to express the inner self, thus experiencing frustration. But any abnormal measure or persistent sense of thwarting and frustration may be dealt with and, by these mental and spiritual methods, eliminated.

First of all an understanding of life is essential, and an unconditional acceptance of everything in life and every experience that may come one's way. With understanding will come a love of life and living, for love and understanding are one and the same; with it also arises the determination no longer to frustrate natural processes but by acceptance to cooperate with nature. The methods of spiritual and mental culture have long held out hope that these inhibitory conditions may be alleviated. Poverty of estate as well as of idea is a life-condition which these techniques have always acknowledged to be amenable to treatment. The usual method is one of such deep and prolonged reflection upon just that mental stimulus, moral quality or material thing which is wanted, that the idea of the need sinks into the so-called subconscious mind. If the barriers leading to the subconscious are penetrated so that the latter accepts the idea of the need, then, so it is said, sooner or later life will inevitably attract one of those things required. But, as with the therapeutic methods, there were so many instances where, despite close adherence to the prescribed techniques, success was not forthcoming. It is my contention, therefore, that they fail for very much the same reasons that their healing efforts fail. In short, it was because there was no true understanding of the interior psycho-dynamic mechanism whereby such effects could be produced. There was no appreciation of the methods by which the dynamic nature of the Unconscious could be stimulated to the extent that the human personality became transformed into a powerful magnet attracting to itself whatever it truly desired or was necessary to welfare.

Whether this procedure is morally defensible is a question I do not wish to discuss at length, though I know it will be raised. But the answer is brief. Whatever faculties we have are meant to be used, and used both for our own advantage and that of others. If we are in a state of constant mental friction, emotional frustration, and excessive poverty, I fail to see in what way we can be of service either to ourselves or our fellow men. Eliminate these restrictions first, improve the mental and emotional faculties so that the spiritual nature is able to penetrate through the personality and manifest itself in practical ways, then we are in a position to be of some service to those with whom we come into contact. The preliminary stimulation of the psycho-spiritual centers within, and then formulating clearly and vividly one's demands upon the universe is capable of attracting almost anything required, so long, naturally, as it exists within the bounds of reason and possibility.

First of all, let me preface my further remarks by stating that from the practical point of view the rudiments of the astrological schema are of untold value in that they offer a concise classification of the broad divisions of things. I am not concerned here with astrology as such, merely that it is convenient to use its schema. Its roots are in the seven principal ideas of planets to which most ideas and things may be referred. To each of these root ideas there is attributed a positive and negative color, and a divine name for the purpose of vibration. I propose naming the planets with their principal attributions:

Saturn. Older people and old plans. Debts and their repayment. Agriculture, real estate, death, wills, stability, inertia. Positive color indigo; negative black. *YHVH Elohim,* pronounced *Yod-Heh-Vav-Heh Eh-loh-heem.*

Jupiter. Abundance, plenty, growth, expansion, generosity. Spirituality, visions, dreams, long journeys. Bankers, creditors, debtors, gambling. Positive color purple; negative blue. *El,* pronounced exactly as written.

Mars. Energy, haste, anger, construction or destruction (according to application), danger, surgery. Vitality and magnetism. Will-power.

Positive and negative colors bright red. *Elohim Gibor*, pronounced *Eh-loh-heem Gibor.*

Sun. Superiors, employers, executives, officials. Power and success. Life, money, growth of all kinds. Illumination, imagination, mental power. Health. Positive color orange; negative color yellow or gold. *YHVH Eloah ve-Daath*, pronounced *Yod-Heh-Vav-Heh El-loh-ah ve-dah-ath.*

Venus. Social affairs, affections and emotions, women, younger people. All pleasures and the arts, music, beauty, extravagance, luxury, self-indulgence. Both colors emerald green.[8] *YHVH Tzavaoth,*[9] pronounced *Yeh-hoh-voh Tzah-va-oth.*

Mercury. Business matters, writing, contracts, judgment and short travels. Buying, selling, bargaining. Neighbors, giving and obtaining information. Literary capabilities and intellectual friends. Books, papers. Positive color yellow; negative color orange.[10] *Elohim Tzavaoth.*

Moon. General public, women. Sense reactions. Short journeys and removals. Changes and fluctuations. The personality. Positive color blue; negative color puce.[11] *Shad-dai El Chai.*

These very briefly are the attributions of the planets under which almost everything and every subject in nature may be classified. This classification is extremely useful because it simplifies enormously one's task of physical and spiritual development. It may be best if before concluding I instance a few simple and elementary examples to illustrate the function and method of employing these correspondences.

---

8. The positive or King Scale color of Venus is green, while the negative or Queen Scale color is actually sky blue. Regardie may be conflating the Queen Scale color of *Netzach* (the seventh Sephirah on the Tree of Life corresponding to Venus) with the King Scale color of the planet Venus.

9. We have changed the Ashkenazic "Tzavoos" to the Sephardic "Tzavaoth" and "Tzabaoth," since the Hebrew letter Beth is used for the sound of "v" as well as "b."

10. The passive color of Mercury is violet. The passive color of the eighth Sephirah of *Hod*, which corresponds to Mercury, is orange.

11. The passive color of the Moon is silver. The passive color of the ninth Sephirah of *Yesod*, which corresponds to the Moon, is violet.

Suppose I am engaged in certain studies requiring books that are not easily obtainable from booksellers. Despite my every demand for them, in spite of widespread advertising and willingness to pay a reasonable price for them, my efforts are unavailing. The result is that for the time my studies are held up. This delay reaches the point when it is excessive and irritating, and I decide to use my own technical methods for ending it. At certain prescribed intervals, preferably upon awakening in the morning and before retiring to sleep at night, I practice the rhythmic breath and the Middle Pillar. By these methods I have made available enormous quantities of spiritual power, and transformed the Unconscious into a powerful storage battery, ready to project or attract power to fulfil my need. This I circulate through the auric system.

My next step consists of visualizing the negative or passive color of Mercury,[12] orange, so that meditating upon it changes the surrounding auric color to that hue. Orange is used because books, which I need, are attributed to Mercury; and I employ the negative color because it tends to make the sphere of sensation open, passive and receptive.[13] Then I proceed to charge and vitalize the sphere by vibrating the divine name again and again, until it seems to my perceptions that all the mercurial forces of the universe react to the magnetic attraction of that sphere. All the forces of the universe are imagined to converge upon my sphere, attracting to me just those books, documents, critics, friends and so on, needed to further my work. Inevitably, after persistent and concentrated work I hear from friends or booksellers quite by chance, so it would seem, that these books are available. Introductions are procured to the right people, and taken by and large my work is assisted. The results occur, however, in a perfectly natural way. One is not to imagine that the use of these methods contravenes the known laws of nature and that miraculous phenomena will occur. Far from it. There is nothing in them that is supernatural. These

12. See footnote 10.

13. See appendix II for more information on the use of positive and negative colors associated with the Qabalistic energy centers.

methods are based upon the use of psychic principles normally latent within man, and which everyone possesses. No individual is unique in this respect. And the use of these psychic principles brings results through quite normal but unsuspected channels.

On the other hand, should I desire to help a patient who has literary aspirations but at a certain juncture finds his style cramped and the free flow of ideas inhibited, I should alter my method in one particular point only. Instead of using orange as before, I should visualize the aura as of a yellow or golden color, though the vibratory name would be the same. Again, instead of imagining the universal forces to have a centripetal motion towards my sphere, I should attempt to realize that the mercurial forces awakened within me by the color visualization and vibration are being projected from me to my patient. If he, too, becomes quiet and meditative at the same hour, my help becomes more powerful since he consciously assists my efforts with a similar meditation. But this need not be insisted upon. For, as shown by telepathy experiments, the greater part of the receiver's impressions are unconsciously received. Therefore, in the case of the patient, his own unconscious psyche will pick up automatically and of necessity the inspiration and power I have telepathically forwarded to him in absentia.

This system combines telepathic suggestion with the willed communication of vital power. I strenuously oppose those partitive apologists who uphold in theory the one faculty to the detriment of the other. Some deny suggestion or telepathy, and argue overenthusiastically on behalf of vital magnetism. Others refuse categorically to admit the existence of magnetism, pressing their proofs exclusively in favor of telepathy and suggestion. Both, to my mind, are incorrect and dogmatic when insisting upon their idea alone as having universal validity or as being the sole logical mode of explanation. Equally, each is right in some respects and in a certain number of cases; there is a place for both in the natural economy of things. The resources of nature are both great and extensive enough to admit the mutual existence of both of them, and innumerable other powers also.

The technical procedure is, as I have shown, extremely simple—even where employed for subjective ends. Suppose the realization suddenly comes to me that instead of being the magnanimous person I had imagined myself to be I am really mean and stingy. Of course I could go through a course of psychoanalysis to discover *why* my nature early in life had become warped so that a habit of meanness was engendered. But this is a lengthy and costly business—bad arguments, possibly, against its necessity. And so much would depend upon the analyst and his relations with myself. Instead, however, I might resort to the following technique. My first steps consist of those described above—rhythmic breathing, the light-shaft formulated from head to foot, and the circulation of force through the aura. Then remembering that a generous outlook upon, and an attitude towards life is a Jupiterian quality, I would surround myself with an azure sphere whilst vibrating frequently and powerfully the divine name *El*. It depends entirely upon one's skill and familiarity with the system whether the names are vibrated silently or audibly, but by either way, powerful Jupiterian currents would permeate my being. I would even visualize every cell being bathed in an ocean of blueness; and I would attempt to imagine currents invading my sphere from every direction, so that all my thinking and feeling is literally in terms of blueness. Slowly a subtle transformation ensues. That is, it would were I really sincere, desirous of correcting my faults, and if I did attempt to become generous enough as to perform the practice faithfully and often.

Likewise, if a friend or patient complained of a similar vice in him, appealing to me for help, in this instance I would use a positive color for projection. I would formulate my sphere as an active dynamic purple sphere, rich and royal in color, and project its generous, healing, and fecund influence upon his mind and personality. With time the fault would be corrected to his satisfaction and thus enhance his spiritual nature.

And so on, with everything else. The few examples will, I am sure, have shown the application of the methods.

It is not enough simply to wish for certain results and idly expect them to follow. Failure only can come from such an idle course. Anything worthwhile and likely to succeed requires a great deal of work and perseverance. The Middle Pillar technique is certainly no exception. But devotion to it is extremely worthwhile because of the nature and quality of the results which follow. Once a day will demonstrate the efficacy of the method. Twice a day would be much better—especially if there is some illness or psychic difficulty to overcome. After a while, the student who is sincere and in whom the spiritual nature is gradually unfolding, will apply himself to the methods quite apart from the promise which I have here held out. Healing powers, freedom from poverty and worry, happiness—all these are eminently desirable. But over and above all of these is the desirability of knowing and expressing the spiritual Self within—though it may be in some cases that this ideal is hardly attainable until some measure of fulfilment in other respects and on other levels has been achieved. When, however, the ideal is realized as desirable, the value of this method will also be realized as supremely effectual to that end.

CORRESPONDENCES FOR HEALING RITUALS

In *The Art of True Healing*, Regardie laid out the basics of the Middle Pillar exercise, in which he divided up the five Qabalistic energy centers located along the center of the human body in accordance with their elemental correspondences. One section of that essay in particular described how the colors of the various energy centers can be utilized for healing, physical and mental regeneration, and inner alchemy.

Regardie suggested using the negative or Queen Scale colors in visualizations that involve the person who is actually performing the exercise. In Regardie's words, "I employ the negative color because it tends to make the sphere of sensation open, passive and receptive."[1] Conversely, if the practitioner is performing the exercise for someone else's benefit, he or she would employ the positive or King Scale color when visualizing the other person, because the act of *projecting energy* to another is a positive, stimulating act. The person receiving the benefit of the exercise can aid the process by remaining receptive and open.

The following is a list of all the basic Qabalistic energies that can be used in this regard, not just the five centers of the Middle Pillar. These are the energies of the ten Sephiroth and the paths assigned to

---

1. See appendix I, page 190.

the twenty-two Hebrew letters. Collectively, they are known as the Thirty-Two Paths of Wisdom, and they are listed here in order.[2]

The Thirty-Two Paths of Wisdom

1. Kether	10. Malkuth	19. Leo	28. Aquarius
2. Chokmah	11. Air	20. Virgo	29. Pisces
3. Binah	12. Mercury	21. Jupiter	30. Sun
4. Chesed	13. Moon	22. Libra	31a. Fire
5. Geburah	14. Venus	23. Water	31b. Saturn
6. Tiphareth	15. Aries	24. Scorpio	32a. Earth
7. Netzach	16. Taurus	25. Sagittarius	32b. Spirit
8. Hod	17. Gemini	26. Capricorn	—– Daath
9. Yesod	18. Cancer	27. Mars	

---

2. Note that numbers 31a and 32b on the list of the Thirty-Two Paths of Wisdom are both assigned to the letter Shin, while 31b and 32a are both assigned to the letter Tau. The final power on the list, Daath, is considered neither a Sephiroth nor a path, but rather a conjunction of the powers of Chokmah and Binah.

The following chart shows the forces of the ten Sephiroth (plus Daath) along with the various correspondences that can be employed in a healing ritual based on Regardie's technique (which appears later in this section).

Sephirotic Energies

Force	King Scale Color (Positive)	Queen Scale Color (Negative)	Divine Name	Body Part
1. Kether	Brilliance	White	Eheieh	Crown of head
2. Chokmah	Soft blue-gray	Gray	Yah	Left temple
3. Binah	Deep red-violet	Black	YHVH Elohim	Right temple
4. Chesed	Deep violet	Blue	El	Left shoulder
5. Geburah	Orange	Red	Elohim Gibor	Right shoulder
6. Tiphareth	Rose pink	Yellow	YHVH Eloah ve-Daath	Heart
7. Netzach	Yellow-orange	Green	YHVH Tzabaoth	Left hip
8. Hod	Violet	Orange	Elohim Tzabaoth	Right hip
9. Yesod	Blue-violet	Violet	Shaddai El Chai	Groin
10. Malkuth	Yellow	Citrine, Olive, Russet, Black	Adonai ha-Aretz	Feet and ankles
—– Daath	Lavender	Gray white	YHVH Elohim	Throat

This next chart shows the forces and correspondences of the five elements.[3]

Elemental Energies

Force	King Scale Color (Positive)	Queen Scale Color (Negative)	Divine Name	Body Part
11. Air	Yellow	Sky blue	YHVH	Throat
23. Water	Blue	Sea green	El	Groin
31a. Fire	Red	Vermillion red	Elohim	Heart
32a. Earth	Citrine, Olive, Russet, Black	Yellow-orange	Adonai	Feet and ankles
32b. Spirit	White	Deep purple	Eheieh	Crown of head

3. A different set of elemental attributions corresponding to the four Qabalistic worlds could also be used, wherein Fire (Yod) would be located at the head and throat and Air (Vav) would be positioned at the heart and lungs.

The following shows the forces and correspondences of the seven planets.

Planetary Energies

Force	King Scale Color (Positive)	Queen Scale Color (Negative)	Divine Name	Body Part
12. Mercury	Yellow	Violet	Elohim Tzabaoth	Respiratory system, brain and central nervous system, thyroid, hands
13. Moon	Blue	Silver	Shaddai El Chai	Groin, reproductive system, stomach, digestive system, lymphatic system
14. Venus	Green	Sky blue	YHVH Tzabaoth	Throat, thymus, kidneys, digestive system, female reproductive system
21. Jupiter	Violet	Blue	El	Liver, thighs, feet, pituitary gland, growth in general
27. Mars	Red	Red	Elohim Gibor	Muscles, arteries, male reproductive system
30. Sun	Orange	Yellow	YHVH Eloah ve-Daath	Heart, spine, vitality in general
31b. Saturn	Blue-violet	Black	YHVH Elohim	Veins, bones, skin, hair, teeth, spleen, immune system

This final chart shows the forces and correspondences of the twelve Zodiac signs.

Zodiacal Energies

Force	King Scale Color (Positive)	Queen Scale Color (Negative)	Divine Name	Body Parts/ Systems	Illnesses
15. Aries	Red	Red	Elohim	Head, face, eyes, brain function	Headaches, eye trouble, fevers, inflammations, wounds, accidents
16. Taurus	Red-orange	Deep blue-violet	Adonai	Neck, ears, throat, thyroid, vocal cords, tonsils	Throat problems
17. Gemini	Orange	Pale mauve	YHVH	Shoulders, arms, hands, lungs, brain, nervous system, respiratory system	Bronchial problems, nerve diseases, pneumonia, asthma

Force	King Scale Color (Positive)	Queen Scale Color (Negative)	Divine Name	Body Parts/ Systems	Illnesses
18. Cancer	Yellow-orange	Maroon	El	Upper abdomen, chest, breasts, ribs, stomach, solar plexus, diaphragm, upper liver, alimentary canal, nutrition in general	Digestion problems
19. Leo	Yellow	Deep violet	Elohim	Heart, liver, spine, spinal column, sides, upper back, vital forces, blood	Heart trouble, poor circulation, blood issues
20. Virgo	Yellow-green	Slate gray	Adonai	Digestive system, lower liver, intestines, spleen, nervous system, absorption in general	Digestive and intestinal troubles
22. Libra	Green	Blue	YHVH	Kidneys, lumbar region, loins, buttocks, skin, small intestine, appendix	Kidney trouble, spine problems

Force	King Scale Color (Positive)	Queen Scale Color (Negative)	Divine Name	Body Parts/ Systems	Illnesses
24. Scorpio	Blue-green	Dull brown	El	Reproductive system, sex organs, bowels, gall bladder, colon, bladder, excretory system	STDs, reproductive problems, colon problems
25. Sagittarius	Blue	Yellow	Elohim	Liver, hips, thighs, sciatic nerve	Gout, rheumatism, sciatica, accidents
26. Capricorn	Blue-violet	Black	Adonai	Skeletal system, joints, knees, upper legs, hair	Skin problems, arthritis, bone issues
28. Aquarius	Violet	Sky blue	YHVH	Lower legs, calves, ankles, circulatory system, teeth	Ankle problems, varicose veins, nervous disorders, blood problems
29. Pisces	Red-violet	Buff, flecked silver-white	El	Feet, toes, lymphatic system, body fat, perspiration in general	Cold, flu, and similar illnesses

The following is a sample healing ritual that shows how these correspondences might be utilized. It specifically deals with the Sephirah of Tiphareth, which can be employed for general healing, convalescence, balance, equilibrium, calmness, illumination, and spiritual growth.

A Healing Ritual of Tiphareth

This exercise can be performed either standing, sitting, or lying down. Begin by establishing a pattern of rhythmic breathing. Follow this with the basic Exercise of the Middle Pillar as follows:

Vibrate the name "Eheieh" (pronounced "Eh-hey-yay," meaning "I am"). Keep vibrating this word until it is the only thought in your conscious mind. Then imagine a shaft of light descending from your Kether center to your Daath center at the nape of the neck.

Form a sphere of light at the Daath center. Vibrate the name "YHVH Elohim" (pronounced "Yode-heh-vav-heh El-oh-heem," meaning "the Lord God"). Intone the name until it is the only thing in your conscious mind.

Bring a shaft of light down from the Daath center to the Tiphareth center around your heart. Form a sphere of light there. Vibrate the name "YHVH Eloah ve-Daath" (pronounced "Yode-heh-vav-heh El-oh-ah v'-Dah-ath," meaning "Lord God of Knowledge") several times until it fills your consciousness.

See the shaft of light descending from Tiphareth into the Yesod center in the genital region. Imagine a sphere of light formed there. Intone the name "Shaddai El Chai" (pronounced "Shah-dye El-Chai,"[4] meaning "Almighty Living God") several times as before.

Visualize the shaft of light descending from Yesod into your Malkuth center at the feet and ankles. Vibrate the name "Adonai ha-Aretz" (pronounced "Ah-doe-nye ha-Ah-retz," meaning "Lord of Earth") a number of times as before.

Imagine the Middle Pillar complete. Then circulate the light you have brought down through the Middle Pillar around the outside of your body to strengthen your aura.

---

4. The "ch" in *Chai* is to be pronounced like the "ch" in the Scottish word "loch."

Using the cycles of breathing, bring the light up one side of the body and down the other, from Malkuth to Kether and back to Malkuth; up the right side of the body (inhale) and down the left side (exhale).

After performing this for a short period of time, imagine the ribbon of light descending down the front of your body and rising up your back.

Still employing rhythmic breathing, visualize the shaft of light rising up the Middle Pillar in the center of your body. When it reaches Kether, imagine a shower of light surrounding the outside of your body as it descends to Malkuth again. Circulate the light in this manner for some time.

Focus some of the energy back into your Tiphareth or heart center, the seat of equilibrium and balance. (This completes the basic Middle Pillar portion of the ritual.)

If you are performing the ritual for your own benefit, visualize your Tiphareth center filled with a bright yellow light. Concentrate on this primary yellow color—the Queen Scale color of Tiphareth—at your heart center. With rhythmic breathing, see this yellow color begin to expand outward from Tiphareth until it fills your entire aura. Imagine yourself within a brilliant yellow egg of light, and circulate the color throughout the entire auric system, inside and out. Vibrate "YHVH Eloah ve-Daath," the divine name of Tiphareth, several times while continuing to visualize the color yellow. Concentrate on those symbols, forces, and aspects of Tiphareth that you wish to attract into your sphere. When you feel that the work of the exercise has been accomplished, complete and seal the ritual by performing the Qabalistic Cross as follows.

The Qabalistic Cross

Stand and face east. Imagine a brilliant white light touching the top of your head. Reach up with the index finger or blade of a dagger to connect with the light and bring it to the forehead.

Touch the forehead and vibrate "Atah" (Ah-tah—*Thou art*).

Touch the breast and bring the dagger blade or index finger down until it covers the groin area, pointing down to the ground. Imagine the light descending from the forehead to the feet. Vibrate "Malkuth" (Mahl-kooth—*The Kingdom*).

Touch the right shoulder and visualize a point of light there. See the shaft of light running through the center of the body to form a horizontal beam of light from your heart center that joins with the point of light at the right shoulder. Vibrate "ve-Geburah" (v'Ge-boo-rah—*The Power*).

Touch the left shoulder and visualize a point of light there. See the horizontal shaft of light extending from the heart center to join this point of light. Vibrate "ve-Gedulah" (v'Ge-doo-lah—*The Glory*).

Imagine a completed cross of light running from head to feet and shoulder to shoulder.

Bring the hands outward, away from the body, and finally bring them together again, clasped on the breast as if praying. Vibrate "Le-Olahm, Amen" (lay-Oh-lahm, Ah-men—*Forever, unto the ages*).

§

If you are performing this ritual for the benefit of another person, perform the preliminary Middle Pillar exercise as described. Visualize your Tiphareth center filled with a bright rose-pink light—the King Scale color of Tiphareth—at your heart center. With rhythmic breathing, see this color of rose-pink begin to expand outward from Tiphareth until it fills your entire aura. Vibrate "YHVH Eloah ve-Daath," the divine name of Tiphareth, several times while continuing to visualize the color rose-pink. Concentrate on those symbols, forces, and aspects of Tiphareth that you wish to project to the other person. When you feel that sufficient energy has been generated, visualize and project the rose-pink energy from your Tiphareth center to the corresponding center of the other person. Visualize his or her aura filling up with this color and its corresponding Tiphareth energy. Then visualize the aura of the other person turning from rose-pink to bright primary yellow as the light transmutes from your projected energy to the receptive energy of the person receiving the beneficial effects of this force. When you feel that the work of the exercise has been accomplished, complete and seal the ritual by performing the Qabalistic Cross.

Using the various correspondences listed in this appendix, similar rites can be devised for a number of different healing rituals.

GLOSSARY

ADONAI: Hebrew word meaning "Lord." Associated with the north and the element of Earth by its connection with the Sephirah of Malkuth.

ADONAI HA-ARETZ: Hebrew phrase for "Lord of Earth." Divine name associated with Malkuth.

ALBERTUS MAGNUS: (1193/1206–1280) Albert the Great. German philosopher, scientist, theologian, and Catholic saint. He was called *Doctor Universalis* ("Universal Doctor") in recognition of his great knowledge. His works on philosophy filled thirty-six volumes when printed in 1890. Along with his student Thomas Aquinus, Albertus was influential in the spread of the "New Science," particularly Aristotelian thought. He was the most prolific writer of his century and wrote on a vast array of subjects, including the Heavens, the natural world, the properties of the elements, meteorology, minerals, metals, life and death, the intellect, and astrology. He established the study of nature as a legitimate science within the Christian tradition. His influence on European philosophy was enormous. His most important work was called *On Alchemy.*

ALBIGENSIANS: Members of a Catharist Christian sect of southern France in the eleventh through thirteenth centuries. They were exterminated for heresy during the Inquisition.

ALCHEMY: A process of transformation, discipline, and purification. There are two types of alchemy, which often overlap. Practical, laboratory, or outer alchemy is concerned with transforming a base material into a higher and more purified substance, such as the turning of lead into gold or the extraction of a medicinal substance from a plant in order to create a healing elixir. Spiritual, theoretical, or inner alchemy is concerned with the transformation of the human soul from a state of baseness to one of spiritual enlightenment. Alchemical texts are often full of allegory and mythological symbolism.

ALEMBICK (or ALEMBIC): A container used for distillation. A still or the upper part of a still; a still-head. Its shape was said to resemble a dancing bear.

ALPHIDIUS: Alchemist cited by Salomon Trismosin in *Splendor Solis.*

AMMONIA: A solvent used in alchemy.

ANALYSAND: A person who is undergoing psychotherapy.

ANALYTICAL PSYCHOLOGY: A term used by Carl G. Jung to describe his particular method of psychotherapy.

ANIMA: According to Jungian psychology, an archetypal "soul image" that is the embodiment of the reflective feminine nature of man's subconscious.

ANIMA MUNDI: Latin for "the Soul of the World." The divine essence that permeates all things.

ANIMALS: In alchemy, animals are often used to symbolize basic component substances and processes.

ARCHETYPE: Often referred to in Jungian psychology to mean an idea, mode of thought, or god-form that has manifested from the collective unconscious of humanity.

ARISTOTLE: (384–322 BCE) One of the greatest Greek philosophers. In terms of influence, only Plato could be named as a peer. Aristotle wrote about two hundred works, of which around thirty-one still survive, on subjects as varied as logic, metaphysics, ethics, political theory, aesthetics, rhetoric, and biology. Aristotle's work was at the forefront of Western thought and philosophy from Late Antiquity through the Renaissance. He taught that the fifth element is aether, that the other four elements are composed of various combinations of hot, cold, wet, and dry qualities, and that all things strive toward perfection of their true natures.

ARISTOTELIAN: A school of philosophy derived from the work of Aristotle, who had an enormous influence on all manner of topics, from language to theology to biology. Aristotelianism featured the use of deductive reasoning and a focus on knowledge either accessible by natural means or derived from reason or experience. Aristotelian metaphysics promoted the four material elements and their qualities, and held that the soul was an inseparable form of each living creature.

ARGENT VIVE: Living Silver. Philosopher's Mercury or Quicksilver. Secret Fire. The Universal Solvent of All Metals.

ARNOLD OF VILLANOVA: (1235–1311) Spanish alchemist, pharmacist, astrologer, physician, and skilled alchemist who translated a number of Arabic texts on medicine, including works by Avicenna. He is credited with the discovery of carbon monoxide and pure alcohol. He claimed to have attained the Philosopher's Stone, and he wrote a medical book on wine entitled *Liber de Vinis*. He also wrote *The Alchemy*, comprised of a handful of short treatises; the most important of them are *The Treasure of Treasures* and *The Philosophers' Rosary*.

ART: A reference to alchemy.

ASHMOLE, ELIAS: (1617–1692) A celebrated antiquarian, historian, occult philosopher, and founding member of the Royal Society, a group dedicated to science and practical scientific research.

ATWOOD, MARY ANNE: (1817–1910) Nineteenth-century English spiritual alchemist who researched spirituality and metaphysics with her father, Thomas South. At her father's request she wrote *A Suggestive Inquiry into the Hermetic Mystery*, published in 1850. Later, both father and daughter became convinced that the book exposed far too many alchemical secrets, and except for a few copies sold or owned by the author, all other copies were destroyed.

AUGOEIDES: A Greek word used by Iamblichus to refer to the transformed spiritual body worn by the initiate who had overcome the materialism of the physical world. Its meanings include "shining one," "glittering one," "light vision," or "bright shape" and refer to the radiant nature of the Higher Self. This word has been a source of confusion because it is sometimes used to mean the Higher Genius in Kether, but other times it is used to mean the Higher Self in Tiphareth.

AULA LUCIS: "The House of Light." A discourse written in 1651 by Thomas Vaughan ("Eugenius Philalethes").

AURA: A shell or layer of astral substance that surrounds and permeates the physical body. Also called the Sphere of Sensation.

AUREA CATENA HOMERI: *The Golden Chain of Homer, or A Description of Nature and Natural Things.* An important book on alchemy, written in Leipzig in 1723 by Dr. Anton Josef Kirchweger.

AVICENNA: (980–1037) Known in Arabic as *Ibn Sīnā*, Avicenna was considered the most famous and influential of the philosopher-scientists of the Islamic world. His major contributions were in the fields of Aristotelian philosophy and medicine. He wrote about one hundred books, the most influential of which was the *Canon of Medicine,* which was used as a medical text in French universities until 1650. Avicenna's ideas on psychology and imagination are found in the *al-nafs* ("soul, self, or psyche") sections of his *Kitab al-shifa' (The Book of Healing)* and *Kitab al-najat (The Book of Deliverance).*

BACON, ROGER: (?1214–?1294) English philosopher, theologian, scientist, educational reformer, and alchemist. He was known as Doctor Mirabilis (Latin: "Wonderful Teacher"). Bacon is created with inventing the telescope and gunpowder. Asked by Pope Clement IV for a treatise on the sciences, Bacon produced the *Opus majus* ("Great Work"), the *Opus minus* ("Lesser Work"), and the *Opus tertium* ("Third Work").

BATH OF THE INNOCENTS: The blood (mineral spirit) of metals, particularly of gold and silver. In alchemy, baths symbolize the process of dissolution wherein metals are cleansed and purified.

BENDIT, LAURENCE J.: (1898–1974) Psychiatrist, author, Theosophist, and parapsychologist. In 1923 he established a psychiatric practice in London. Bendit and his wife, Phoebe, were prolific writers; they collaborated on a number of important texts, including *Man's Latent*

Powers (1938), *This World and That* (1948), and *The Psychic Sense* (1943). Bendit specialized in the question of psychic ability in relation to psychological problems.

BERNHEIM, HIPPOLYTE: (1840–1919) French physician and neurologist. One of the founders of the Nancy School of hypnotherapy. He was known for his theory of suggestibility in relation to hypnotism.

BERTHELOT, PIERRE EUGÈNE MARCELLIN: (1827–1907) French chemist who synthesized a number of organic compounds from inorganic substances. Berthelot translated many old Greek and Arabic alchemical treatises.

BHAGAVAD GITA: Sanskrit for "Song of the Lord." An influential Indian religious text composed in the first or second century CE and commonly known as the *Gita*. It comprises chapters 23 to 40 of book 6 of the *Mahabharata* and takes the form of a dialogue between Prince Arjuna and Krishna.

BINAH: Hebrew word for "understanding," referring to the third Sephirah on the Tree of Life.

BODHIDHARMA: (sixth century CE) A Buddhist monk credited with establishing the Zen branch of Mahayana Buddhism.

BRAID, JAMES: (1796–1860) Scottish-born physician who coined the term *hypnosis* and as a result is considered by many to be the "Father of Hypnosis." Braid's interest in the subject started in 1841 after seeing a performance by Swiss magnetizer Charles Lafontaine. Trying to find a scientific reason for the trance state, Braid believed that it was a result of a fatigue of the eyes. Concluding that the phenomenon was a form of sleep, Dr. Braid named the phenomenon *hypnosis* after Hypnos, the Greek god of sleep and dreams. After a time, he realized that the trance state could be achieved without sleep; however, the terms "hypnosis" and "hypnotism" had already taken hold in the common vernacular.

BRAMWELL, DR. JOHN MILNE: (1852–1925) Scottish physician, author, and hypnotherapist who collected the works of Dr. James Braid and maintained Braid's legacy in Great Britain.

BUDDHA-NATURE: Buddha Principle. A Mahayana Buddhist term that refers to the seed of Buddhahood in all beings. It is that which allows sentient beings to become Buddhas. One's Buddha-nature is activated when all illusions, ignorance, and defilements are overcome.

BULL: A symbol of elemental Earth.

CALCINE: (See *CALCINATION.*)

CALCINATION: The process of using fire to reduce plant material to a fine ash.

CALL, ANNIE PAYSON: (1853–1940) Author of *Power Through Repose* (1891). Call wrote several articles and books on mental health.

CARRINGTON, HEREWARD: (1880–1958) British investigator of psychic phenomena. After emigrating to the United States, he joined the American branch of the Society for Psychical Research at age nineteen. He published more than one hundred books and pamphlets on the paranormal and psychical research, stage magic, and alternative medicine.

CHARCOT, JEAN-MARTIN: (1825–1893) French neurologist and instructor at the Salpêtrière School. He was known as "the founder of modern neurology" and was famous for his work with hypnosis and hysteria.

CHESED: Hebrew word for "mercy," referring to the fourth Sephirah on the Tree of Life. Also called Gedulah, which means "greatness, magnificence, glory."

CHOKMAH: Hebrew word for "wisdom," referring to the second Sephirah on the Tree of Life.

COAGULATION: The process of reducing a fluid to solid form.

COLLECTIVE UNCONSCIOUS: in Jungian psychology, those mental patterns and primordial images that are shared by all of humanity.

CONSCIOUS: The component of waking awareness. The state of being awake and perceptive.

CORPUS HERMETICUM: The "Hermetic body of writings." Eighteen tracts said to have been written by Hermes Trismegistus and translated into Latin by Marsilio Ficino in 1471.

CROOKES, SIR WILLIAM: (1832–1919) A British chemist and physicist who specialized in spectroscopy—the study of the interaction between matter and radiated energy. Crookes was a Spiritualist, a theosophist, and a member of the Society for Psychical Research. He joined the Hermetic Order of the Golden Dawn in 1890, taking on the motto *Ubi Crux, Ibi Lux* ("Where the Cross is, there is Light").

CROWLEY, ALEISTER: Former member of the original Golden Dawn, whose Order motto was *Perdurabo*, "I will endure." He later went off to assume authority of his own Order, the *Ordo Templi Orientis* (or O.T.O.) and took on the name *To Mega Therion*, "The Great Beast." He wrote a number of books, including *Magick in Theory and Practice*, *The Book of Thoth*, and *Book Four*.

CRYPTOGRAM: A message or writing in code or cipher. An occult symbol or figure that has a hidden significance.

DAVID-NEEL, ALEXANDRA: (1868–1969) Belgian-French explorer, Buddhist, theosophist, feminist, anarchist, and writer. David-Néel was the first European woman to reach the Tibetan capital of Lhasa, forbidden to outsiders, in 1924. She wrote over thirty books about Eastern religion and philosophy, including *With Mystics and Magicians in Tibet*.

DE INSOMNIIS: "On Dreams." The title of a book by Synesius of Cyrene. The text explains why dreams allow the soul to reach higher realms, as well as the importance of investigating one's dreams.

DEATH: In alchemy, the substance that is to be changed, that dies to an old existence and is transformed or reborn into a new existence. It is resurrected to a higher existence. "Except a corn of wheat fall into the ground and die, it abideth alone: but if it die, it bringeth forth much fruit." From this biblical passage was derived the alchemical axiom "No generation without prior corruption."

DECOCTION: The extraction of a substance (a chemical, drug, or flavor) through boiling. The digestion of a substance in the flask without adding any other substance.

DELBOEUF, JOSEPH: (1831–1896) A Belgian-French psychologist who studied hypnosis and somnambulism.

DISINTEGRATION: The breaking down of a substance into separate parts.

DISTILLATION: Also called *circulation* or *rectification,* because it entails a continuous cycle (rising and falling). Purifying a substance through heat and evaporation. The process of boiling a liquid until it vaporizes and is then recondensed by cooling. The rising vapor is considered the spirit of the substance. Considered the primary tool of the alchemist.

DRAGON: Death, putrefaction, decay. Winged dragons represent the volatile principle; dragons without wings represent the fixed principle. Ouroboros, or the dragon biting its own tale, represents the fundamental unity of all things.

DUALISM: A theory that the universe is ruled by two opposing principles.

EARTH: One of the four elements whose properties include manifestation, solidity, and material creation. In practical alchemy, metals are often referred to as Earth.

EGO: That portion of the psyche that is conscious, most directly governs thought and behavior, and is most concerned with outer reality. Also called the *conscious self.*

ELEMENTS: The five magical substances or divisions of nature: Fire, Water, Air, Earth, and the ruling fifth element of Spirit. These are the basic modes of existence, energy, and action, as well as the basic building blocks of everything in the universe. The four basic elements are each assigned a combination of two of the four qualities of heat, cold, dryness, and moisture.

ELIXIR: A liquid medicine obtained through alchemy.

ELIXIR OF LIFE: Derived from the Philosopher's Stone, the elixir of life is a universal medicine, a refined tincture said to confer immortality and restore youth.

EMPIRICIST: One who holds the philosophy that all knowledge originates in experience.

ENANTIODROMIA: A Jungian idea stating that the superabundance of any force inevitably produces its opposite. The changing of something into its opposite.

ENLIGHTENMENT: In Buddhism and Hinduism, this refers to the awakening to ultimate truth. A transcendent divine experience that rises above all desire and suffering.

EVANS-WENTZ, WALTER: (1878–1965) American anthropologist and writer who was a pioneer in the study of Tibetan Buddhism. He is best known for helping compile and edit *The Tibetan Book of the Dead*.

FAECES (or FECES): Residue left over from alchemical operations.

FERMENTATION: Soaking a plant in water to create a tincture. Sometimes refers to adding the required precious metal as a yeast to the Philosopher's Stone, enabling it to transmute base metals into this particular precious metal. It is associated with putrefaction and decay, but also with the work of transformation and regeneration. In mystical alchemy, fermentation implies the liberation of intuitive powers and the creation of dreams.

FIRE: Fire is one of the four elements of alchemy, whose properties include activity and transformation. It is associated with the operation of calcination and is represented by the metal lead.

FIRST MATTER: "The primal one thing" that is at the core of manifestation. The beginning of the work, the base metal. The first state of unformed matter. The elementary substance of inherent possibilities that contains the germs, seeds, or potencies of all things. It is a fusion of the four elements. Once the First Matter was known and purified, it became the Philosopher's Stone. Also called *Hyle*.

FIXATION: The process of stabilizing and incarnating a substance. To make a volatile subject fixed or solid.

FLAMEL, NICOLAS: (1330–1418) French notary and alchemist. According to his own account, Flamel came across a book filled with alchemical symbolism called the *Book of Abraham the Jew*. Flamel and his wife, Perenelle, began a series of alchemical experiments, and after consulting a Jewish alchemist, they set about preparing the First Matter. After a few years, the couple had converted mercury into silver and gold.

After this, Flamel became wealthy and founded at least fourteen hospitals. Many myths and a good deal of speculation surround Flamel.

FLOWER OF MIND: (Greek: *anthos nou*) That part of the soul that is the most divine and makes union with God possible.

FLUDD, ROBERT: (1574–1637) English physician, astrologer, and mathematician. He wrote several books on Hermetic medicine and alchemy, but his major contribution was a huge encyclopedia of Renaissance occult philosophy called *Utriusque cosmi maioris scilicet et minoris metaphysica, physica atqve technica historia,* or *The Metaphysical, Physical, and Technical History of Both Universes, That Is, the Greater and the Lesser.* Fludd was a staunch defender of Rosicrucianism.

FODOR, DR. NANDOR: (1895–1964) Hungarian-born British and American psychologist and paranormal researcher. Considered one of the leading authorities on poltergeists. His magnum opus was the *Encyclopedia of Psychic Science* (1934).

FRATER ALBERTUS: (1911–1984) Frater Albertus Spagyricus, whose real name was Dr. Albert Richard Riedel, founder of the Paracelsus Research Society, which later became the Paracelsus College. His works include *The Alchemist's Handbook* (1960) and *The Seven Rays of the QBL* (1981).

FREE ASSOCIATION: A spontaneous, logically unconstrained and undirected association of ideas, emotions, and feelings. A psychoanalytic technique in which a patient's articulation of free associations is encouraged in order to reveal unconscious thoughts and emotions, such as traumatic experiences that have been repressed.

FREEMASONRY: An international fraternal order with many historical links to occultism. The most influential of the fraternal orders in the West, Freemasonry is the source of a large number of esoteric ideas on degrees, initiations, lodges, symbolism, etc.

FREUD, SIGMUND: (1856–1939) Austrian neurologist and founder of psychoanalysis. Freud developed the theory that the conscious mind is only a small part of our composition, and our motivations are caused, for the most part, by factors that we are unaware of. Freud postulated that the psyche is divided into three distinct factions: the *id,* the *ego,* and the *super-ego.* Human beings, according to Freud, are motivated by vital animal instincts—primarily the sexual drive, which he called the *libido*. Other elements of psychology uncovered by Freud were the ideas of the Oedipus complex and infantile sexuality.

FREUDIAN: (See *FREUD, SIGMUND*.)

GARSTIN, E. J. LANGFORD: (1983–1955) A prominent member of the Alpha et Omega, a spinoff of the Golden Dawn. He was the author of two published works on spiritual alchemy: *Theurgy, or the Hermetic Practice* (1931) and *The Secret Fire* (1932).

GEBER: (c. 720–c. 810) Latinized version of the name Abu Musa ibn Hayyan (Jabir ibn Hayyan). An Arabic alchemist who practiced in Baghdad and is considered the father of both Islamic and European alchemy. He had a large role in designing alchemical furnaces; however, his major contribution was the sulphur-mercury (masculine-feminine) theory of the formation of metals. During the fourteenth century, an unknown Spanish alchemist wrote several alchemical treatises using Geber's name, including the *Summa Perfectionis (Sum of Perfection)* and *Liber Fornacum (Book of Furnaces)*.

GEBURAH (or GEVURAH): Hebrew word for "power." Often referred to as "severity," Geburah is the fifth Sephirah on the Tree of Life. The phrase *ve-Geburah*, meaning "and the power," is used in the Qabalistic Cross.

GUATAMA BUDDHA: (563–483 BCE) Also known as Siddhartha Gautama. The founder of Buddhism.

GNOTHI SEAUTON: Greek for "Know Thyself." Maxim inscribed above the door to the temple of Apollo at Delphi.

GNOSTIC: (See *GNOSTICISM*.)

GNOSTICISM: Concerning *gnôsis*, the Greek word for "knowledge" or "insight." The name given to a loosely organized religious movement that flourished in the first and second centuries CE. Gnostics believe that gnosis was arrived at by way of interior, intuitive revelation.

GOLD: The most perfect of all the metals. The goal of the Great Work. Perfection and harmony. Complete balance of masculine and feminine. A symbol of perfection of all matter on any level, including mind, spirit, and soul.

GOLDEN FLOWER: In Buddhism and Taoism, the golden flower symbolizes the quintessence. The blossoming or opening up of the light of the mind. The awakening of the real self and its hidden potential.

GREAT WORK: A term borrowed from alchemy's magnum opus. It refers to the esoteric path of human spiritual evolution, growth, and illumination, which is the goal of theurgy. The attainment of the highest possible degree of perfection.

GRODDECK, GEORG: (1866–1934) German physician who was a pioneer in psychosomatic medicine. His treatment was a combination of psychoanalysis, naturopathy, hypnosis, and suggestion. One of his most influential works was *The Book of the It* (1923).

HALI: An Islamic alchemist. May refer to Hali Abenragel, an Arabian astrologer of the tenth and early eleventh centuries.

HARTMANN, FRANZ: (1838–1912) German physician, occultist, theosophist, and astrologer. He wrote several books on esoteric subjects, including *Magick: White and Black, In the Pronaos of the Temple of Wisdom,* and *Alchemy and Astrology.*

HELLENISTIC: Relating to post-Classical Greek history and culture in and Mediterranean world, from the death of Alexander the Great (323 BCE) to the death of Cleopatra (30 BCE).

HELMONT, JAN BAPTISTE VAN: (1579–1644) Flemish physician, mystic, and chemist who advanced scientific understanding of the physical properties of gases and coined the word "gas."

HERACLEITUS: (540–480 BCE) Greek philosopher who posited that the element of Fire forms the basic material principle of the universe.

HERMES: Greek messenger god, equated with the Egyptian Thoth. Patron deity of Hermeticism and alchemy.

HERMES TRISMEGISTUS: "Hermes the Thrice-Great." The Greek god Hermes and the Egyptian god Thoth merged into one figure who was said to be the first and greatest magician. Hermes Trismegistus was reputed to be an ancient Egyptian priest and magician who was credited with writing forty-two books, collectively known as the Hermetic literature. These books, including the *Emerald Tablet* and the *Divine Pymander*, describe the creation of the universe, the soul of humanity, and the way to achieve spiritual rebirth.

HERMETIC: Relating to Hermes Trismegistus or the works ascribed to him. Having to do with the occult sciences, especially alchemy, astrology, and magic deriving from Western sources (Egyptian, Judeo-Christian, and Graeco-Roman).

HERMETICISM: An ancient spiritual, philosophical, and magical tradition that originated in the Hellenistic Period. Hermeticism takes its name from the god Hermes Trismegistus. Hermeticism is the primary basis of the Western Esoteric Tradition that embraces the Perennial Philosophy, or the Ageless Wisdom.

HIGH PLACE: A hilltop place of worship.

HILDEGARD VON BINGEN: (1098–1179) Hildegard of Bingen, also known as Saint Hildegard, was a Christian mystic, composer, and philosopher.

HOD: Hebrew word for "splendor," referring to the eighth Sephirah on the Tree of Life.

HOLLANDER, BERNARD: (1864–1934) London psychiatrist and prominent phrenologist. His works include *Positive Philosophy of the Mind* (1891), *The Mental Function of the Brain* (1901), and *Scientific Phrenology* (1902).

HOLY GHOST: (See *HOLY SPIRIT*.)

HOLY SPIRIT: Ruach Qadesh. The mysterious power of God, conceived of as the mode of God's activity, manifested especially in a supernatural manner or revelation to certain individuals. The third person of the Christian Trinity.

HSUEH-FENG: Chinese monk and influential Zen master. He appears in many classical koan.

HYDRARGYRUM: An obsolete name for mercury.

HYLE: First Matter. (See *FIRST MATTER*.)

HYPNOSIS: A sleeplike state usually induced by another person in which the individual may experience suppressed or forgotten memories, hallucinations, and increased suggestibility.

HYPNOTISM: (See *HYPNOSIS.*)

I CHING: The *Book of Changes*, one of the oldest of the Chinese classic texts. The text contains a complete system for divination and comprises a set of oracular statements represented by sixty-four sets of six horizontal lines, each called hexagrams.

ILLUMINATION: Spiritual enlightenment.

IMAGO: Image.

IMBIBE: To absorb.

INDIVIDUATION: The process by which a person becomes self-realized or differentiated as a separate indivisible unity or "whole" that contains all aspects of the self. The development of an integrated personality.

IOSIS: In alchemy, the fourth and final stage of the Great Work, represented by a reddening or purpling of the substance.

JAMES, WILLIAM: (1842–1910) Influential American physician, philosopher, and psychologist who discussed hypnosis and various states of mind in his book *The Principles of Psychology* (1890).

JANET, PIERRE: (1859–1947) One of the primary founders of the analytical tradition in psychology. Janet was the source for much of Carl G. Jung's writings on the dissociation theory.

JEHOVAH: A Latinized version of the Hebrew godname YHVH, the Tetragrammaton, or "four-lettered name," which is substituted for the true name of God, which is both unknown and unpronounceable. A more correct version of the godname YHVH would be Yahweh.

JUNG, CARL GUSTAV: (1875–1961) Swiss psychologist/psychiatrist who founded analytical psychology. Jung developed the concepts of the collective unconscious and the archetypes, which he held were fundamental to the study of the psychology of religion. According to Jung, archetypes are instinctive patterns, have a universal character, and are expressed in human behavior and images. The psychology that Jung gradually developed was described by him as *Heisweg*, a German word that means "sacred way" and a "method of healing." Jung's idea of the psyche was based upon a separation between the *conscious* and the *unconscious*—the personal unconscious being a tributary of the greater river of the *collective unconscious*. After discovering that alchemical symbols and ideas appeared in the dreams and behaviors of his patients, Jung began a lifelong study of alchemy and concluded that alchemical images uncover the archetypal origins of the human mind and are key to a process of transformation and self-individuation.

KETHER: Hebrew word for "crown," referring to the first Sephirah on the Tree of Life.

KHEPHRA: Egyptian god of the rising sun, represented by a scarab beetle.

KILNER, WALTER JOHN: (1847–1920) Doctor of electrotherapy for St. Thomas' Hospital in London. Author of a book on the human aura called *The Human Atmosphere* (1883), based on his studies.

KOAN: In Zen Buddhism a paradoxical story or riddle used to aid meditation and to provoke enlightenment.

KRISHNA: In Hinduism, the eighth incarnation of Lord Vishnu. Krishna takes on various roles, including God-child, mischief-maker, ideal lover, divine hero, and Supreme Being.

KUNDALINI: Sanskrit word meaning "serpent power." A fiery, transformative power said to reside in the base chakra.

KUNDALINI-SHAKTI: Divine spiritual power within every human being. The universal energy of consciousness. (See *KUNDALINI*.)

LAMEN: A magical symbol suspended from a collar and worn on the chest.

LANKAVATARA SUTRA: An important text of Mahayana Buddhism.

LIBIDO: According to Freud, the libido is the sexual urge, but according to Jung, it is the total of psychic energy and vitality, and its expression is through instinct, desire, and function.

LIÉBEAULT, AMBROISE-AUGUSTE (or LIÉBAULT): Founder of the Nancy School of hypnotherapy, which taught that hypnosis was induced by suggestion and not by magnetism or hysteria. Considered by many to be the father of modern hypnotherapy, Liébeault was an influence on Sigmund Freud, who studied at the Nancy School.

LION: Heat, fire, and sulphurous or solar action. Symbol of the living force that must be sought in the First Matter. The beginning of the work. A green lion indicates the Fire of Venus and the raw, unpurified or untamed energy of nature. A red lion indicates this same fiery energy, but mixed with gold and brought under control of the Will. In other words, the red lion has been tamed or trained through Will.

LODGE, SIR OLIVER: (1851–1940) A British physicist, Christian Spiritualist, and member of the London-based Society for Psychical Research who wrote more than forty books about the afterlife, electromagnetic theory, and other topics.

LULLY, RAYMOND: (1232/33–1315) Also called Ramon Llull. Spanish mystic and poet whose writings had a major influence on Neoplatonic philosophy and mysticism throughout medieval and seventeenth-century Europe. After experiencing a vision, Lully developed a system of contemplative philosophy with strong similarities to Qabalah that became known as the Lullian Art, described in his book *Ars Magna*. Lully was reputed to have written more than ninety works on alchemy; however, many of these were probably penned by Ramon de Tarrega.

LUMEN VESTIMENTI: The Light of the Vestment, or Vehicle of Light. The Robe of Glory that awaits the soul in its higher state.

MAGIC: Derived from the Greek *mageia*. The science and religion of the priests of Zoroaster. The art of causing change to occur in one's environment and one's consciousness. Willpower, imagination, intention, and the use of symbols and correspondences play a major role in this art. (See *THEURGY*.)

MAGNESIA: In alchemy, magnesia is a word often used to describe the primordial transforming substance in the universe. Talc. A mixture of metals.

MAGNETISM: The power to attract, fascinate, or influence. German physician Franz Mesmer described animal magnetism as an invisible natural force exerted by living beings. This force could have physical effects, including healing.

MAGNUM OPUS: Latin for the "Great Work." The alchemical process.

MAHAYANA: Sanskrit for "Great Vehicle." One of two major Buddhist traditions. A major principle of Mahayana practice is the bodhisattva, or "wisdom being," who works for the enlightenment of all sentient beings.

MALKUTH: Hebrew word for "kingdom," referring to the tenth Sephirah on the Tree of Life.

MEDITATION: In Eastern practice, meditation involves emptying the mind of all thoughts in order to silence the mind. In Western practice, meditation involves concentrating on a specific topic while blocking out all thoughts that are unrelated to the topic. Both practices induce a specific mode of conscious awareness.

MERCURY: A liquid metal, mercury is sometimes called quicksilver. In alchemy, Mercury refers to one of the three alchemical principles or heavenly substances that comprise all things in the universe (Mercury, Sulphur, and Salt). This is a watery, feminine principle that relates to the concept of consciousness. It is also sometimes described as Airy. Mercury is the universal Spirit or vital life-force that permeates all living matter. This fluid and creative principle is symbolic of the act of transmutation—it is the transforming agent of the alchemical process. Mercury is the essential *Spirit*, the most important of the three principles, which mediates between the other two, modifying their extreme tendencies. In practical alchemy, Mercury has two states, both of which are liquid. The first (volatile) state is prior to the removal of Sulphur. The second (fixed) state is after the Sulphur has been returned. This final and stabilized state is sometimes referred to as The Secret Fire, Refined Mercury, Prepared Mercury, Mercury of the Philosophers, and Mercury of the Wise. In plant alchemy, Mercury is alcohol; in mineral alchemy, it is metallic mercury; in animal alchemy, it is blood.

MESMER, FRANZ ANTON: (1734–1815) Swiss physician and occultist who developed the theory of animal magnetism, a type of subtle life-force energy connected with animal life that could be manipulated for the purpose of healing. His method become known as *mesmerism*, which, unlike hypnotism, focused on energy work and not mental processes. Mesmer explained his theories in the book *Mémoire sur la découverte du magnétisme animal* (*Dissertation on the Discovery of Animal Magnetism*, 1779). Mesmer's ideas were highly popular in occult circles and had a huge influence on nineteenth-century French occult revivalists such as Eliphas Levi, whose ideas on the Astral Light were nearly identical with Mesmer's theory of animal magnetism.

MESSIANISM: The belief in a messiah or savior.

METALS: To the alchemist, metals are living, breathing substances, in a constant state of progression, each one having as its component parts of Mercury, Sulphur, and Salt, the difference in varying proportions. The metals are seven in number and are therefore aligned with the seven planets and their various qualities.

METAPHYSICS: The branch of philosophy that examines the nature of reality, including the relationship between mind and matter, substance and attribute, fact and value. A priori speculation upon questions that are unanswerable to scientific observation, analysis, or experiment.

MIDDLE PILLAR: The central pillar on the Qabalistic Tree of Life. The Exercise of the Middle Pillar is a Golden Dawn technique for awakening the Sephiroth or *Galgalim* of the Middle Pillar within the magician's sphere of sensation. More than anyone else, Israel Regardie understood the wide range of magical and therapeutic applications inherent to this exercise.

MOON: The planetary name for silver. In alchemy, it refers to the feminine.

NEOPLATONISM: The last school of Greek philosophy, founded in the third century CE by Plotinus. Neoplatonism dominated Greek thought until the sixth century CE. It combined the doctrines of Plato with East Asian mysticism. Neoplatonists believed that reason alone could not satisfy the human soul.

NETZACH: Hebrew word for "victory," referring to the seventh Sephirah on the Tree of Life.

NEUROSIS: Any of various mental or emotional disorders arising from no apparent organic lesion or change and involving symptoms such as insecurity, anxiety, depression, and irrational fears. Because a neurosis is not as detrimental as psychosis, a person with a particular neurosis can otherwise function normally.

NEUROTIC: (See *NEUROSIS*.)

OSIRIS: Egyptian god of the afterlife.

OVERSOUL: The spiritual essence or vital force in the universe that transcends individual consciousness and in which all souls partake.

PARACELSUS: (1493–1541) Born Philippus Aureolus Theophrastus Bombastus von Hohenheim, he changed his name to Aureolus Paracelsus to show that he was "beyond Celsus," the renowned first-century Roman physician. A German-Swiss alchemist and physician, Paracelsus introduced the concept of disease to medicine. Paracelsus believed that disease was the result of external agents attacking the body, and promoted the use of chemicals against illness-causing agents. He is considered the father of modern medicine and a forerunner of homeopathy, microchemistry, and chemotherapy. Paracelsus maintained the Hermetic view that human life in inseparable from that of the universal mind. The basic idea of purifying gold of its gross components is behind much of Paracelsus's work.

PHAEDRUS: Written around 370 BCE and considered one of Plato's greatest literary works. The text takes the form of a dialogue between Plato's main protagonist, Socrates, and Phaedrus.

PHILOSOPHER'S STONE: *Lapis Philosophorum*. The Stone of the Wise. The Magnum Opus. The Celestial Ruby. Symbol of the transmutation of humanity's lower nature into the Higher Self. True spiritual attainment and illumination. The search for the Philosopher's Stone is the search for ultimate Truth and Purity. Also called the Elixir of Life, or Tincture. In physical alchemy, the Stone is the manufacture of gold from a base metal. In mystical alchemy, it is the transmutation of the lower into the higher.

PHILOSOPHICAL MONTH: Forty days.

PHOENIX: The bird of rebirth and reoccurrence. A symbol of alchemical resurrection. Indicates the preparation of the red tincture of the solar forces, philosophic sulphur. The phoenix is also a symbol of elemental Fire and of the idea of freeing the spirit from the bonds of the physical.

PLATO: (427–347 BCE) Greek philosopher and follower of Socrates, Plato founded his academy (in 386 BCE), where he taught and wrote for most of his life. Plato is universally accepted as one of the all-time geniuses who presented his ideas in the form of dramatic dialogues, as in *The Republic*. He created a profound philosophy concerned with humanity's social and personal conduct. Plato believed that the material world was a lower and inferior reflection of a higher truth—a higher world of ideas or archetypes. He also believed there were three parts to the human soul: reason, will, and desire.

PLATONIC: (See *PLATONISM*.)

PLATONISM: The philosophy of Plato, which emphasized that corporeal things are simply copies of transcendent ideas. These abstract ideas are the objects of true knowledge obtained through reminiscence.

PLEROMA: Greek word meaning "fullness." The totality of divine powers.

PLOTINUS: (205–270 CE) Hellenistic follower of Plato and founder of the Neoplatonic School in the third century CE. Most of what is known about him comes from his student Porphyry, who compiled the works of Plotinus in *The Enneads*.

PORTMANTEAU: A word or morpheme whose form and meaning are derived from a blending of two or more distinct words.

POWER COMPLEX: The psychological term for a basic pattern of emotions, perceptions, memories, and desires present in an individual's personal unconscious organized around the theme of power.

PRANA: In yoga, the vital life force that courses through the *nadis* of the human body. Spirit.

PRANAYAMA: Sanskrit word for "the breath way." Yogic techniques for breath control and vital energy manipulation.

PRATUM: In alchemy, a meadow or garden of ideas, symbolic of the unconscious.

PRIMA MATERIA: The "first matter," or the original material from which the universe is created.

PROCLUS (PROCLUS LYCAEUS): (412–485 CE) Influential Greek Neoplatonist nicknamed "the Successor," Proclus was one of the last great classical Greek philosophers as well as a theurgist and initiate of various mystery cults.

PROJECTION: An alchemical process. After the creation of the Philosopher's Stone, projection would be utilized to transform a lower substance into a higher one. The powder of projection was a powder used by alchemists to transmute base metal into gold. The process of adding a ferment or tincture to a substance to effect a transformation.

PRYSE, JOHN MORGAN: (1859–1942) Theosophist and author.

PSYCHE: The Greek word for "soul." The mind functioning as the center of thought, emotion, and behavior and consciously or unconsciously adjusting or mediating the body's responses to the social and physical environment.

PSYCHIATRY: The branch of medicine that deals with the diagnosis, treatment, and prevention of mental and emotional disorders.

PSYCHIC HEAT: (See *TUMO*.)

PSYCHOLOGY: The study of the mind, mental processes, and human behavior.

PSYCHOSIS: A severe mental disorder, with or without organic damage, characterized by derangement of personality and loss of contact with reality and causing deterioration of normal social functioning.

PSYCHOTHERAPY: The healing of the psyche. The treatment of mental disorders with methods that revolve around the interpersonal relationship between therapist and client. Psychoanalysis and analytical psychology are two forms of psychotherapy.

PSYCHOTIC: Relating to psychosis, a mental illness marked by loss of contact with reality, delusional thinking, and hallucinations.

PTOLEMAIC: Having to do with Claudius Ptolemy, mathematician, astrologer, and astronomer (second century BCE).

PTOLEMAIS: A town in Cyrenaica (eastern Libya).

PUFFERS: False alchemists who swindled clients.

PUTREFACTION: In alchemy, the first stage of the fermentation process. Decomposition.

PYTHAGORAS: Sixth-century-BCE Greek philosopher who is considered the first true mathematician. Pythagoras believed in reincarnation of the human soul and the idea that the essence of everything in the universe is numbers. He coordinated the religious thought of his predecessor, Orpheus, into a complete system of philosophy.

QABALAH: Hebrew word meaning "tradition." It is derived from the root word *qibel*, meaning "to receive." This refers to the ancient custom of handing down esoteric knowledge by oral transmission. What the word Qabalah encompasses is an entire body of ancient Hebrew mystical principles that are the cornerstone and focus of the Western Esoteric Tradition.

QABALIST: One who studies the Qabalah.

QABALISTIC TREE: (See *TREE OF LIFE.*)

QUICKSILVER: (See *MERCURY.*)

QUINTESSENCE: The "fifth element," which unites and rules over the other four elements. The essential animating Spirit and purest essence of life force.

RA: The Egyptian god of the Sun.

RENAISSANCE: The period of European history that followed the Middle Ages from about the fourteenth to the seventeenth century, marked by humanistic revival of classical art, architecture, literature, and philosophy.

RIEDEL, ALBERT: (See *FRATER ALBERTUS.*)

RAVEN'S HEAD: *Caput corvi.* Decapitation as a symbol of the nigredo, or blackening phase. Putrefaction, decomposition.

REDUCTION: Reducing a substance to first principles.

REICH, WILHELM: (1897–1957) Austrian psychologist who created a form of therapy that focused on the autonomic nervous system. At the end of the 1930s, Reich believed he had discovered a new type of energy that he called *orgone,* or life force of the universe (similar to *prana*).

REICHIAN: (See *REICH, WILHELM.*)

ROSICRUCIAN: A mystical and philosophical movement that emerged in the seventeenth century and spawned several secret organizations or orders concerned with the study of religious mysticism, alchemy, Qabalah, and professing esoteric spiritual beliefs. The symbolism of Rosicrucianism is primarily Christian, and the Rosicrucian path emphasizes the way of transformation through the Christ impulse. A member of the Rosicrucian Brotherhood.

ROSICRUCIANISM: (See *ROSICRUCIAN*.)

RUBIFICATION: Reddening.

RUBY: Another name for the Philosopher's Stone.

SAL AMMONIAC: Ammonium chloride. The earliest known salt of ammonia. Albertus Magnus said that there were two kinds of sal ammoniac: natural and artificial. The natural form was sometimes white and sometimes red.

SALT: In alchemy, salt is one of the three alchemical principles (Mercury, Sulphur, and Salt). This is the principle of substance or form, conceived of as a heavy, inert mineral body that is part of the nature of all metals. It is the hardening, fixed, contractive tendency, as well as crystallization. Salt refers to the vehicle in which the properties of Sulphur and Mercury are grounded. Salt is the essential corpus, or *body*. It is sometimes referred to as Earth. Salt represents the final manifestation of the Philosopher's Stone.

SAMADHI: Sankrit for "with God." Complete self-integration and the goal of all yoga.

SATORI: Buddhist word for understanding, comprehension. Enlightenment.

SCHIZOPHRENIA: A mental disorder characterized by a breakdown of thought processes. Those who have this condition often experience hallucinations.

SECRET FIRE: The hidden or elemental Fire. Philosophic Mercury, described as a "fiery water" or "philosophic vinegar." It is the root of metals which harmonizes with them and is the medium that combines the tinctures. There are four divisions of the Secret Fire, each named after Zodiac signs: *Sun of Aries* (original stage), *Sun of Taurus* (black stage),

Sun of Gemini (white stage), and *Sun of Leo* (red stage). Cosmic energy, magnetic in character, within and around the cells of the human body, that forms the aura. Kundalini energy or spiritual forces (as opposed to prana, or vital life-force energy).

SENDIVOGIUS, MICHAEL: (1566–1636) Polish physician, philosopher, diplomat, and one of the last major figures in Renaissance alchemy. In 1604 he was said to have transmuted base metal into gold in the presence of Rudolf II and others. During the same year, he published his most famous work, *Novum Lumen Chymicum* (*A New Light of Alchemy*), written in a coded alchemical language that could only be deciphered by other alchemists. The book greatly enhanced his reputation as an alchemist.

SEPHIRAH: One of the Sephiroth.

SEPHIROTH: Hebrew word meaning "numbers, spheres, emanations." Refers to the ten divine states or god-energies depicted on the Qabalistic Tree of Life. The singular form is *Sephirah*.

SERPENT: A symbol of the kundalini.

SILBERER, HERBERT: (1882–1923) Austrian psychoanalyst who moved in the same circles as Sigmund Freud and Carl Jung. In 1914 he wrote his most important work, *Probleme der Mystik und ihrer Symbolik* (*Problems of Mysticism and Its Symbolism*), an exploration of alchemical imagery and modern psychology.

SILVER: One of the seven metals of alchemy, silver corresponds to the Moon and the feminine.

SOCIETAS ROSICRUCIANA IN AMERICA: An American Rosicrucian Order founded in 1907 by Sylvester C. Gould and George Winslow Plummer, both prominent Freemasons and Rosicrucians. In 1916 the Order began to admit women and dropped its Masonic requirement.

SOCRATES: (470–399 BCE) Classical Greek philosopher who is considered one of the founders of Western philosophy. The teachings of Socrates are known mainly through the accounts of later classical writers such as Plato and Xenophon.

SOLUTION: An alchemical process that involves reducing a substance to a liquid after the spirit has been extracted.

SOLVENT: A substance, usually a liquid, capable of dissolving another substance.

SOMA HELIAKON: The "Golden Body of the Solar Man." The "Solar Body." The shining form of the soul, self-realized.

SOPHIA: Greek term for "wisdom," often personified and honored as a goddess by the Gnostics.

SOUL: The personal part of an individual, regarded as separate from the body and the spirit. The middle part of the threefold constitution of body, soul, and spirit. The soul is the mediator between the body and the spirit.

SOUL OF THE WORLD: (See *ANIMA MUNDI*.)

SPAGYRIC ART: "The separative art." A term for alchemy, in which the fusion of duality is a constant theme. Specifically used to refer to plant alchemy.

SPECTRUM: The range of colors contained in a ray of light can be separated into the seven visible colors of the rainbow (red, orange, yellow, green, blue, indigo, and violet).

SPEIREMA: Serpent power. Kundalini energy.

SPIRIT: The transcendent fifth element, which unites and governs the other four elements of Fire, Water, Air, and Earth. The vital principle or animating force within living beings. Also, a sentient, incorporeal entity. In alchemy, it refers to Mercury. In inner alchemy, Spirit is the divine presence that strives toward perfection and seeks material manifestation for expression. The Ultimate Reality of the universe.

STELLA MATUTINA. The "Morning Star." An initiatory magical order directly descended from the Golden Dawn.

SUBLIMATION: The vaporization of a solid substance directly from the solid to the gas phase without melting, fusing, or passing through a liquid phase. Purification of a substance through dissolution and reduction to its principles.

SULPHUR (or SULFUR): The dynamic, expansive, volatile, acidic, unifying, masculine, paternal, and fiery principle. Sulphur is the emotional, feeling, and passionate urge that motivates life. It is symbolic of the desire for positive change and of vital heat. The entire act of transmutation depends upon the correct application of this vibrant principle. Fire is the crucial element in the science of alchemy. Sulphur is the essential *Soul*. In practical alchemy, Sulphur, or oil, is usually extracted from Mercury by distillation. Sulphur is the stabilizing aspect of Mercury, from which it is extracted and dissolved back into.

SUN (or SOL): The planetary name for gold. In alchemy, it refers to the masculine.

SUTRA: The Sanskrit word for a Buddhist, Hindu, or Tantric scripture.

SUZUKI, DAISETZ TEITARO: (1894–1966) Japanese author of several influential books and essays on Buddhism and Zen, who was instrumental in spreading knowledge of these philosophies to the West.

SYNESIUS OF CYRENE: (373–414) Bishop of Ptolemais. Libyan philosopher and student of Hypatia who struggled with his Christian faith and his philosophical Greek education. Synesius's writings were a mixture of Orthodox Christianity and Neoplatonism. *The True Book* was written by an unknown alchemist who took the name of Synesius.

TANTRA: An Indian style of meditation that sees the physical world as spiritual. Tantra examines all aspects of existence, including sexuality.

TAO: A Chinese word meaning "way," "path," or "route." In Taoist philosophy, it implies a basic eternal principle and a natural order that underlies all substance and activity of the universe. The absolute or noumenal reality.

TAOISM: A Chinese philosophical tradition founded by Lao-Tzu in the sixth century BCE. Taoism promotes living a life of simplicity and noninterference with the course of natural events, the end result of which is a happy existence in harmony with the Tao.

THEURGY: Greek word meaning "God-working." Magic used for personal growth and spiritual evolution and for becoming closer to the Divine.

TIBETAN BOOK OF THE DEAD: Written by a Tibetan monk, the *Book of the Dead* chronicles the religious experiences and stages of death and rebirth from the Tibetan point of view.

TINCTURE: The part of a substance that is extracted by a solvent.

TIPHARETH: Hebrew word for "beauty," referring to the sixth Sephirah on the Tree of Life.

TRANCE STATE: A hypnotic state. Intense mystic absorption that causes a temporary loss of consciousness at the earthly level.

TREE OF LIFE: In Hebrew, *Etz ha-Chayim*. A glyph or symbol that is central to the Qabalah. It is a symmetrical drawing of ten circles or spheres known collectively as Sephiroth, arranged in a certain manner, with twenty-two connecting paths running between the spheres. It is considered a blueprint for understanding all things and relationships in the universe, including the essence of God and the soul of humanity. (See *SEPHIROTH*.)

TREVISAN, BERNARD: (1406–1490) Bernard of Treviso. The name refers to one or more enigmatic Italian alchemists.

TRISMOSIN, SALOMON: The alleged teacher of Paracelsus and author of the German text *Splendor Solis* ("The Splendour of the Sun"), one of the most beautiful of all illuminated alchemical manuscripts (1582), which described the philosophy of alchemy.

(THE) TRUE BOOK: In the context of Regardie's book, this refers to *The True Book of the Learned Greek Abbot Synesius Taken Out of the Emperor's Library*.

TUMO: Psychic heat, inner fire. A form of yoga that has as its goal control over body processes.

UNCONSCIOUS: The division of the mind in psychoanalytic theory containing elements of psychic makeup, such as memories or repressed desires, that are not subject to conscious perception or control but that often affect conscious thoughts and behavior.

UNION WITH GOD: Christian mystical experience. *Theosis*. Also called divinization, deification, or transforming union. Partaking in God's divinity.

UNIVERSAL AGENT: The substance from which all forms arise. The universal spirit or energy. The animating principle. Mercury.

URAEUS: The sacred winged cobra of Egypt. A symbol of divine energy and royal authority.

VALENTINE, BASIL: (late fifteenth or early sixteenth century) Basilius Valentinus. German alchemist, Benedictine monk, and author of many influential texts on alchemy, including *The Triumphal Chariot of Antimony* (1604) and *The Twelve Keys* (1599).

VAUGHAN, HENRY: (1621–1695) Welsh doctor, author, and esoteric poet. Twin brother of alchemist Thomas Vaughan.

VAUGHAN, THOMAS: (1621–1665) Welsh philosopher and mystic heavily influenced by Agrippa. Vaughan wrote about natural magic under the pen name Eugenius Philalethes, a name chosen out of respect for his teacher Eirenaeus Philalethes. In 1650 he wrote *Coelum Terrae*.

VENUS: The planetary name for copper. The feminine.

VINEGAR: Acetic acid, or acid distilled or fermented out of metals or minerals.

VIRGIN'S MILK: The mercurial medium of conjunction for the union of Sol and Luna. The pure white texture created by the albedo which can transform based metals into silver. The white philosophical mercury, mercurial water, or the "water of life."

WAITE, ARTHUR EDWARD: (1875–1940) Christian mystic, occultist, and member of the original Hermetic Order of the Golden Dawn. A prolific author, Waite wrote several books, including *The Secret Doctrine in Israel* and *The Holy Kabbalah*.

WATER: One of the four elements of alchemy. Properties of Water include cleansing and purification.

WATER OF THE WISE: Philosopher's Mercury. Other names for this include Celestial Water, Aqua Vitae, Water of Chaos, Water of the Wise, Dew of May, Alkahest, Honey, Vinegar, and Azoth.

WESTCOTT, WILLIAM WYNN: (1843–1925) Primary founder of the Hermetic Order of the Golden Dawn, established in 1888 as "a Hermetic Society whose members are taught the principles of Occult Science and the Magic of Hermes." His Order mottos were *Sapere Aude,*

"Dare to be wise," and *Nom Omnis Moriar,* "I shall not wholly die." Author of *An Introduction to the Study of the Kabalah* and *Numbers: Their Occult Power and Mystic Virtues,* Westcott also compiled and published a number of Hermetic texts in his *Collectanea Hermetica.*

WILHELM, RICHARD: (1873–1930) German scholar, theologian, and translator of important Chinese texts including *The Secret of the Golden Flower* and the *I Ching.*

WORLD OF IDEAS: A theory by Plato stating that non-material abstract forms (ideas) comprise the highest level of reality.

YANG: In Chinese Taoism the positive, active, male principle.

YESOD: Hebrew word for "foundation," referring to the ninth Sephirah on the Tree of Life.

YHVH: Four letters, *Yod Heh Vav Heh* or YHVH, which stand for the highest Hebrew name for God, whose real name is considered unknown and unpronounceable. These letters are also attributed to the four elements of Fire, Water, Air, and Earth. Often referred to as the Tetragrammaton or the "four-lettered name." Sometimes incorrectly referred to as Jehovah.

YHVH ELOHIM: Divine Hebrew name of Binah, meaning "the Lord God." Associated with Daath in the Exercise of the Middle Pillar.

YIN: In Chinese Taoism, the negative, passive, female principle.

YOGA: Sanskrit word meaning "union." The Eastern science of physical, mental, and spiritual integration.

ZAZEN: Seated meditation. A discipline at the heart of Zen Buddhist practice.

ZEN: A Japanese school of Mahayana Buddhism that focuses on acquiring enlightenment by direct intuition through meditation.

ZOSIMOS OF PANOPOLIS: (300 BCE) Gnostic alchemist in Alexandria, said to have founded the main Greek school of alchemy. Author of the oldest known books on "alchemy," a term that first appears in his writings.

BIBLIOGRAPHY

Atwood, Mary Anne. *A Suggestive Inquiry into the Hermetic Mystery, with a Dissertation on the More Celebrated of the Alchemical Philosophers Being an Attempt Towards the Recovery of the Ancient Experiment of Nature.* London: Trelawney Saunders, 1850. www.rexresearch.com/atwood/cont.htm.

Bogert, L. Jean. *Dietetics Simplified: The Use of Foods in Health and Disease.* New York: The MacMillan Company, 1940.

Bramwell, J. Milne. *Hypnotism: Its History, Practice and Theory.* London: J. B. Lippincott, Co., 1903.

Call, Annie Payson. *Power Through Repose.* Boston: Little, Brown, and Co., 1891. Available through Google Books.

Cicero, Chic, and Sandra Tabatha Cicero. *The Essential Golden Dawn.* St. Paul, MN: Llewellyn Publications, 2003.

———. *Self-Initiation into the Golden Dawn Tradition.* St. Paul, MN: Llewellyn Publications, 1998.

Cicero, Sandra Tabatha. *The Book of the Concourse of the Watchtowers: An Exploration of Westcott's Enochian Tablets.* Elfers, FL: H.O.G.D. Books, 2012.

Coster, Geraldine. *Yoga and Western Psychology.* London: Motilal Banarsidass, 1934.

Councell, R. W. *Apollogia Alchymiae: A Restatement of Alchemy.* London: John M. Watkins, 1925. Online text at www.levity.com /alchemy/counsel1.html, www.rexresearch.com/alchemy2/councell .htm, and www.alchemywebsite.com/counsell.html.

Crowley, Aleister. *The Holy Books.* Dallas, TX: Sangreal Foundation, 1972. http://hermetic.com/crowley/libers/lib65.html.

———. *Magick in Theory and Practice.* New York: Dover Publications, 1976.

David-Néel, Alexandra. *Magic and Mystery in Tibet.* New York: Dover Publications, 1971.

Evans-Wentz, Walter Y., ed. *The Tibetan Book of the Dead.* London: Oxford University Press, 2000.

———. *Tibetan Yoga and Secret Doctrines: Seven Books of Wisdom of the Great Path.* London: Oxford University Press, 1978.

Fitzgerald, Augustine. *The Essays and Hymns of Synesius of Cyrene, Including the Address to the Emperor Arcadius and the Political Speeches.* London: Oxford University Press, 1930.

Goddard, Dwight. *A Buddhist Bible.* 1932. www.sacred-texts.com /bud/bb.

Hollander, Bernard. *Methods and Uses of Hypnosis and Self Hypnosis.* London: George Allen & Unwin Ltd., 1928. www.pnl-nlp.org /courses/ebooks/book_model/METHODS%20AND%20USES%20 OF%20HYPNOSIS%20AND%20SELF-HYPNOSIS.

Hopkins, Arthur John. *Alchemy, Child of Greek Philosophy.* New York: Columbia University Press, 1934. http://babel.hathitrust.org/cgi /pt?id=uc1.b4566948.

Humphreys, Christmas, ed. *The Sutra of Wei Lang.* Shanghai: Yu Ching Press.

Ingalese, Richard. *Golden Manuscripts: They Made the Philosopher's Stone.* Kila, MT: Kessinger Publishing, 1992.

Jowett, Benjamin, ed. *The Dialogues of Plato, Translated into English with Analyses and Introductions.* London: Oxford University Press, 1871.

Judge, William Quan. *Bhagavad Gita.* Recension of text. 1890. www.theosociety.org/pasadena/gita/bg-eg-hp.htm.

Jung, Carl G. *Modern Man in Search of a Soul.* Translated by W. S. Dell and C. F. Baynes. New York: Harcourt, Brace & World. nd.

———. *Psychology and Alchemy.* Princeton, NJ: Princeton University Press, 1980.

Kelly, Edward. *The Stone of the Philosophers.* Hamburg: 1676. www.levity.com/alchemy/kellystn.html.

Kilner, Walter J. *The Human Atmosphere: or the Aura Made Visible by the Aid of Chemical Screens.* New York: Rebman Co., 1911. www.sacred-texts.com/eso/tha.

Kirchweger, Anton Josef. *Aurea Catena Homeri.* 1723. www.levity. com /alchemy/catena1.html.

Langford Garstin, E. J. *The Secret Fire: An Alchemical Study.* Laguna Niguel, CA: Rosicrucian Order of the Golden Dawn, 2009.

———. *Theurgy, or the Hermetic Practice: A Treatise on Spiritual Alchemy.* Berwick, ME: Nicolas-Hays, Inc., 2004.

Morienus. *The Book of Morienus: Being the Revelations of Morienus to Khalid Ibn Yazid Ibn Mu'Awiyya, King of the Arabs of the Divine Secrets of the Magisterium and Accomplishment of the Alchemical Art.* Paris, 1559. www.rexresearch.com/alchemy3/morienus.htm.

Philalethes, Eirenaeus. *Ripley Revived: or An Exposition upon Sir George Ripley's Hermetico-Poetical Works.* London: Tho. Ratcliff and Nat. Thompson, 1677. www.rexresearch.com/riplrevv/riply revv.htm.

Pryse, James M. *The Apocalypse Unsealed: Being an Esoteric Interpretation of the Initiation of Iôannês.* New York: 1910.

Regardie, Israel. *The Art of True Healing: A Treatise on the Mechanism of Prayer, and the Operation of the Law of Attraction in Nature.* London: Leaf Studio, 1937.

———. *The Eye in the Triangle: An Interpretation of Aleister Crowley.* Las Vegas, NV: Falcon Press, 1989.

———. *The Middle Pillar: The Balance Between Mind and Magic.* Woodbury, MN: Llewellyn Publications, 1998.

———. *The Philosopher's Stone: Spiritual Alchemy, Psychology, and Ritual Magic.* Woodbury, MN: Llewellyn Publications, 2013.

Shields, Christopher. "Aristotle's Psychology," *Stanford Encyclopedia of Philosophy* (Spring 2011). Edited by Edward N. Zalta. http://plato .stanford.edu/archives/spr2011/entries/aristotle-psychology.

Silberer, Herbert. *Hidden Symbolism of Alchemy and the Occult Arts.* New York: Dover Publications, 1971.

Suzuki, Daisetz Teitaro. *Essays in Zen Buddhism.* New York: Rider and Co., 1950.

———. *An Introduction to Zen Buddhism.* New York: Grove Press, 1963.

———. *The Zen Koan as a Means of Attaining Enlightenment.* Rutland, VT: Charles E. Tuttle Co., Inc., 1994.

Synesius of Cyrene, Saint. *On Dreams.* Translated with notes by Isaac Myer. Philadelphia, PA: 1888.

———. *On Dreams.* Translated by Augustine Fitzgerald. www.livius .org/su-sz/synesius/synesius_dreams_01.html.

Trismosin, Salomon. *Splendor Solis: Alchemical Treatises of Salomon Trismosin, Adept and Teacher of Paracelsus.* London: Kegan Paul, Trench, Trubner & Co., Ltd. www.rexresearch.com/splsol /trismosin.htm.

Updegraff, Robert R. "The Conscious Use of the Subconscious Mind." *Reader's Digest* 33, no. 198 (October, 1938). Condensed from *Forbes* (September 15, 1938). www.infocitybd.com/?p=293.

Valentine, Basil. *Triumphal Chariot of Antimony*. Kila, MT: Kessinger Publishing, 1992. Available online at www.levity.com/alchemy /antimony.html, www.sacred-texts.com/alc/antimony.htm, and http://openlibrary.org/books/OL24342370M/Basil_Valentine_his _triumphant_chariot_of_antimony.

———. *Trois traitez de la philosophie naturelle non encore imprimez*. Translated by P. Arnauld. www.archive.org/stream/troistraitez dela00arna#page/n1/mode/2up.

Vaughan, Thomas. *Aula Lucis*. 1651. www.levity.com/alchemy/aula _lucis.html and http://archive.org/details/aulalucisorhouse00vaug.

———. *Lumen de Lumine*. 1651. Available online at www.levity.com /alchemy/lumen.html, www.rexresearch.com/alchemy2/vaughan4 .htm, and http://archive.org/details/lumendelumineorn00vaug.

Waite, Arthur Edward. *The Hermetic Museum: Containing Twenty-Two Most Celebrated Chemical Tracts*. York Beach, ME: Samuel Weiser, 1991. www.sacred-texts.com/alc/hm1/hm104.htm.

———. *The Magical Writings of Thomas Vaughan*. London: George Redway, 1888.

———. *The Secret Tradition in Alchemy: Its Development and Records*. London: Kegan Paul, Trench, Trubner & Co., Ltd., 1926.

———. *The Works of Thomas Vaughan: Eugenius Philalethes*. London: Theosophical Publishing House, 1919.

Westcott, William W., ed. *Collectanea Hermetica, Vol. III: A Short Enquiry Concerning the Hermetic Art*. London Theosophical Publishing Society, 1894.

Wilhelm, Richard, trans. *The Secret of the Golden Flower: A Chinese Book of Life*. London: Kegan Paul, Trench, Trubner & Co., 1962.

Wilkins, Charles, trans. *The Bhagvat-Geeta, or Dialogues of Kreeshna and Arjoon*. Bangalore: Wesleyan Mission Press, 1846.

INDEX

To Write to the Authors

If you wish to contact the author or would like more information about this book, please write to the author in care of Llewellyn Worldwide Ltd. and we will forward your request. Both the author and publisher appreciate hearing from you and learning of your enjoyment of this book and how it has helped you. Llewellyn Worldwide Ltd. cannot guarantee that every letter written to the author can be answered, but all will be forwarded. Please write to:

Chic Cicero and Sandra Tabatha Cicero
℅ Llewellyn Worldwide
2143 Wooddale Drive
Woodbury, MN 55125-2989
Please enclose a self-addressed stamped envelope for reply,
or $1.00 to cover costs. If outside the U.S.A., enclose
an international postal reply coupon.

Many of Llewellyn's authors have websites with additional information and resources. For more information, please visit our website at http://www.llewellyn.com.